Series Authors

Rev. Richard N. Fragomeni, Ph.D.
Maureen Gallagher, Ph.D.
Jeannine Goggin, M.P.S.
Michael P. Horan, Ph.D.

Scripture Co-editor and Consultant

Maria Pascuzzi, SSL, S.T.D.

Multicultural Consultant

Angela Erevia, MCDP, M.R.E.

The Ad Hoc Committee to Oversee the Use of the Catechism, National Conference of Catholic Bishops, has found this catechetical series, copyright 2002, to be in conformity with the Catechism of the Catholic Church.

Allen, Texas

Contributing Writer
Janie Gustafson, Ph.D.

Contributing Authors
Family Time: Steve and Kathy Beirne
We Care: Richard Reichert, M.A.
Feasts and Seasons: Marianne K. Lenihan
Our Catholic Heritage: Pat Enright

Advisory Board
William C. Allegri, M.A., Patricia M. Feeley, SSJ, M.A., Edmund F. Gordon, Patricia A. Hoffmann, Cris V. Villapando, D.Min.

Consultants
Margaret J. Borders, M.R.S., Kelly O'Lague Dulka, M.S.W., Diane Hardick, M.A., Debra Schurko, Linda S. Tonelli, M.Ed. Joy Villotti-Biedrzycki

Music Advisor
GIA Publications: Michael A. Cymbala, Alec Harris, Robert W. Piercy

Nihil Obstat
M. Kathleen Flanagan, S.C., Ph.D.
Ellen Joyce, S.C., Ph.D.
Censors Librorum

Imprimatur
✠ Most Reverend Frank J. Rodimer
Bishop of Paterson
January 26, 2001

The *nihil obstat* and *imprimatur* are official declarations that a book or pamphlet is free of doctrinal and moral error. No implication is contained therein that those who have granted the *nihil obstat* and *imprimatur* agree with the contents, opinions, or statements expressed.

Acknowledgments

Excerpts from *The New American Bible* © 1970 by the Confraternity of Christian Doctrine, Washington, DC, including the revised *New Testament* © 1986 by the Confraternity of Christian Doctrine, Washington, DC, used with permission. All rights reserved.

All adaptations of Scripture are based on *The New American Bible* © 1970 and 1986.

Excerpts from the English translation of the *Rite of Baptism for Children* © 1969, International Committee on English in the Liturgy, Inc. (ICEL); excerpts from the English translation of the *Rite of Confirmation,* Second Edition © 1975, ICEL; excerpts from the English translation of *The Roman Missal,* Second Edition © 1985, ICEL. All rights reserved.

Music selections copyrighted and/or administered by GIA Publications are used with permission of GIA Publications, Inch. 7404 So. Mason Avenue, Chicago, Illinois 60638-9927. Please refer to songs for specific copyright dates and information.

Arrangement of "Now Thank We All Our God," by Margaret W. Mealy, © 1981, GIA Publications, Inc. Used with permission.

In Appreciation: Blessed Kateri Church, Sparta, NJ; Church of the Assumption, Morristown, NJ; Our Lady of Mercy Church, Whippany, NJ; Our Lady of the Lake Church, Sparta, NJ; Saint Ann's Church, Parsippany, NJ; Saint Joseph's Church, Croton Falls, NY; Saint Peter the Apostle Church, Parsippany, NJ; Saint Thomas More Church, Convent Station, NJ; OCP Publications, Portland, OR; ILP Publications, Nashville, TN; GIA Publications, Inc., Chicago, IL; WLP Publications, Schiller Park, IL

Credits

DESIGN: Lusignan Design and Scott Foresman

COVER: Gene Plaisted, OSC/The Crosiers

SCRIPTURE ART: Diane Paterson

ALL OTHER ART: 19 Lyn Martin; 19 Bernard Adnet; 21 Tom Sperling; 23 Amanda Harvey; 34 Susan Gaber; 34 Roman Dunets; 35 Jennifer De Cristoforo; 39 Emily Thompson; 43a Ron Magnes; 43b–d Tom Sperling; 47 Freddie Levin; 48, 49 Beth Foster Wiggins; 55 Kristina Stephenson; 56 Pat Hoggan; 59a Laura Huliska-Beith; 59b–d Anthony Lewis; 63 Jill Dubin; 66 Roman Dunets; 66 Winifred Barnum-Newman; 67 Jill Dubin; 75 Terra Muzick; 82 Diane Paterson; 83 Gershom Griffith; 87 Freddie Levin; 88 Beth Foster Wiggins; 90 Shelley Dieterichs; 99 George Hamblin; 99 Patti Greene; 103 Louise M. Baker; 106 Roman Dunets; 107 Daniel L. Grant; 111 Jill Dubin; 115 Patti Greene; 122 Cindy Rosenheim; 122 Diane Paterson; 127 Freddie Levin; 128, 129 Beth Foster Wiggins; 135 Lyn Martin; 139 Patti Greene; 146 Diane Paterson; 147 Amanda Harvey; 163 Morella Fuenmayor; 167 Freddie Levin; 170 Beth Foster Wiggins; 178, 179 Jill Dubin; 183 Jane Conteh Morgan; 187 Gregg Valley; 195 Randy Chewning; 207 Freddie Levin; 208, 210 Beth Foster Wiggins; 211 Freddie Levin; 211 Amanda Harvey; 213 Anthony Lewis; 214 Amanda Harvey; 215 Bernard Adnet; 217 Anthony Lewis; 218, 219 Diane Paterson; 220 Freddie Levin; 221 Terra Muzick; 223 Phyllis Pollema-Cahill; 225 Morella Fuenmayor; 226 Phyllis Pollema-Cahill; 227 Diane Paterson; 232 Jamie Smith; 257, 258 Cindy Rosenheim; 268 Elizabeth Wolf

PHOTOS: 11 Micha Bar'Am/© Magnum Photos; 11 Nancy Pierce/Black Star/PictureQuest; 14 Michael St. Maur Sheil/Corbis; 15 Paul Barton/The Stock Market; 22 Scibilia/Art Resource, NY; 27 James L. Shaffer; 27 Victoria and Albert Museum, London/Art Resource, NY; 28 Tom Till/Stone; 30 Art Resource, NY; 31 Elyse Lewin Studio Inc./Image Bank; 31 J. Carini/Image Works; 31 Jennie Woodcock/Corbis; 36 Gerrad Del Vecchio/Stone; 38 Photri, Inc.; 39 Jim Zuckerman/Corbis; 42 Myrleen Ferguson Cate/PhotoEdit; 44 Stephen Simpson/FPG International LLC; 51 ©Sonia Halliday Photographs; 51 Bob Daemmrich/Stock Boston; 54 Neg. No. 323703, (Photo by John S. Nichols), Courtesy Dept. of Library Services/American Museum of Natural History/Department of Library Services, Neg. No.; 60 ©Terry Donnelly; 62 SuperStock; 68 Tom Blagden/© Larry Ulrich Stock; 70 Erich Lessing/Art Resource, NY; 76 NRNPNX/Index Stock Imagery; 79 © Charles Gupton/Stock, Boston/PictureQuest; 84 Werner H. Muller/Peter Arnold, Inc.; 85, 86 Milt & Joan Mann/Cameramann International, Ltd.; 91 Rene Burri/© Magnum Photos; 91 Jim Whitmer; 95 Mary Kate Denny/PhotoEdit; 95 John Terence Turner/FPG International/PictureQuest; 102 The Pierpont Morgan Library/Art Resource, NY; 104 SuperStock; 106 Saint Katharine Drexel Guild; 108 CP George/Visuals Unlimited; 110 Zev Radovan; 116 SuperStock; 119 Jim Whitmer; 119 Robin Rudd/Unicorn Stock Photos; 119 Myrleen Ferguson Cate/PhotoEdit; 124 SuperStock; 131 Z. Radovan, Jerusalem; 131 Myrleen Cate/Photo Network/PictureQuest; 139 David Young-Wolff/PhotoEdit; 140 Robert Landau/Corbis; 142 Gene Plaisted, OSC/The Crosiers; 143 George Kamper/Stone; 143 Benjamin Fink/FoodPix; 143 David Young-Wolff/PhotoEdit; 144 Gene Plaisted/The Crosiers/Catholic News Service; 148 Erich Lessing/PhotoEdit; 150 Abegg-Stiftung; 151 Bob Daemmrich/Image Works; 156 Tony Arruza/Corbis; 159 © Lynne Siler/Focus Group/ PictureQuest; 162 Edwin Pacheco Courtesy Mr. and Mrs. Edwin Pacheco; 164 Gene Plaisted, OSC/The Crosiers; 171 Thomas Nebbia/NGS Image Collection; 171 Myrleen Ferguson Cate/PhotoEdit/PictureQuest; 173 Lawrence Migdale/Stock Boston; 174 P. Vauthey/Corbis Sygma; 175 Laura Dwight/PhotoEdit; 175 Ellen Senisi/Image Works; 188 Alfred B. Thomas/Animals Animals/Earth Scenes; 190 Marquette University Archives; 191 Brooks Kraft/Corbis Sygma; 191 Christopher Morris/Black Star; 191 AFP/Corbis; 194 © Frank Fournier/Contact Press Images/PictureQuest; 196 PhotoDisc; 198 Brent Jones; 199 / Milt & Joan Mann/Cameramann International, Ltd.; 199 PhotoDisc; 216 Mryleen Ferguson Cate/PhotoEdit; 222 Luis Elvir/AP/Wide World; 228 Skjold Photographs; 229 IT Stock International/Index Stock Imagery/PictureQuest; 235 Myrleen Ferguson/PhotoEdit; 239 Gene Plaisted, OSC/The Crosiers; 240 Bill and Peggy Wittman © W.P. Wittman; 241 Gene Plaisted/Gene Plaisted, OSC/The Crosiers; 241 Bill & Peggy Wittman © W.P. Wittman; 241 Bob Daemmrich/Image Works; 247 Bill and Peggy Wittman © W.P. Wittman; 248 Bob Daemmrich/Stock Boston; 249 Myrlenn Ferguson Cate/PhotoEdit; 251 Gene Plaisted, OSC/The Crosiers; 253 Alan Odie/ PhotoEdit; 254 Myrleen Cate/Stone; 255 Myrleen Cate/PhotoEdit; 256 Mary Kate Denny/Stone; 256 Myrleen Cate/Stone; 258 Jim Whitmer

ALL OTHER PHOTOS: Scott Foresman and Pearson Learning

S6301 ISBN 978-0-7829-1270-8

12 13 14 15 16 17 • 13 12 11 10 09 08

Our Commitment Prayer

Name ______________________

Leader: God, our Creator, you made all things to show your love for us.

All: **We will take care of the gifts of your creation.**

Leader: God, our Father, the stories in the Bible teach us about your love for all people.

All: **We will listen carefully to your holy words.**

Leader: Loving God, you sent your own Son, Jesus, into the world.

All: **We will follow Jesus by showing our love for others.**

Leader: God, you sent the Holy Spirit to Jesus' first followers, and the Catholic Church was born.

All: **We will ask the Holy Spirit to help us learn more about you this year.**

CONTENTS

UNIT 4 The Holy Spirit

UNIT 5 Jesus' Church of Followers

FEASTS AND SEASONS

OUR CATHOLIC HERITAGE

Blest Are We

Words and Music by David Haas
Spanish translation by Ronald F. Krisman

REFRAIN
Blest are we, ho - ly chil - dren of light — are — we! —
¡Ben-de-ci - dos, so - mos san - tos hi - jos de la luz! —
Blest are we, cho - sen peo - ple of God! —
¡Ben - de - ci - dos y e - le - gi - dos por Dios! —
Blest are we, God has plans — for you and me! —
¡Ben - de - ci - dos, Dios nos quie - re ser cual Je - sús!
Fine
Blest — are we! — We are the chil - dren of God! —
¡Ben - de - ci - dos, so - mos los hi - jos de Dios! —
VERSE
1. For our world, — each sis - ter and broth - er:
1. Por el mun - do, por to - dos sus pue - blos:
We — are called, — called — to serve! —
¡So - mos lla - ma - dos pa - ra ser - vir! —
We are here to love — one an - oth - er:
Nos a - me - mos los u - nos a los o - tros; —
D.C.
We — are called, — called — to serve! —
¡So - mos lla - ma - dos pa - ra ser - vir! —

2. For the poor, the meek and the lowly:
We are called, called to serve!
For the weak, the sick and the hungry:
We are called, called to serve!

3. For all those who yearn for freedom:
We are called, called to serve!
For the world, to be God's kingdom:
We are called, called to serve!

2. Por los pobres, los mansos y humildes:
¡Somos llamados para servir!
Por los enfermos, hambrientos, y débiles:
¡Somos llamados para servir!

3. Por los que sufren y quieren ser librados:
¡Somos llamados para servir!
Venga a nosotros el Reino de los Cielos:
¡Somos llamados para servir!

LET US PRAY

Sign of the Cross

In the name of the Father,
and of the Son,
and of the Holy Spirit.
Amen.

Señal de la Cruz

En el nombre del Padre,
y del Hijo,
y del Espíritu Santo.
Amén.

The Lord's Prayer

Our Father, who art
in heaven,
hallowed be thy name;
thy kingdom come;
thy will be done on earth
as it is in heaven.
Give us this day
our daily bread;
and forgive us our trespasses
as we forgive those
who trespass against us;
and lead us not
into temptation,
but deliver us from evil.
Amen.

Hail Mary

Hail Mary, full of grace,
the Lord is with you.
Blessed are you among
women,
and blessed is the fruit
of your womb, Jesus.
Holy Mary,
Mother of God,
pray for us sinners,
now, and at the hour
of our death.
Amen.

Glory Be to the Father

Glory be to the Father,
and to the Son,
and to the Holy Spirit.
As it was in the
beginning, is now,
and will be forever.
Amen.

I Believe

I believe in God, the Father almighty,
  creator of heaven and earth.

Prayer to My Guardian Angel

Angel of God, my guardian dear,
  to whom God's love commits me here.
Ever this day be at my side
  to light and guard, to rule and guide.
Amen.

Grace Before Meals

Bless us, O Lord,
and these your gifts,
which we are about to receive
from your goodness,
through Christ our Lord.
Amen.

Grace After Meals

We give you thanks for all your gifts,
almighty God,
living and reigning
now and forever.
Amen.

Morning Prayer

Loving God, bless the work we do.
Watch over us and guide us in school
and at home.
Help us realize that everything we do
gives praise to you.
We make this prayer in Jesus' name.
Amen.

EveningPrayer

Parent:	May God bless you and keep you.
Child:	May he guide you in life.
Parent:	May he bless you this evening.
Child:	And keep us in his sight.
Parent:	May God be with you,(name).
Child:	And also with you.
Together:	In the name of the Father, and of the Son, and of the Holy Spirit.
	Amen.

My Prayer

AMEN.

UNIT 1

Our Church Community

With our families, we belong to our parish church community. We come together to thank and praise God. We care for one another's needs.

I am the Good Shepherd. I know you by name. I care about you. You belong to me.

Based on John 10:14–15

Jesus cares for each of us just as the shepherd in the picture cares for his sheep. We follow Jesus when we care for people in our church community.

UNIT
1
SONG

We Praise You

Words by Mike Balhoff

Music by Darryl Ducote and Gary Daigle

REFRAIN

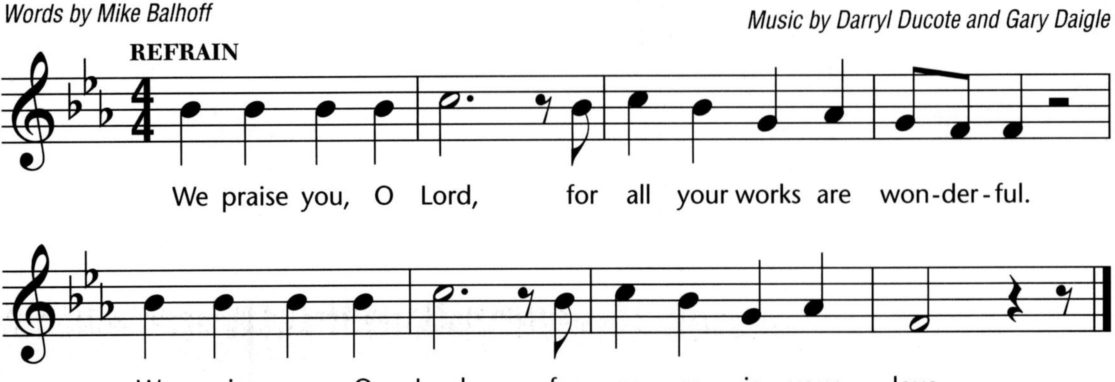
We praise you, O Lord, for all your works are won-der-ful.
We praise you, O Lord, for ev - er is your love.

VERSE

1. Your wisdom made the heavens and the earth, O Lord;
   You formed the land then set the lights;
   And like your love the sun will rule the day,
   And stars will grace the night.

Getting ready for Chapter 1

A choice of things to do at home

We Belong to Jesus' Church

In this first chapter your child will learn to appreciate belonging to your family, will realize that the family belongs to Jesus' community, the Church, and will learn to pray the Sign of the Cross. To understand that Jesus' Church is like a family, your child needs to understand that your family includes your relatives, near and far, living and deceased.

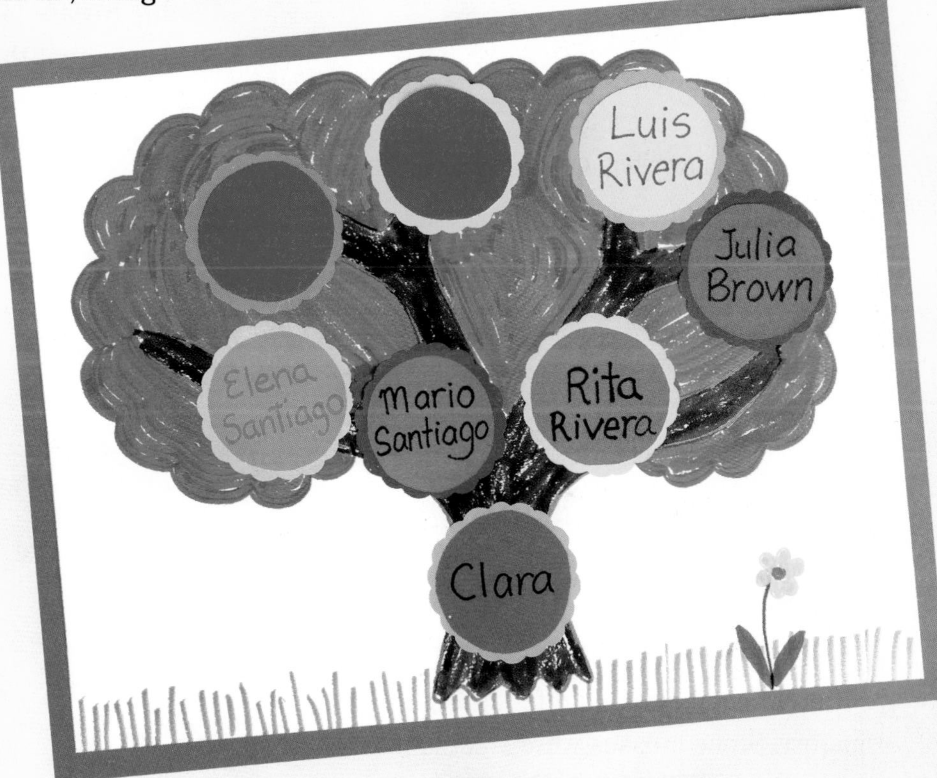

Draw a family tree

To help your child think about the larger family, draw a family tree and label the "branches" with the names of all the relatives you know both living and deceased.

Make a family collage

Help your child understand that relatives, such as grandparents, aunts, uncles, and cousins, are part of your family, even though they do not live in your home. Together, make a collage of family photos.

Share stories

Tell stories about grandparents or other older relatives your child may know. Hearing stories about your family will pave the way for hearing stories about the Church's saints.

A Prayer for the Week

Lord, bless
our family as we start
this day. You know our names.
You call us to follow Jesus
in all we do and say.
Amen.

FAMILY TIME

Something to Do . . .

On Sunday

Notice that the Mass begins with the Sign of the Cross. It is a sign we share as Catholics, no matter what language we speak.

Through the Week

Try to make the Sign of the Cross at least once a day—at mealtime, when you awaken, or before you go to bed.

Visit Our Web Site

www.blestarewe.com

Something to Think About . . .

The Good Shepherd

I am the good shepherd, and I know mine and mine know me.
John 10:14

Jesus calls himself the Good Shepherd because he knows what a hard job it is to be a shepherd. Being out in all kinds of weather and watching to make sure the sheep are protected is a difficult and sometimes dangerous job. As the shepherd risks his life to care for his sheep, Jesus' love for us is so great that he gave his life for us.

Jesus calls each of us by name to follow him as sheep follow their shepherd. Jesus cares for each of us as a shepherd cares for his sheep.

Jesus' Church is like a family to which we belong. Jesus calls us to follow him as members of the Catholic Church.

Something to Know About . . .

Our Heritage

There are many different crosses from different countries and different times in history. Stone crosses were erected in Ireland during the Viking invasion—a time of great destruction. The Irish needed a symbol of Christianity that would endure and that would tell stories from Scripture. Many of these Celtic crosses still stand today as a reminder to the Irish people of their strong Christian faith.

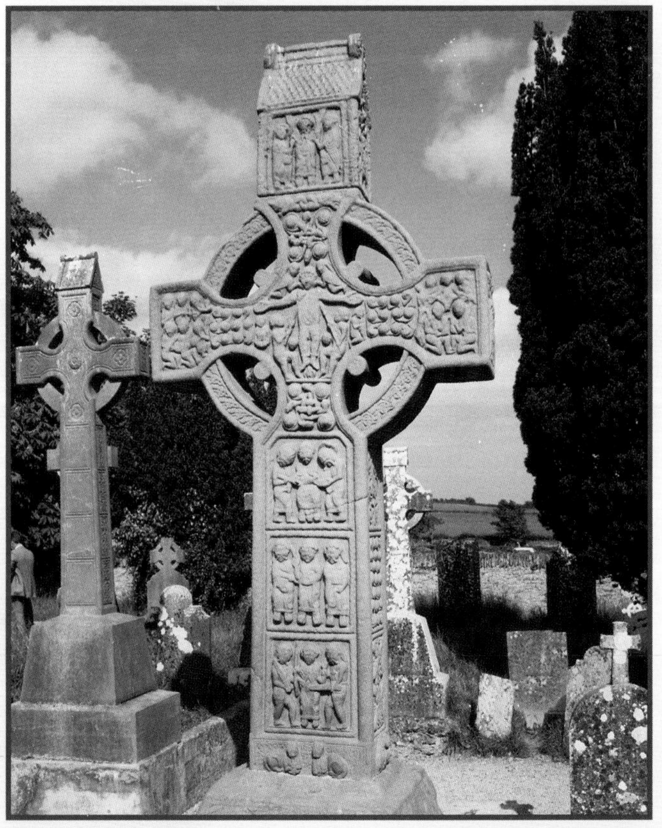

1 We Belong to Jesus' Church

I call you by name. You are mine.

Based on Isaiah 43:1

Share

Everyone belongs to a family.
Families like doing things together.
Look at the picture of a picnic.
Tell about the families you see.

Draw yourself with your family at the picnic.

What other groups do you belong to?

The Good Shepherd

Shepherds take care of sheep. A good shepherd knows each sheep by name. The sheep come when they hear the shepherd's voice.

One day, Jesus said to his friends, "I am the Good Shepherd. I know you by name. I care for you. You belong to me."

Based on John 10:2–14

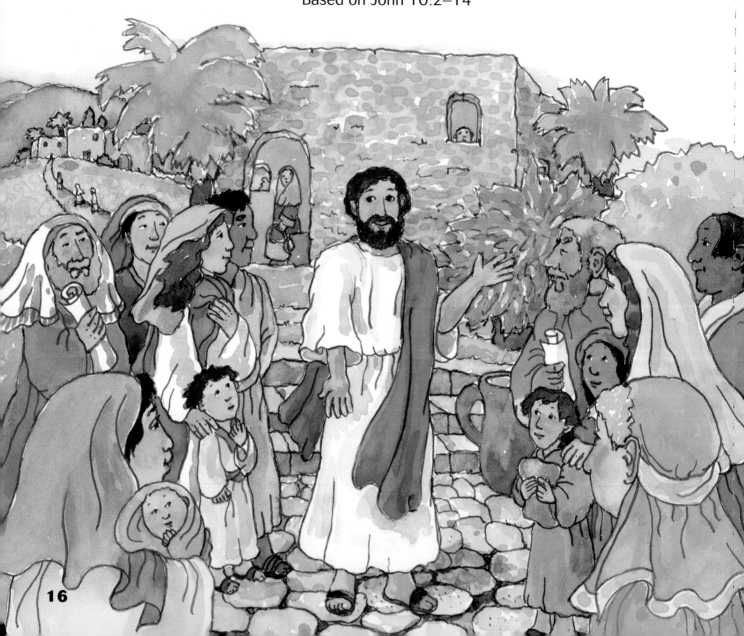

We Follow Jesus

Jesus is like a good shepherd. We are like the sheep. Jesus calls us by name to follow him. We are Jesus' followers. We belong to the **Catholic Church**. We are called Catholics.

Our Church Teaches

The Catholic Church is a **community**. The Church is made up of many kinds of people. There are different kinds of families in our church community. We care for each other. We care for other people, too.

We Believe

The Church is a community of Jesus' followers. Sometimes the Church is called Jesus' true family.

Faith Words

Catholic Church
The Catholic Church is the community of Jesus' followers to which we belong.

community
A community is a group of people who belong together.

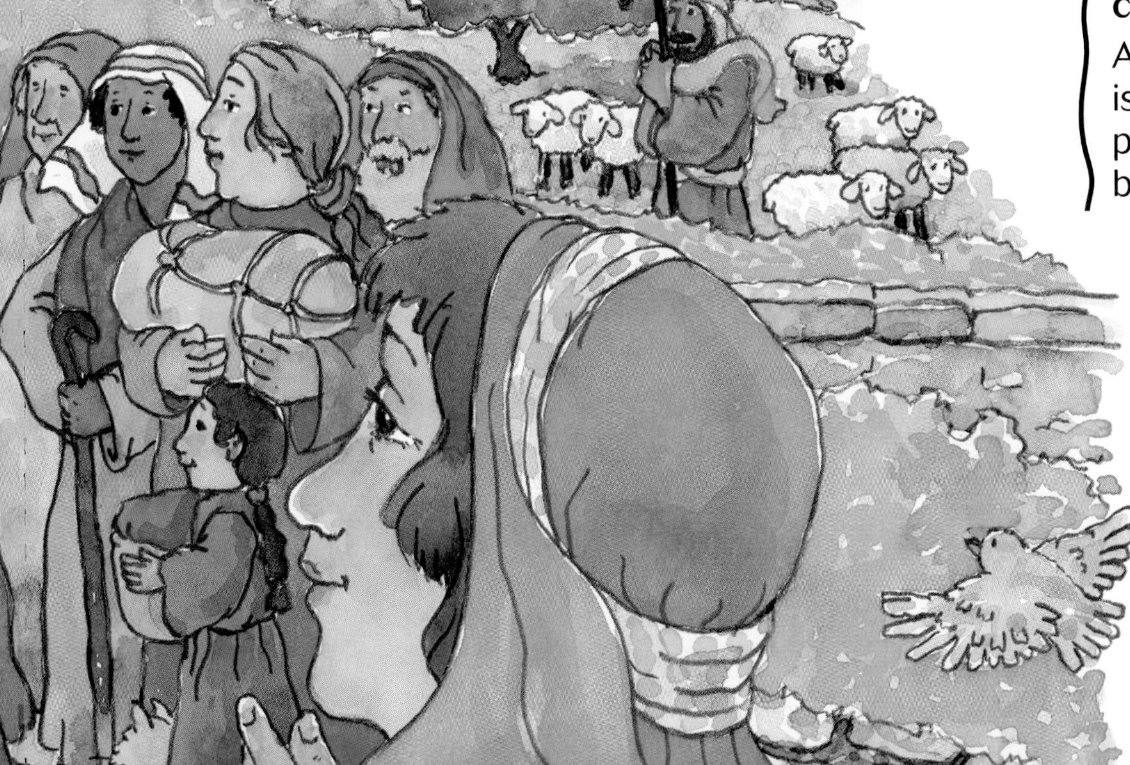

What are some things Catholics do?

Respond

One Sunday Morning

One Sunday morning, Sam and his parents walked to church. They saw other families going to church, too.

"Why are people smiling?" Sam asked.

"They know Jesus loves them," his mother said. "We are all Jesus' followers. We are like a big family."

That morning, Sam prayed with his church community. He listened to the words from the Bible. Soon Sam was smiling, too.

? Why do you think Sam was smiling?

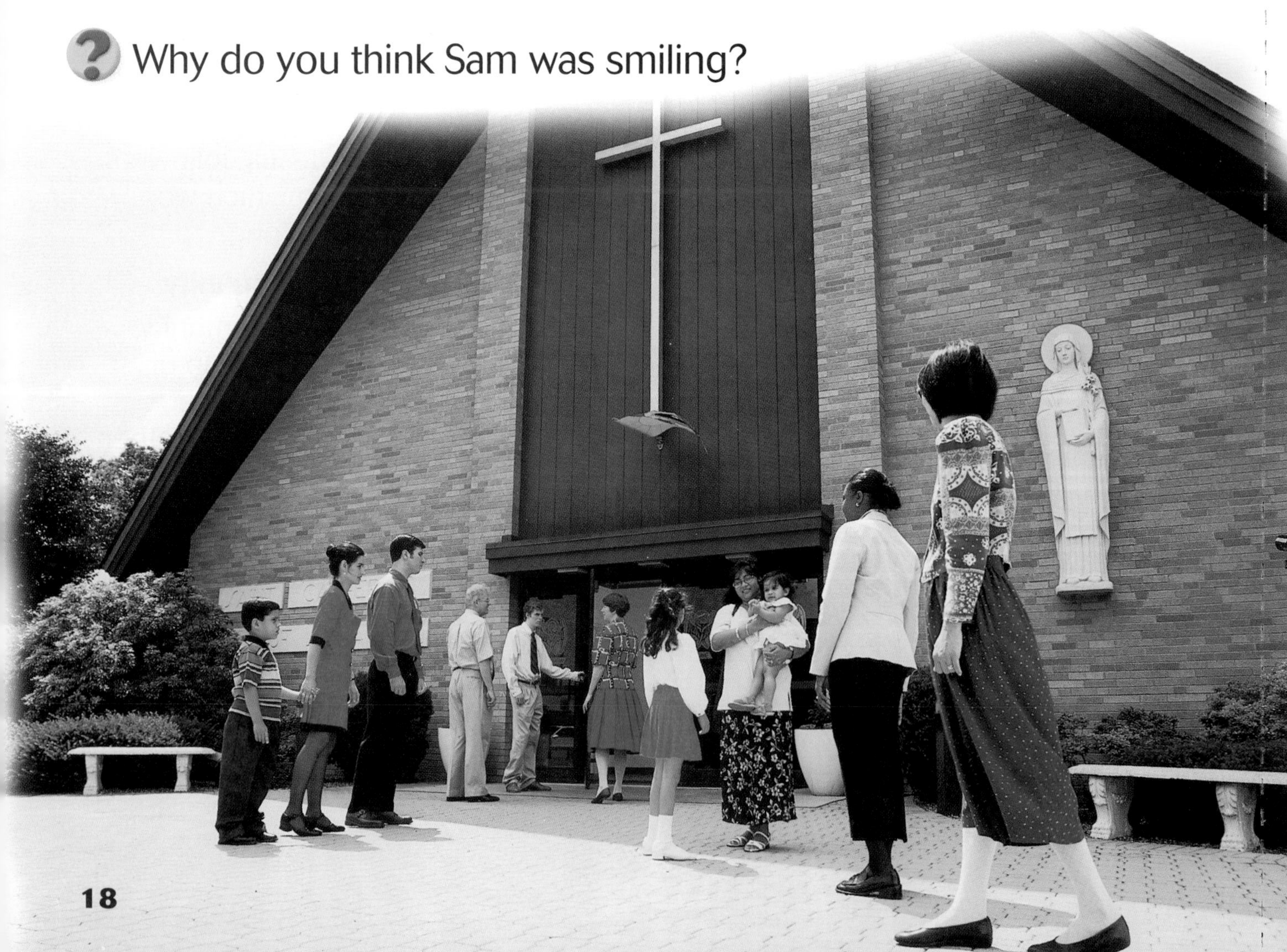

Activities

1. Tell how these people follow Jesus.
Draw a line from each picture to its word.

help

care

listen

pray

2. Write your first name here.

How can we show that we are Catholics?

Prayer Celebration

The Sign of the Cross

We use a special sign to show that we belong to the Catholic Church. Say the words and use your right hand to make the Sign of the Cross.

In the name of the Father,

and of the Son,

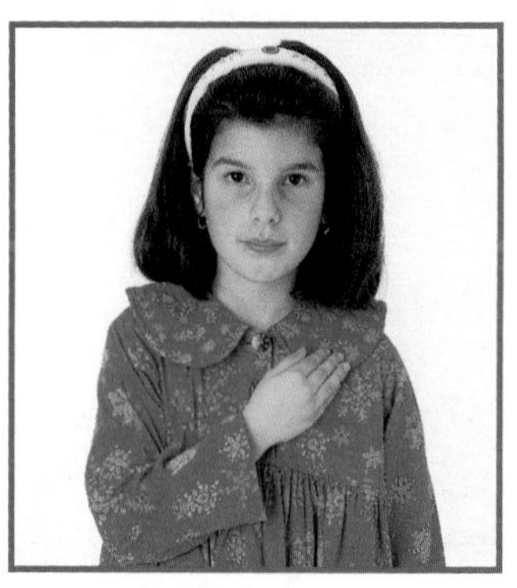

and of the Holy

Spirit.

Amen.

Getting ready for Chapter 2

A choice of things to do at home

We Gather to Celebrate Mass

In this chapter your child will learn that the church building is where the community gathers to celebrate Mass. Like the house or the apartment you live in, where your family and friends come together on happy or sad occasions, the church is a building where our faith family gathers. Your child will also learn about objects found in church. These objects, such as the crucifix and the altar table, help us pray and celebrate Mass, which is a time to thank and bless God.

Dinner table talk

While sitting at your table one night this week, try naming objects you see in your church, beginning with each letter of the alphabet from **A** to **W**.

Cause for celebration

Discuss celebrations with your child and help your child draw a picture of a favorite family occasion, such as a birthday or Christmas celebration.

"Here's the church..."

Do you know the fingerplay "Here's the church, here's the steeple, open the doors and see all the people"? If you know it, teach it to your child and have your child teach it to someone else. If you don't know it, find someone to teach it to you first. Then teach it to your child.

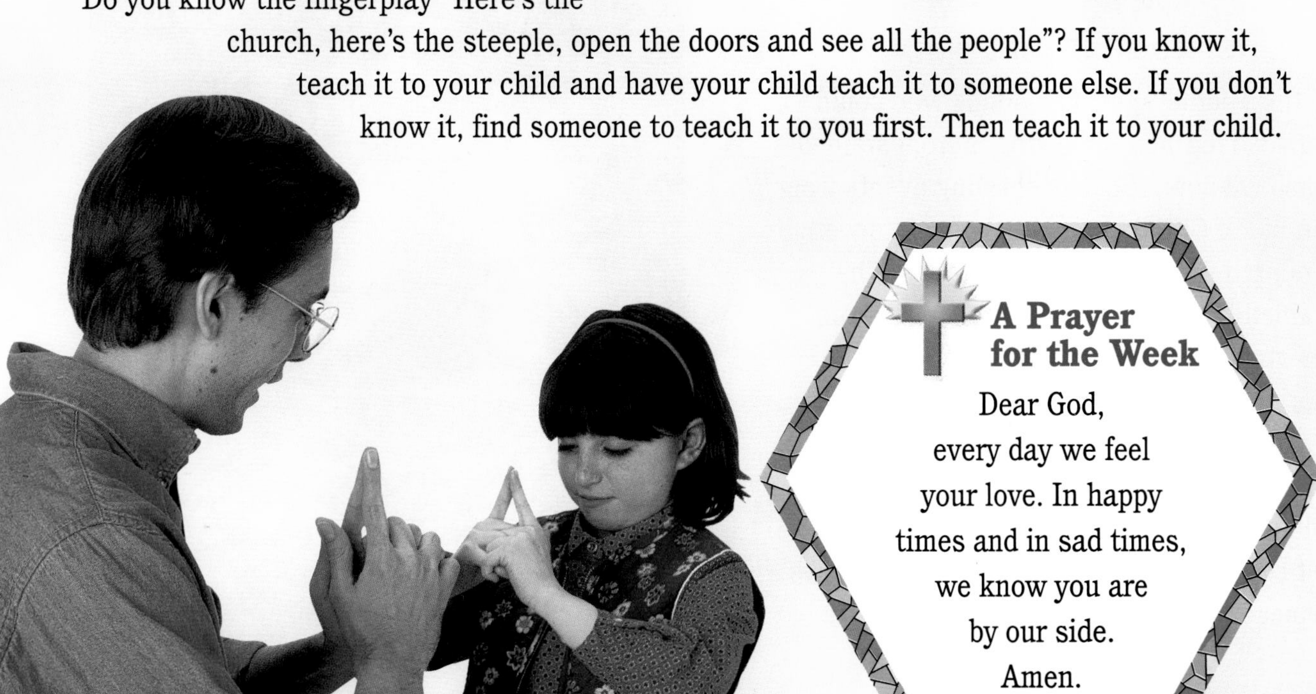

A Prayer for the Week

Dear God,
every day we feel
your love. In happy
times and in sad times,
we know you are
by our side.
Amen.

FAMILY TIME

Something to Do . . .

On Sunday

Arrive at church early. Notice how the area around the altar is decorated. Watch to see what is put on the altar as the priest celebrates Mass.

Through the Week

Set up a prayer table with a cloth, Bible, candle, and plant. Read Bible stories to each other.

Visit Our Web Site

www.blestarewe.com

Something to Know About . . .

Our Heritage in Art

In the Middle Ages, Christians who could not read learned Bible stories from stained-glass windows. Scenes showing events from the life of Christ and stories of saints were rendered in beautiful colored glass. The stained-glass window shown here is from Chartres Cathedral in France. It tells the story of Noah and the Flood.

Your church may have stained-glass windows, too. Check to see what stories are told in the windows of your church. If you're not certain what the stained-glass windows depict ask a member of your parish staff.

Something to Think About . . .

Giving Thanks to God

Let us give thanks to the Lord our God.
Eucharistic Prayer

"Thank God!" is an expression that is very popular. You might hear someone say, "We just made it on time, thank God" or "Thank God I didn't oversleep this morning." Even though we say it often, do we really mean it? How often does your family thank God for all the good things you have? How often do you thank one another for being part of your family? Being **grateful** feels **great**! When you go to church to celebrate Mass, do you remember to give thanks to God?

2 We Gather to Celebrate Mass

When you gather in my name, I am with you.

Based on Matthew 18:20

Share

Catholics gather together in church.
Look at these churches.
How are they alike?
How are they different?

Circle the cross on each church. Then follow the dots to draw the cross in the middle of the page.

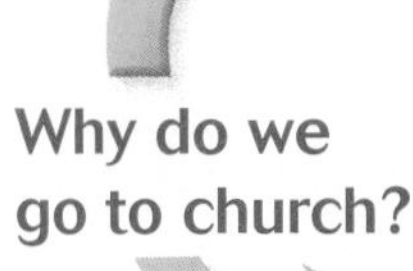

Why do we go to church?

Hear & Believe

We Gather Together

Each week our Catholic community, or **parish**, gathers to celebrate **Mass**. We pray together in our parish **church**. We thank and bless God for giving us Jesus. We ask God to bless us.

The Mass begins with a song. Then the priest and people pray these prayers.

Priest: In the name of the Father, and of the Son, and of the Holy Spirit.

People: Amen.

Priest: The grace and peace of God our Father and the Lord Jesus Christ be with you.

People: And also with you.

Introductory Rites

The Greeting

The priest begins the greeting with the Sign of the Cross. He says the words and we make the sign with our right hand. Then the priest prays that God will bless us with peace. We ask God to bless the priest.

Our Church Teaches

When we gather in our parish church, Jesus is with us. He is with us when we pray with our church community. He is with us at Mass in a special way. Jesus is with us when we thank and bless God who is our Father.

We Believe

The church building is the place where the parish community gathers. Mass is celebrated in the parish church.

Faith Words

parish
A parish is a community of Jesus' followers who belong to the same local Catholic church.

How can we take part in our parish?

Respond

Maria's Parish

Every Sunday, Maria goes to church with her family. She belongs to Saint Ann's parish. Maria likes to sing and pray with her church community. She likes to see her friends. She likes to hear about ways her parish helps people. Maria is proud to belong to Saint Ann's parish.

What do you like about your parish?

Activity

Write the name of your parish church.

Inside a Catholic Church

Parish churches look different on the outside. But they have many things the same on the inside. These things help us to pray. They help us to celebrate Mass. Here are some of the things in Maria's church.

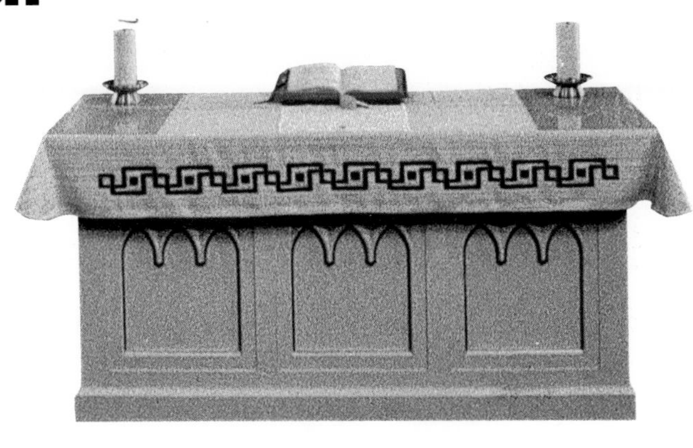

altar table

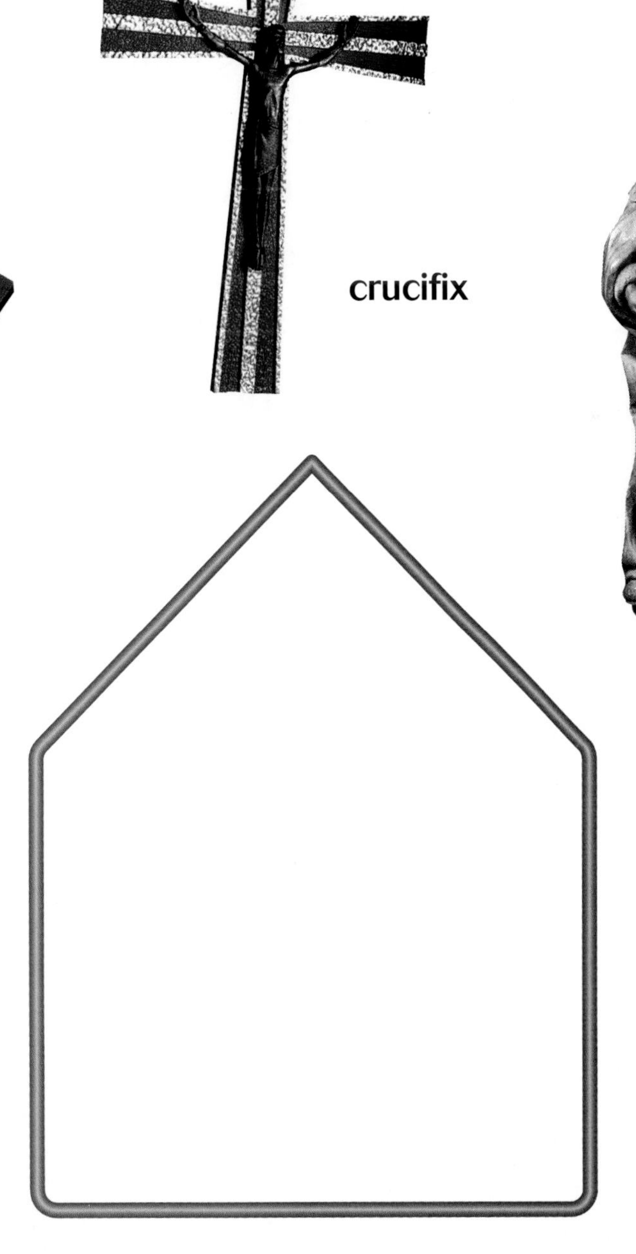

crucifix

statue

baptismal font

Activity

Draw something else that is in your church.

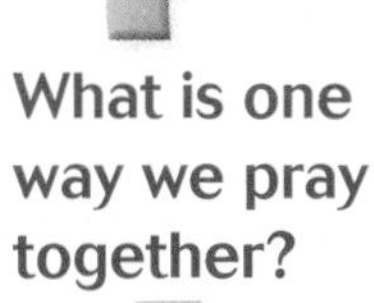

What is one way we pray together?

Prayer Celebration

Blessed Be God

God loves us and gives us many gifts. These gifts are called blessings. Think of a special gift that God has given you. Then pray this **blessing** prayer together. Add the name of your gift, or blessing, to the prayer.

Leader: For our parish community,

All: Blessed be God.

Leader: For our families and friends,

All: Blessed be God.

Leader: For the gift of Jesus,

All: Blessed be God.

Child: For (name a gift),

All: Blessed be God.

Getting ready for Chapter 3

A choice of things to do at home

God's Word Teaches Us

This chapter teaches that the readings at Mass come from a special book called the Bible. The books of the Bible preserve the story of God's care for his people. God speaks to us when we listen to his word at Mass. To highlight the presence of God's word in your family, take time this week to read from your Bible.

Bible story update

Tell a Bible story that parallels with an event that happened in your family. For example, the story of the flood could be paralleled with a flood in your basement. Tell about the event and explain the parallel.

Favorite story

Do you have a favorite story from the Bible? If so, share it with your child and tell why you like it. Then ask your child to tell about a favorite Bible story. Find out why your child thinks the story is special.

Drawing Bible stories

Help your child draw a picture of a favorite Bible story and write a title for the drawing. Place the picture on the refrigerator or in another place where your child will see it throughout the week.

A Prayer for the Week

We thank you for
giving us the Bible, Lord.
Help us learn how you want
us to speak and act
by reading your
holy word.
Amen.

FAMILY TIME

Something to Do . . .

On Sunday

Listen to the Gospel story and the homily. On your way home, invite family members to talk about what they would have said if they were the priest.

Through the Week

Try to relate the Gospel reading and the homily to your daily life.

Visit Our Web Site

www.blestarewe.com

Something to Think About . . .

The Power of God's Word

Then Philip opened his mouth and, beginning with this scripture passage, he proclaimed Jesus to him.

Acts 8:35

There is a story in the Acts of the Apostles about an Ethiopian man who is reading the book of the prophet Isaiah. The apostle, Philip, asks him if he understands what he is reading. The Ethiopian answers that he needs someone to help him. Philip explains to him how Jesus was the fulfillment of Isaiah's prophecies. The man asks to be baptized. The word of God and Philip's explanation changed the Ethiopian's life.

We already know the story of Jesus, thanks to the writers of the New Testament. This week try to remember the excitement of the man who heard about Jesus for the first time. Try to live as a family who has truly heard the Good News!

Something to Know About . . .

Our Heritage in Art

During the Middle Ages, monks from northern Africa, the Near East, and Europe made books by hand-copying every word. European monks became well known for copying the Bible many times. Painters, called illuminators, illustrated the Bibles using bright colors and lavish gold to create beautiful pictures called illuminations.

These Bibles are treasures. They represent the monks' love for the word of God. They are unique gifts from the monks to us. They are extraordinary works of art, and holy keepsakes of our Catholic tradition. The page shown is from *The Book of Kells* and contains the genealogy of Christ. This book is on display at Trinity College in Dublin, Ireland.

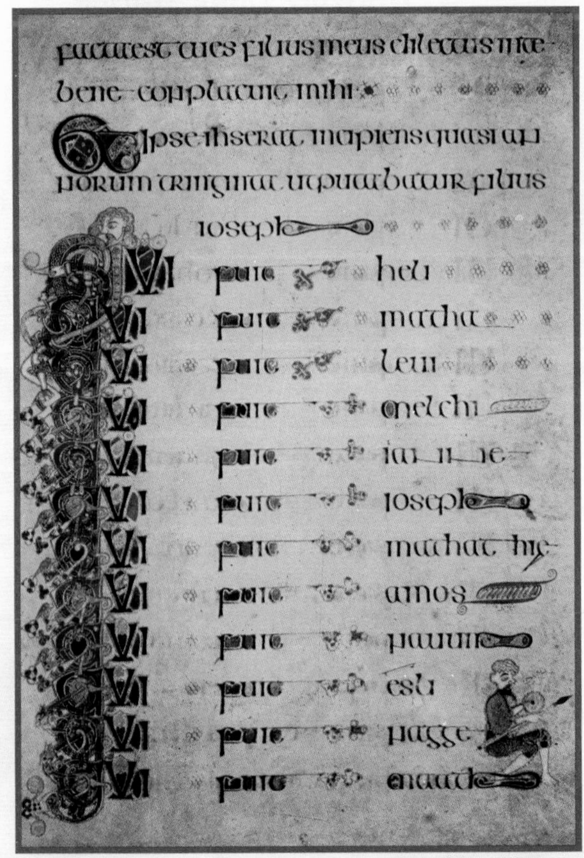

3 God's Word Teaches Us

Hear God's word and keep it.
Then you will be blessed.

Based on Luke 11:28

Share

We learn in many ways.
Look at the pictures.
Tell how each child learns.
Circle your favorite way to learn.

How can we learn about God?

Learning About God

A man was riding home to Africa in his chariot. He was reading a story about God in his Bible. Philip saw him and ran next to the chariot.

"Do you understand the meaning of the story?" Philip asked.

"No," the man said. "I need help."

Philip got into the chariot. He taught the man about God's love. The man also learned about Jesus. From then on, the man followed Jesus. He became a member of the Church.

Based on Acts 8:26–40

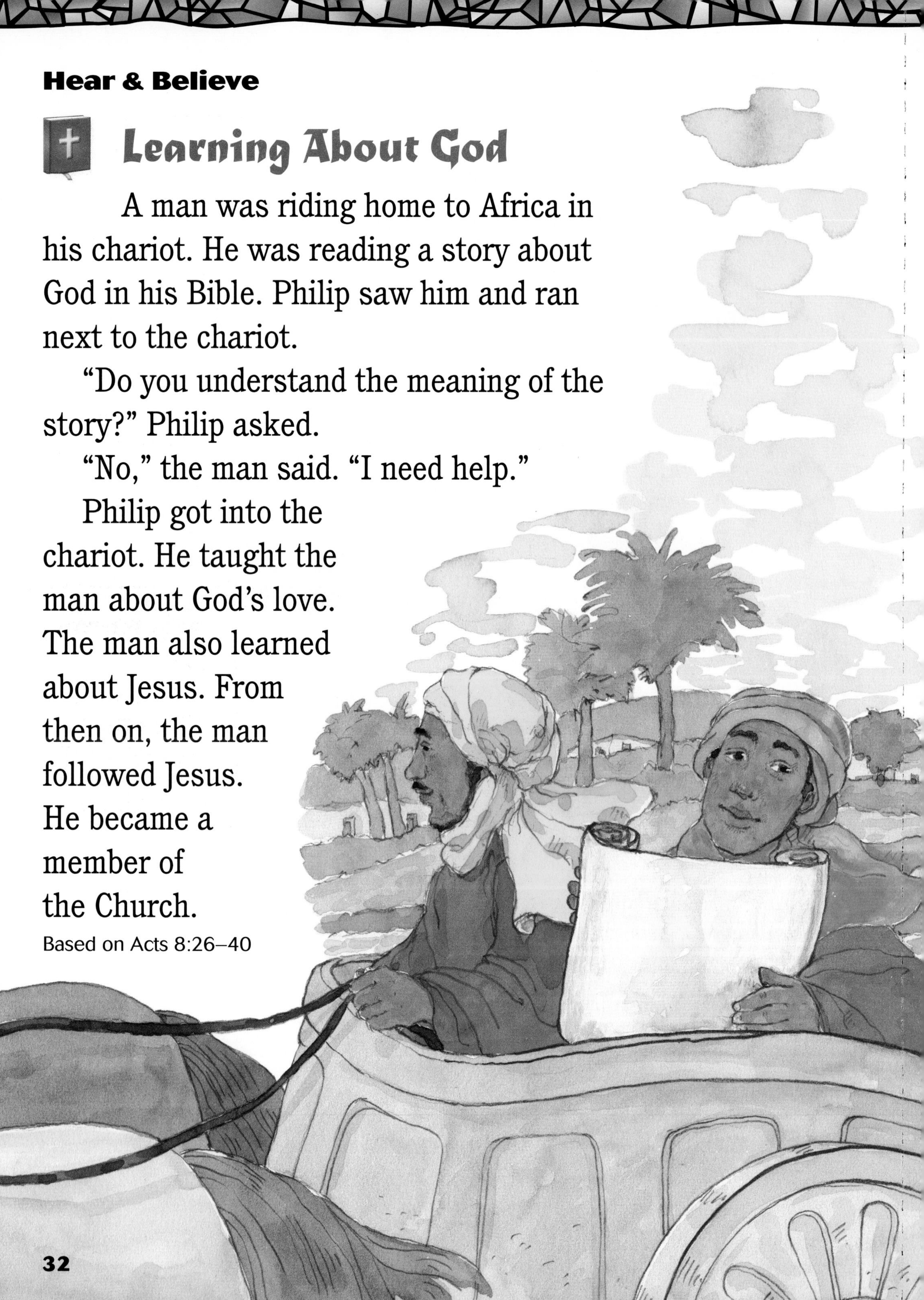

How God Speaks to Us

God speaks to us in many ways. One way is through a special book called the **Bible**. Philip helped the man in the chariot understand the Bible. We listen to readings from the Bible at Mass. The priest or deacon talks about the readings. He helps us understand what God is saying.

We Believe

God speaks to us through the Bible. The readings at Mass teach us about God's love and help us learn how to follow Jesus.

Our Church Teaches

The Bible is the word of God. The stories in the Bible teach us about God. We learn about God's love for people. We learn about their love for God. When we listen to the word of God, we believe we are listening to God.

Faith Words

Bible
The Bible is the written word of God. God chose special people to write the Bible.

How can we hear God's word?

Respond

Saint Augustine

When Augustine was young, he often got into trouble. He did many selfish things.

One day, Augustine was sitting in the garden. He was very sad because his friend had died. Then he heard a neighbor's child sing, "Take and read!" Augustine saw his mother's Bible on the table next to him. He started to read it. He heard God speaking to him.

Augustine listened carefully to God's word. He changed his life. He stopped doing selfish things. He began to follow Jesus.

? How did the word of God change Augustine?

Activities

1. Read each pair of sentences.
   Draw a line under the true sentence.

At Mass I  God's word.

I 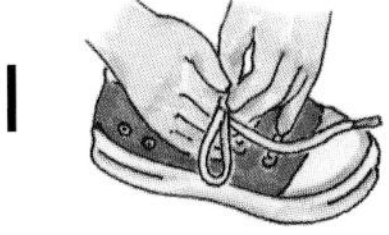 at Mass.

In the story Philip ate an  .

The man from Africa joined the  .

The  tells us about God's love.

Augustine read the  and did not follow Jesus.

---

2. How can you hear God's word?
   Trace the dots to find out.

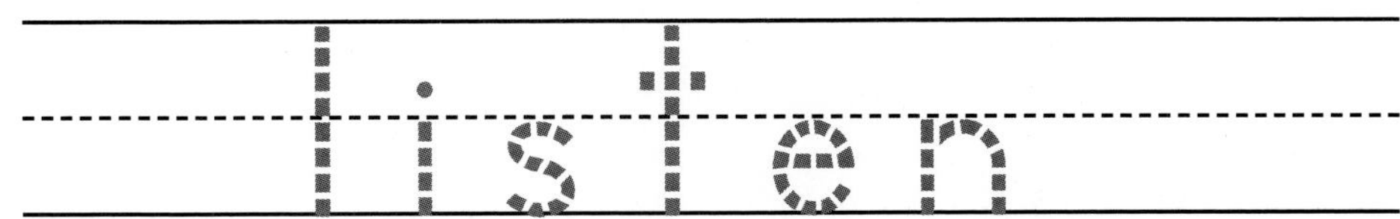

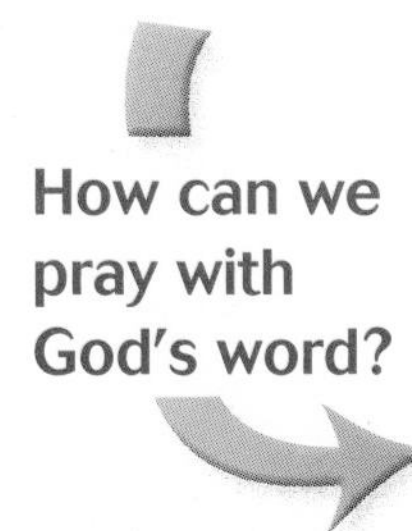

How can we pray with God's word?

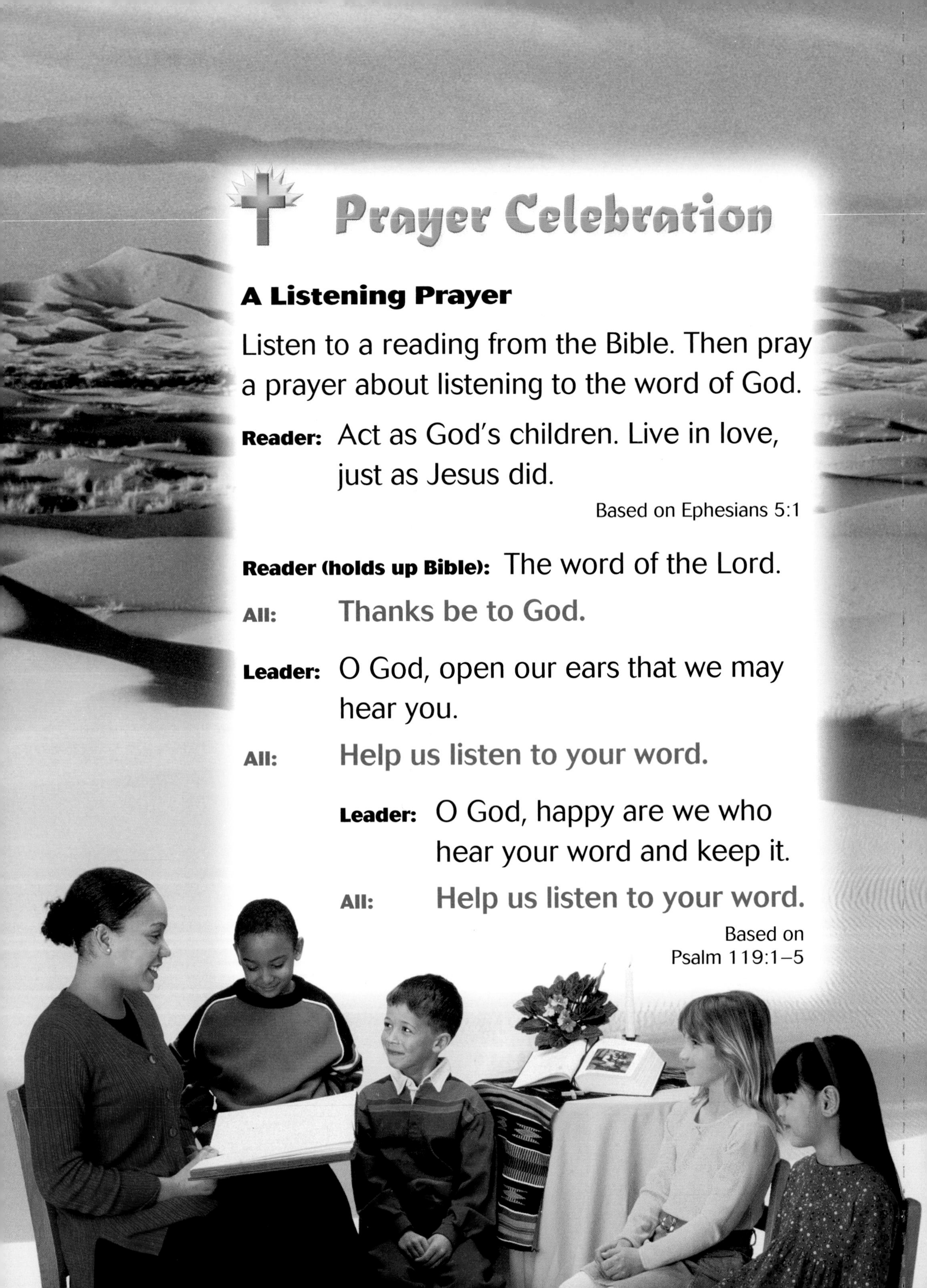

Prayer Celebration

A Listening Prayer

Listen to a reading from the Bible. Then pray a prayer about listening to the word of God.

Reader: Act as God's children. Live in love, just as Jesus did.

Based on Ephesians 5:1

Reader (holds up Bible): The word of the Lord.

All: **Thanks be to God.**

Leader: O God, open our ears that we may hear you.

All: **Help us listen to your word.**

Leader: O God, happy are we who hear your word and keep it.

All: **Help us listen to your word.**

Based on Psalm 119:1–5

Getting ready for Chapter 4

A choice of things to do at home

We Give Praise to God

Learning to offer prayers of praise to God is the focus of this chapter. The children will come to understand that the church building is a special place to pray and that we praise God when we celebrate Mass. The prayers we learn find an echo in the praise we give to our family members.

Make a badge

Together, create a "badge of praise." Give it to a family member who shows a praiseworthy quality, such as bravery, patience, or helpfulness. Each day, give it to another family member. Continue until everyone in the family has received the badge of praise.

Take a walk

Take a walk with your child and look for praiseworthy things in your community. Are the streets clean? Do buses have lifts for wheelchairs? Is there a bike path? Are street signs easy to spot? Find three things you are proud of in your community.

Collect family symbols

With your child, set up a table or shelf with objects that symbolize the goodness or talents of your family. Possible examples of objects include a cookbook, an artwork, or a sport's team photo. Then make a sign saying, "Our family gives praise."

A Prayer for the Week

Dear Lord,
we praise you for all
your wonderful works.
We give you glory
for your goodness.
Amen.

FAMILY TIME

Something to Do . . .

On Sunday

The Gloria of the Mass is a prayer full of praise for God. How many expressions of praise do you hear in that prayer?

Through the Week

Look for the good things the people in your family do. When you see them doing something good, praise them.

Visit Our Web Site

www.blestarewe.com

Something to Think About . . .

Prayers of Praise

Praise him, sun and moon;
praise him, all you shining stars.
Psalm 148:3

Praising God was very important to the writers of the psalms. They wrote many prayers dedicated to praising God. It may be harder than we think to praise God. We are used to asking and thanking God for things. We often put ourselves and our needs at the center of our prayer. But when we praise God, we make God the center of our prayer. Because we live in a world that keeps telling us that we are the most important persons around, it is sometimes difficult for us to give God praise.

Something to Know About . . . Our Heritage

Graffiti is something we usually think of as unsightly and messy. However, the early Christians in Rome created paintings and wrote messages of respect and remembrance in the form of blessings on the catacomb walls by the tombs of the martyrs. After a while, the "graffiti" became standardized. Messages from one Christian to another were sent in a code known only to other believers. Certain symbols were used over and over again and have taken on meanings for all time.

4 We Give Praise to God

I will praise God with all my heart.

Based on Psalm 111:1

Share

We praise others when they are good. We say, "Great job!" We say, "You are wonderful!" Look at the picture. Tell how someone is showing praise.

Draw how your face looks when someone praises you.

Why do we praise God?

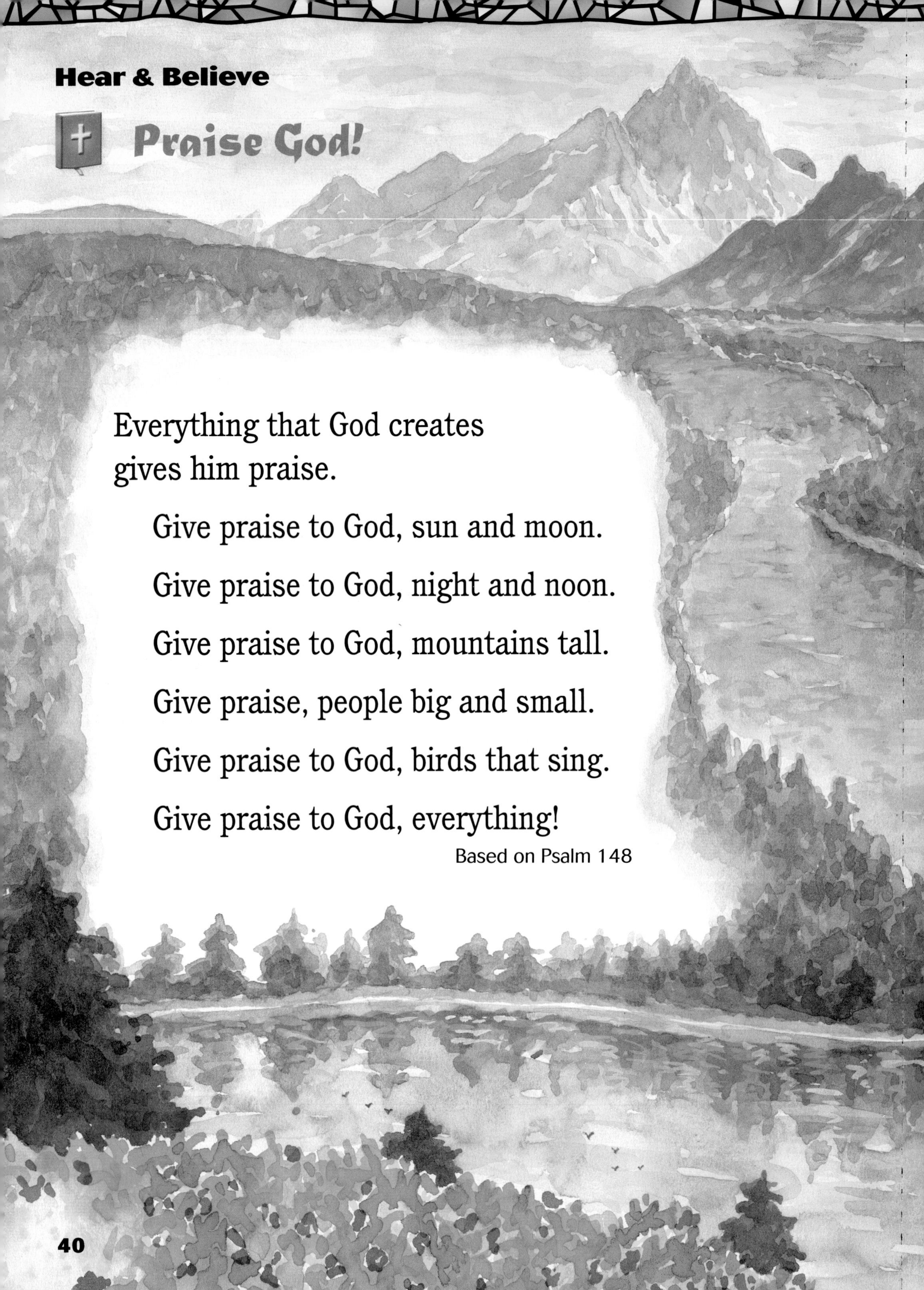

Praise God!

Everything that God creates
gives him praise.

Give praise to God, sun and moon.
Give praise to God, night and noon.
Give praise to God, mountains tall.
Give praise, people big and small.
Give praise to God, birds that sing.
Give praise to God, everything!

Based on Psalm 148

One Kind of Prayer

God is wonderful! God is good! Everything God made gives him **praise**. Praise is one kind of **prayer**. When we pray, we listen to and talk to God. Some prayers of praise are in the Bible. We can praise God anywhere. We can praise God any time.

Our Church Teaches

The church building is a special place to pray. We praise God with our church community at Mass. We can visit a church at other times, too. We can pray silently, knowing that Jesus is with us.

We Believe

We listen to and talk to God when we pray. A church is a special building where we give praise to God.

Faith Words

praise
Praise is a kind of prayer that celebrates God's goodness.

prayer
Prayer is listening to and talking to God.

How do Catholics praise God?

Respond

Glory to God

Joey learned about God even before he started school. He learned that God loves us. He learned that all good things come from God.

Now Joey is in the first grade. Each week he goes to Mass with his family. They praise God with their parish community. Sometimes they sing a prayer called the **Gloria**. Joey's favorite words are "Glory to God in the highest, and peace to his people on earth" (The Order of Mass).

Why do you think Joey likes to sing the Gloria?

Activities

1. Learn to sign the words "Sing praise to the Lord."

sing praise Lord

2. Color the picture. What do the words say?

1 2 3 4 5 6

Glory to God

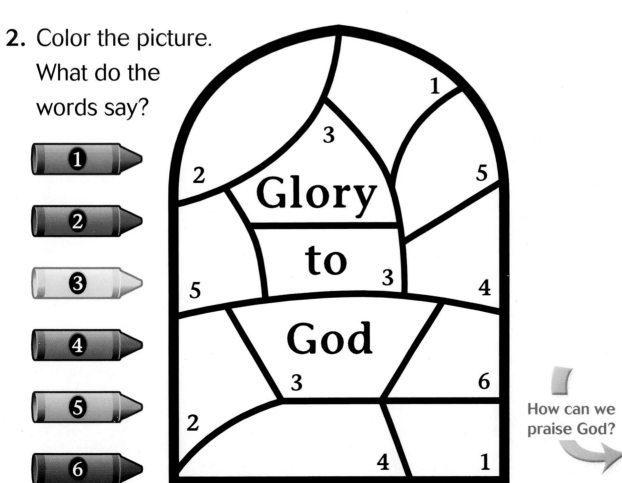

How can we praise God?

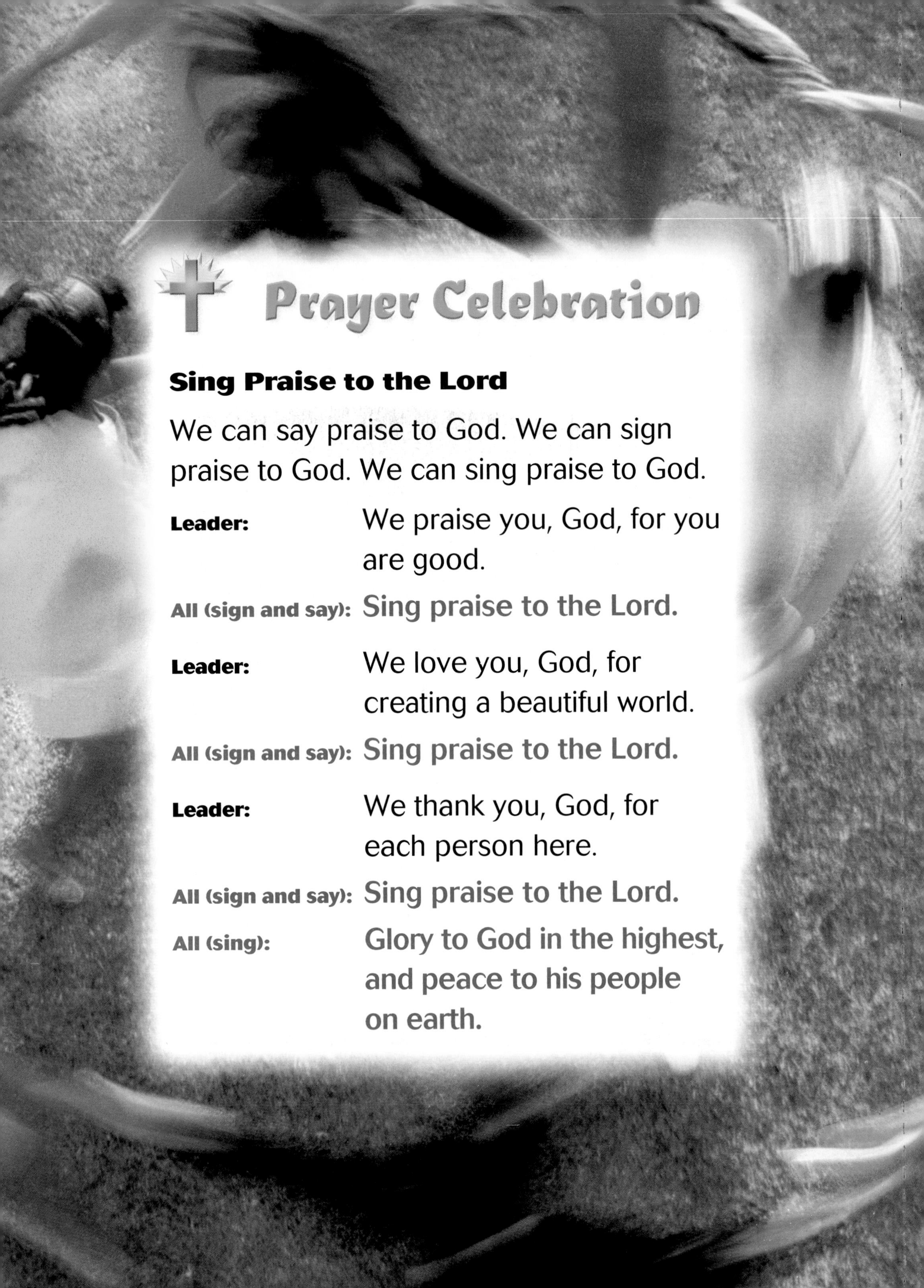

Prayer Celebration

Sing Praise to the Lord

We can say praise to God. We can sign praise to God. We can sing praise to God.

Leader: We praise you, God, for you are good.

All (sign and say): Sing praise to the Lord.

Leader: We love you, God, for creating a beautiful world.

All (sign and say): Sing praise to the Lord.

Leader: We thank you, God, for each person here.

All (sign and say): Sing praise to the Lord.

All (sing): Glory to God in the highest, and peace to his people on earth.

The Ugly Duckling

Once upon a time a mother duck adopted a baby swan. She cared for it along with her own ducklings.

The baby swan was not as cute as the ducklings. It had big feet and a long neck. It was very clumsy. So the ducklings made fun of the swan. They thought it was just an "ugly duckling." This made the little swan very sad.

But swans grow up to be big, beautiful, graceful birds. That is just what the baby swan did. Then the ducklings knew that they had made a big mistake.

What mistake did the ducklings make?

Think About It

Some people are like the baby swan.
Some people are like the ducklings.

Use a ✔ to show what you think.

- ☐ It is hard to see good in some people.
- ☐ I like it when people make fun of me.
- ☐ Some people are not good on the inside.
- ☐ Everyone has beauty on the inside.

Learn About It

God made you good and beautiful. Some people do not see the goodness and beauty inside of you. But they are there. So believe in your goodness and beauty.

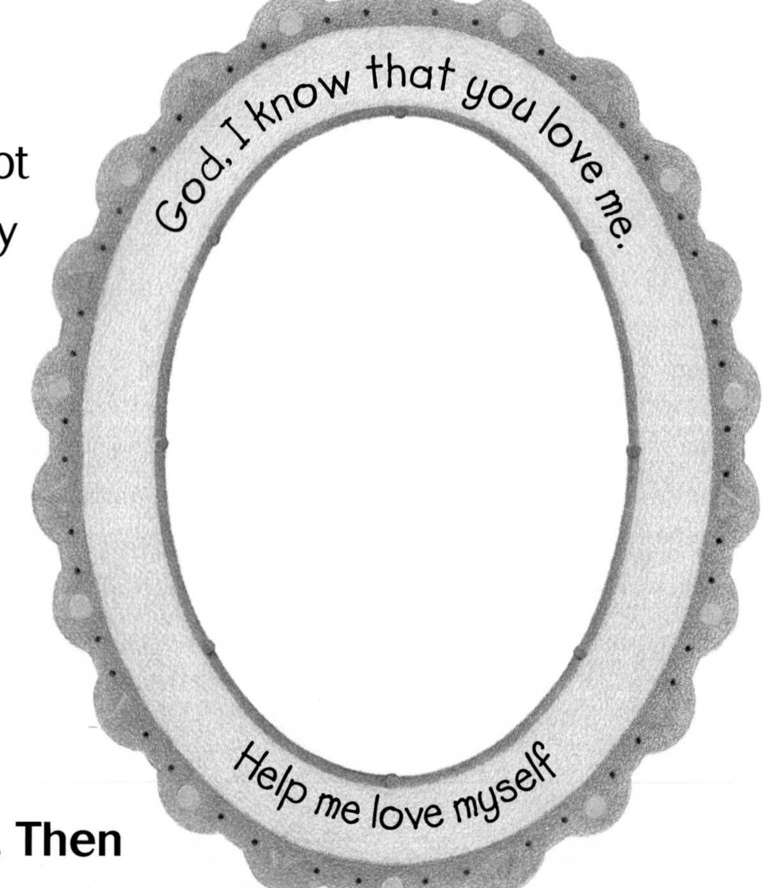

God, I know that you love me.
Help me love myself

Do Something About It

Love yourself. Then you will be able to love others.

Draw a picture of yourself. Then pray the prayer around your picture.

UNIT 1

Organizer

Look at the church windows.
Read the directions below.

1. We belong to Jesus' Church.
   Find the window that says CHURCH.
   Color the top blue.

2. We gather to celebrate Mass.
   Find the window that says MASS.
   Color the top green.

3. God's word teaches us.
   Find the window that says GOD'S WORD.
   Color the top red.

4. We give praise to God.
   Find the window that says PRAISE.
   Color the top yellow.

UNIT 1

Review

A Look at the words on the tree.
Write the best word to complete each sentence.

followers

Father

pray

Mass

1. A church is a building where Catholics ______________ gather to ______________.

2. The parish is a community of Jesus' ______________.

3. We come to the parish church to ______________ celebrate ______________.

4. Jesus is with us when we thank and bless ______________ God, our ______________.

UNIT 1 Review

B Draw a line to the word that completes each sentence.

1. Jesus is like a good •	• **Catholic Church.**
2. Our church is the •	• **shepherd.**
3. A group of people who belong together is a •	• **Catholics.**
4. The Sign of the Cross shows that we are •	• **community.**

C Circle the correct answer.

1. The Bible is the word of God.	Yes	No
2. God speaks to us through the Bible.	Yes	No
3. We listen to the word of God at ball games.	Yes	No
4. We listen to the word of God at Mass.	Yes	No

UNIT 1

Review

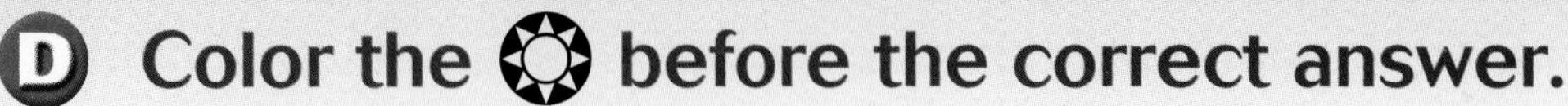

D Color the ❂ before the correct answer.

1. Praise is one kind of __.

❂ **food** ❂ **prayer**

2. When we pray we listen and talk to __.

❂ **God** ❂ **our pets**

3. Everything God made gives him __.

❂ **money** ❂ **praise**

4. A prayer called the Gloria is sung at __.

❂ **parties** ❂ **Mass**

E Draw pictures of three things that give God praise.

UNIT 2

Our Loving God

Jesus taught us that we are all God's special children. God has given us the gift of his wonderful creation. We thank God for all the gifts we have received.

Children, let us love one another.

Based on 1 John 4:7

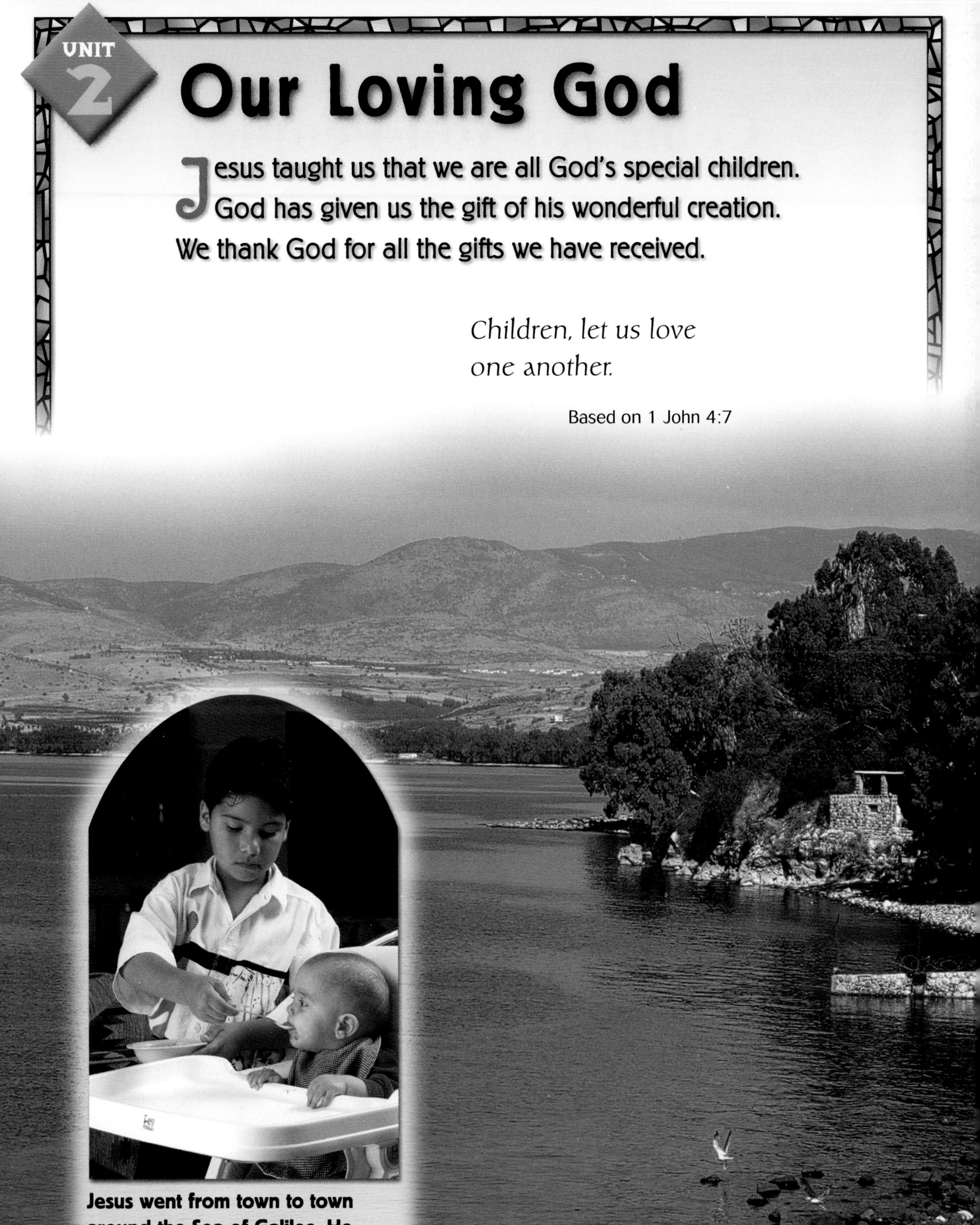

Jesus went from town to town around the Sea of Galilee. He taught people about our loving God. When we show our love for others we follow Jesus.

UNIT
2
SONG

Come All You People

Words and Music by Alexander Gondo
Arranged by John L. Bell
Come all you peo - ple, come and praise your Mak - er,
Come all you peo - ple, come and praise your Mak - er,
Come all you peo - ple, come and praise your Mak - er,
3
Last time
Come now and wor - ship the Lord.

Getting ready for Chapter 5

A choice of things to do at home

God Is Our Loving Father

We look around us at all that God created, and see signs of a loving Father. God not only gave us the gift of life, but continues to care for us. In this chapter the children will learn about God the Father's love for us and for all creation. They will also learn that God gives each of us a guardian angel to protect and guide us.

I love you

Encourage members of your family to include the phrase "I love you" in their conversations. Use it when you talk to each other on the phone, when you leave for school or work in the morning, and before you go to bed at night.

Pick a card, any card

Use the fours, threes, twos, and aces from a deck of cards. Shuffle the cards and put them face down in a pack. Have each person in your family take a card and name different things God has given us. For example, if a four is turned over, name four things; if an ace is turned over, name one thing.

Our family cares

Create a list of ways your family shows that you are partners with God in caring for the earth. For example, do you recycle paper, cans, and glass?

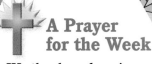

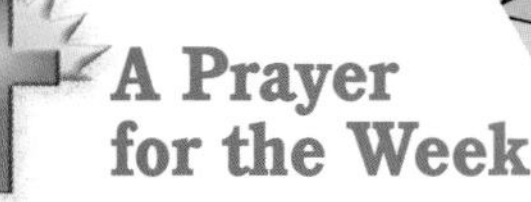

We thank and praise
you God our Creator, for the
wonderful world you have created.
Give us the strength to be
your partners in caring
for your world.
Amen.

FAMILY TIME

Something to Do . . .

On Sunday

At Mass we give thanks for all God's gifts. On the way to church, ask yourselves, "For what gifts are we thankful?"

Through the Week

Spend time outdoors with your family. Notice things that put your family in touch with God's creation.

Visit Our Web Site

www.blestarewe.com

Something to Think About . . .

Remembering God's Goodness

The LORD God then took the man and settled him in the garden of Eden, to cultivate and care for it.

Genesis 2:15

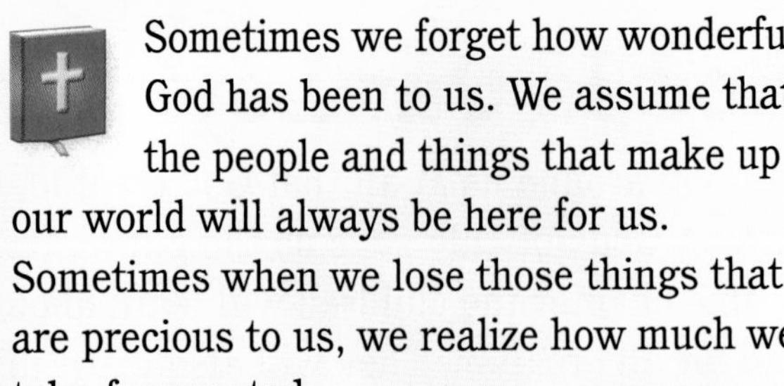

Sometimes we forget how wonderful God has been to us. We assume that the people and things that make up our world will always be here for us. Sometimes when we lose those things that are precious to us, we realize how much we take for granted.

We also live in a society and culture that tells us we need more. We are told that the keys to happiness are more clothes, a bigger house, more toys, and more possessions. Developing a grateful heart begins in a family that believes it is people, not things, that bring true happiness.

Something to Know About . . .

Our Heritage in Science

Many people think there is a conflict between believing in the Bible and believing in evolution. They believe that if God created the world, then evolution could not have taken place. A French Jesuit priest in the early twentieth century tried to help us see God's hand in the scientific universe. Pierre Teilhard de Chardin believed that evolution was the ongoing work of God. He once wrote that he wanted to teach people how to see God everywhere, even in the most hidden places in the world.

5 God Is Our Loving Father

O God, everything you made is wonderful!
Your love will last forever.

Based on Psalm 136:4

Share

God made all things.
All things show God's love.
Look at the picture.
Tell how each thing
shows God's love.

Draw something you like that
shows God's love.

Why did
God make
the world?

Hear & Believe

God Creates the World

God made the 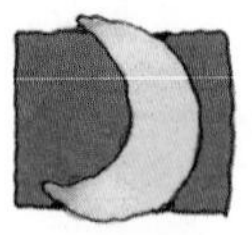 and  at night. God made the  for warmth and light. And on the land, God planted , while in the sky flew  and . The  sprang up from the earth. Sweet  and  came to birth. The  and 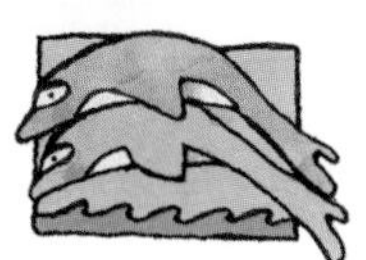 swam in the seas. And on the land were . Soon  and  did appear, with  and ,  and deer.

Based on Genesis 1:1–25

God Creates People

God saw that everything he made was good. Then God made people to be like himself. God told the people to take care of everything. He blessed the people and all that he had made.

Based on Genesis 1:26–31

We Believe

God created all things to show his love for us.

Our Church Teaches

God is our loving Father and **Creator**. God created all things and people out of love. God cares for us and all creation. God gives us each a guardian **angel**. Guardian angels protect and guide us.

Faith Words

Creator
God made everything in the world. God is our Creator.

angel
An angel is a helper or a messenger from God. Guardian angels protect and guide us.

How can we care for God's creation?

Respond

Caring for Creation

Anna often played in her backyard. She really liked the flower garden. Best of all, Anna liked the little statue of Saint Francis. Anna knew that Francis loved everything in the world. He took good care of plants. He was kind to animals. Francis helped people in need.

Anna smiled as she picked up the watering can. "Thank you, God, for making our world," she prayed. Then she began to water the flowers.

How did Anna care for God's creation?

Activities

1. Draw yourself in the heart.

God Loves Me.

God Made Me.

2. Here are some ways we care for God's creation. Draw a line from each way to its matching picture.

Help people in need.

Be kind to animals.

Share God's gifts.

How can we thank God for loving us?

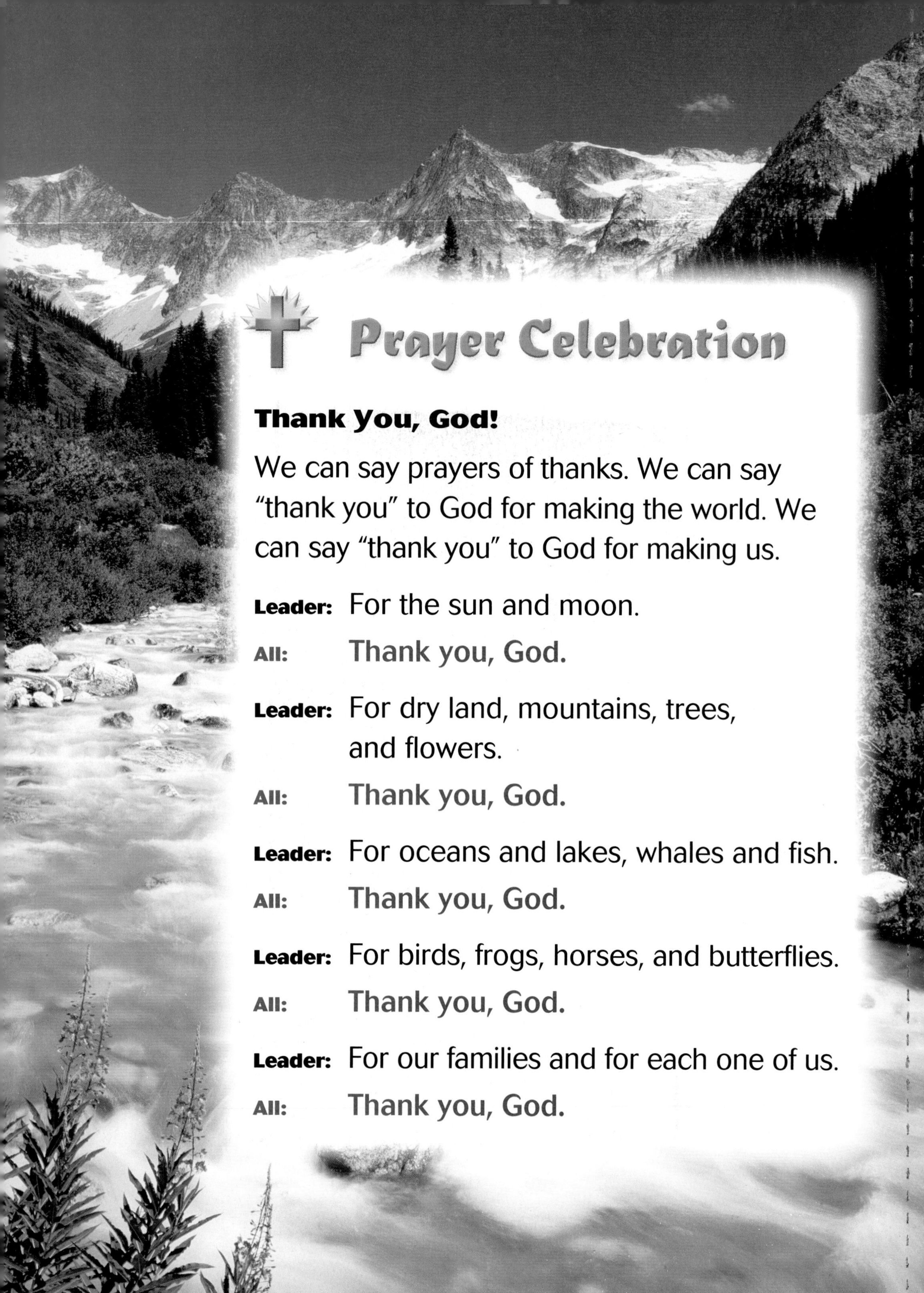

Prayer Celebration

Thank You, God!

We can say prayers of thanks. We can say "thank you" to God for making the world. We can say "thank you" to God for making us.

Leader: For the sun and moon.

All: Thank you, God.

Leader: For dry land, mountains, trees, and flowers.

All: Thank you, God.

Leader: For oceans and lakes, whales and fish.

All: Thank you, God.

Leader: For birds, frogs, horses, and butterflies.

All: Thank you, God.

Leader: For our families and for each one of us.

All: Thank you, God.

Getting ready for Chapter 6

A choice of things to do at home

Baptism Is a Wonderful Gift

We have each received the wonderful gift of Baptism. This chapter discusses Baptism as a celebration of becoming a member of the Christian community and a follower of Jesus Christ. The children will learn that holy water is a sign of our new life with Jesus.

Holy water

If you have holy water in your home, bless your child by making a sign of the cross on his or her forehead. Say the words, "God be with you." Remind your child that God is there to help and that your family is there to listen and to give support.

Water talk

Before dinner, invite your family to wash their hands. During dinner, talk about the many ways your family uses water. Be sure to serve water with your meal.

Remembering your baptism

Was everyone in your family baptized in the same church? If not, tell why each church was chosen. Make or mark a map showing the faith journey of your family. Label each place with the name of the church.

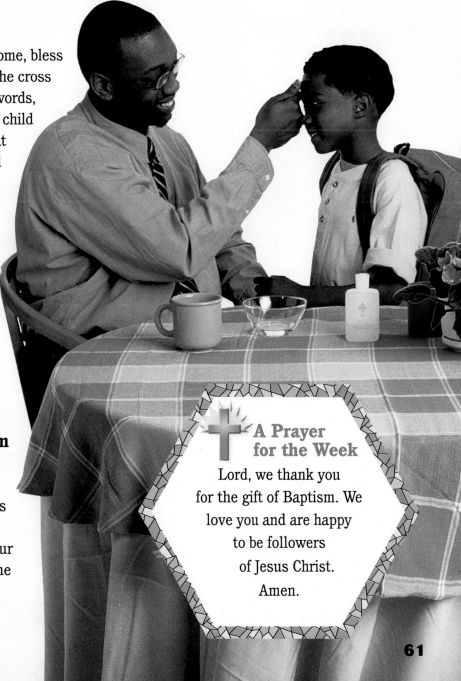

A Prayer for the Week

Lord, we thank you
for the gift of Baptism. We
love you and are happy
to be followers
of Jesus Christ.
Amen.

Something to Do . . .

On Sunday

Listen to the words of the creed. This prayer states what we believe as Catholics. Discuss the meaning of a phrase from the creed on the way home.

Through the Week

Practice living as a follower of Christ. Help someone at school or at work.

Visit Our Web Site

www.blestarewe.com

Something to Think About . . .

The Purpose of Baptism

The Christian community welcomes you.
Rite of Baptism

In addition to cleansing, the waters of baptism initiate the person into the community of faith. We become citizens of our country when we are born, but we do not get to exercise all of our rights until we are older. When we are baptized, we become members of Christ's Church and part of its circle of caring. Baptism gives us the right to the other sacraments, and it gives us our true vocation, which is to be a follower of Christ.

Whatever our job is and whatever our way of life, we should always remember that our first responsibility is to show that a follower of Christ is loving and helpful.

Something to Know About . . .

Our Heritage in Art

Places where people are baptized are called *baptisteries*. In some churches they are very elaborate and beautiful. Some baptisteries have been constructed separate from the church building itself and are richly decorated.

One of the oldest baptisteries is in Rome at the Basilica of St. John Lateran. Construction began during the reign of Constantine, the fourth-century emperor.

One of the most beautiful baptisteries stands opposite the Florence Cathedral in Italy. Legend has it that Michelangelo called the baptistery's third pair of bronze doors "the Gates of Paradise."

6 Baptism Is a Wonderful Gift

The Church welcomes us with joy.
We belong to Jesus Christ.

Based on the Rite of Baptism

Share

We say "Welcome!" in many ways.
We put up signs. We bring gifts.
We shake hands. We share food.

Draw your own welcome picture.

How does the Church welcome us?

Baptism Welcomes Us

Each time a person joins the Catholic Church, there is a welcome celebration.

The priest or deacon says, "The Christian community welcomes you with great joy. In its name I claim you for Christ our **Savior** by the sign of his cross."

During the celebration, the priest or deacon places the person in water three times. He says, "I baptize you in the name of the Father, and of the Son, and of the Holy Spirit."

Rite of Baptism

The Celebration of Baptism

Jesus invites us to belong to the Catholic Church. The Church welcomes new members in a special celebration. We call this celebration **Baptism**.

Our Church Teaches

In Baptism the priest or deacon pours holy water over us. Sometimes he places the new church member in the water. The holy water is a sign of belonging. We receive the gift of new life in Jesus. We belong to the Catholic Church. We are followers of Jesus **Christ**. We are called **Christians.**

We Believe

Through Baptism we become members of Christ's Church.

Faith Words

Baptism

Baptism is a celebration of welcome into the Catholic community.

Christ

Christ is another name for Jesus. It tells us that he was sent by God to save all people.

How do Christians try to live?

Respond

Blessed Kateri Tekakwitha

Kateri was a young Native American girl. A terrible sickness came to her village. Her parents died. The sickness left Kateri almost blind.

One day, a priest came. He told everyone about Jesus. Kateri wanted to be a follower of Jesus. She wanted to belong to the Church.

Kateri celebrated Baptism. She prayed to God every day. She helped people in need.

After Kateri died, many other Native Americans joined the Church. They wanted to live like Kateri and follow Jesus.

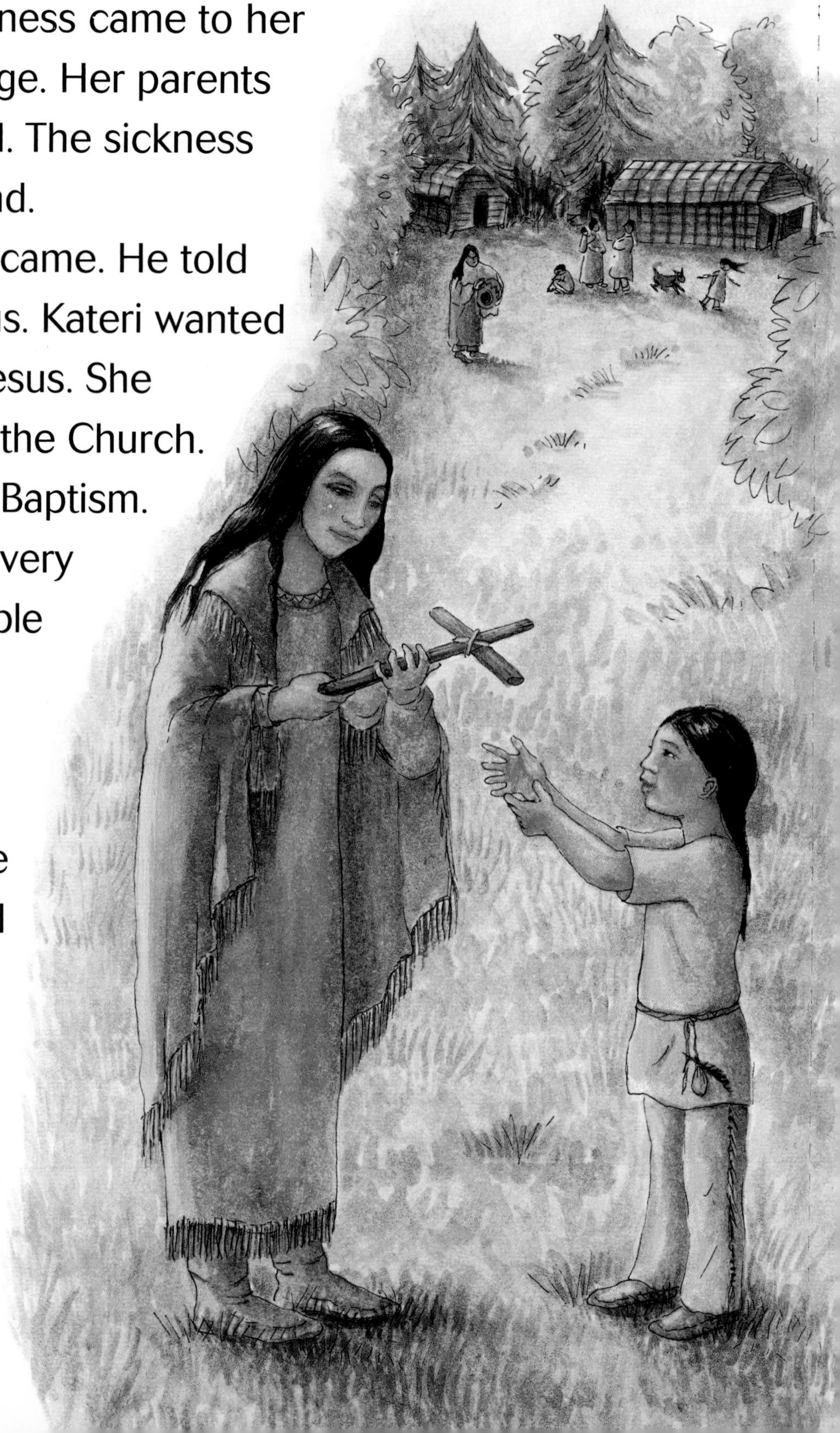

? Why did Kateri want to be baptized?

Activity

Circle the pictures that show people acting as Christians.

How can we celebrate our new life with Jesus?

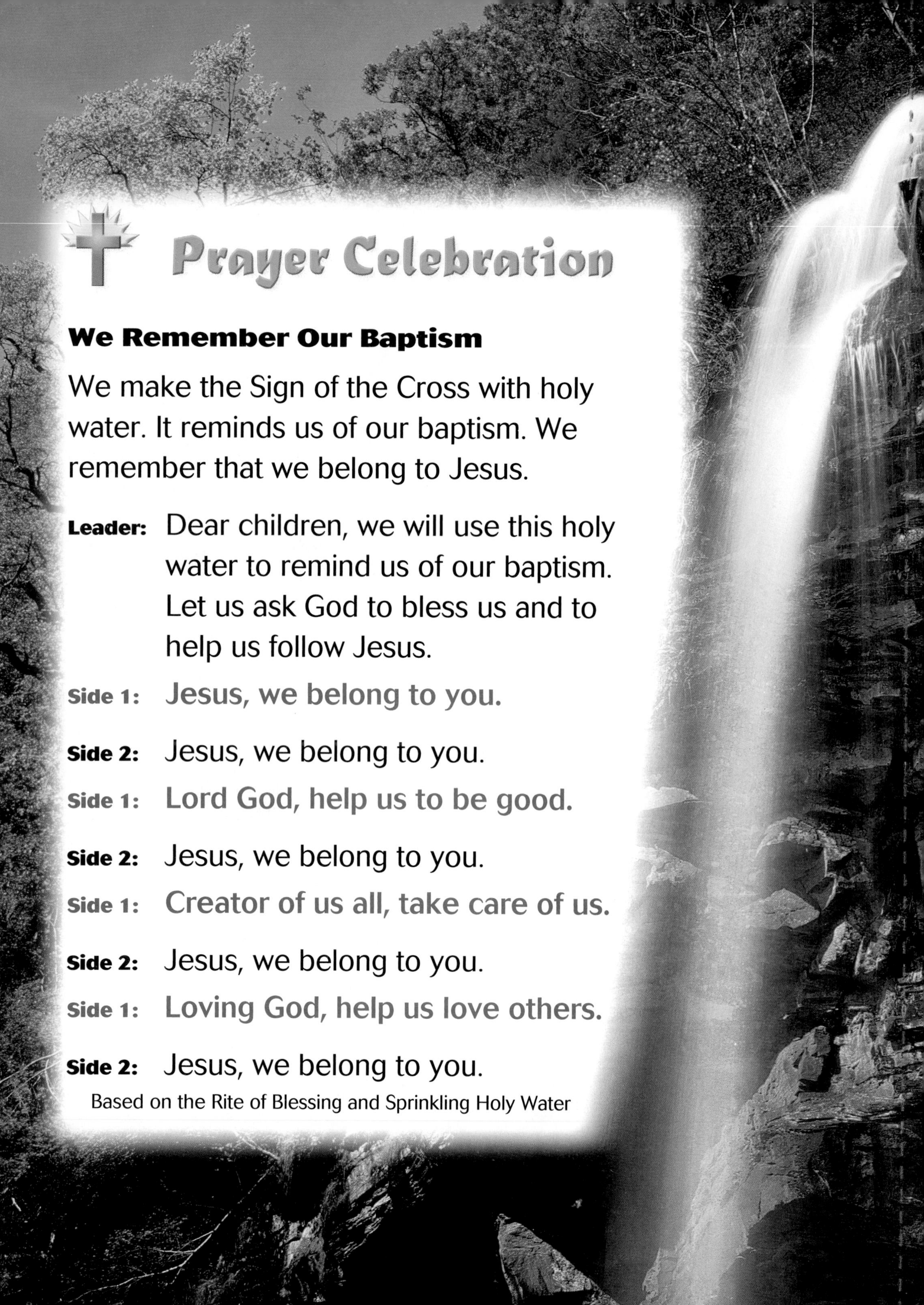

Prayer Celebration

We Remember Our Baptism

We make the Sign of the Cross with holy water. It reminds us of our baptism. We remember that we belong to Jesus.

Leader: Dear children, we will use this holy water to remind us of our baptism. Let us ask God to bless us and to help us follow Jesus.

Side 1: **Jesus, we belong to you.**

Side 2: Jesus, we belong to you.

Side 1: **Lord God, help us to be good.**

Side 2: Jesus, we belong to you.

Side 1: **Creator of us all, take care of us.**

Side 2: Jesus, we belong to you.

Side 1: **Loving God, help us love others.**

Side 2: Jesus, we belong to you.

Based on the Rite of Blessing and Sprinkling Holy Water

Getting ready for Chapter 7

A choice of things to do at home

God Made Us to Be Good and Holy

In this chapter children will understand that God made us to be loving people. We are called to love God, other people, and ourselves. By loving as Jesus did, we recognize God's image in others, and we become holy. God wants us to be happy with him forever in heaven.

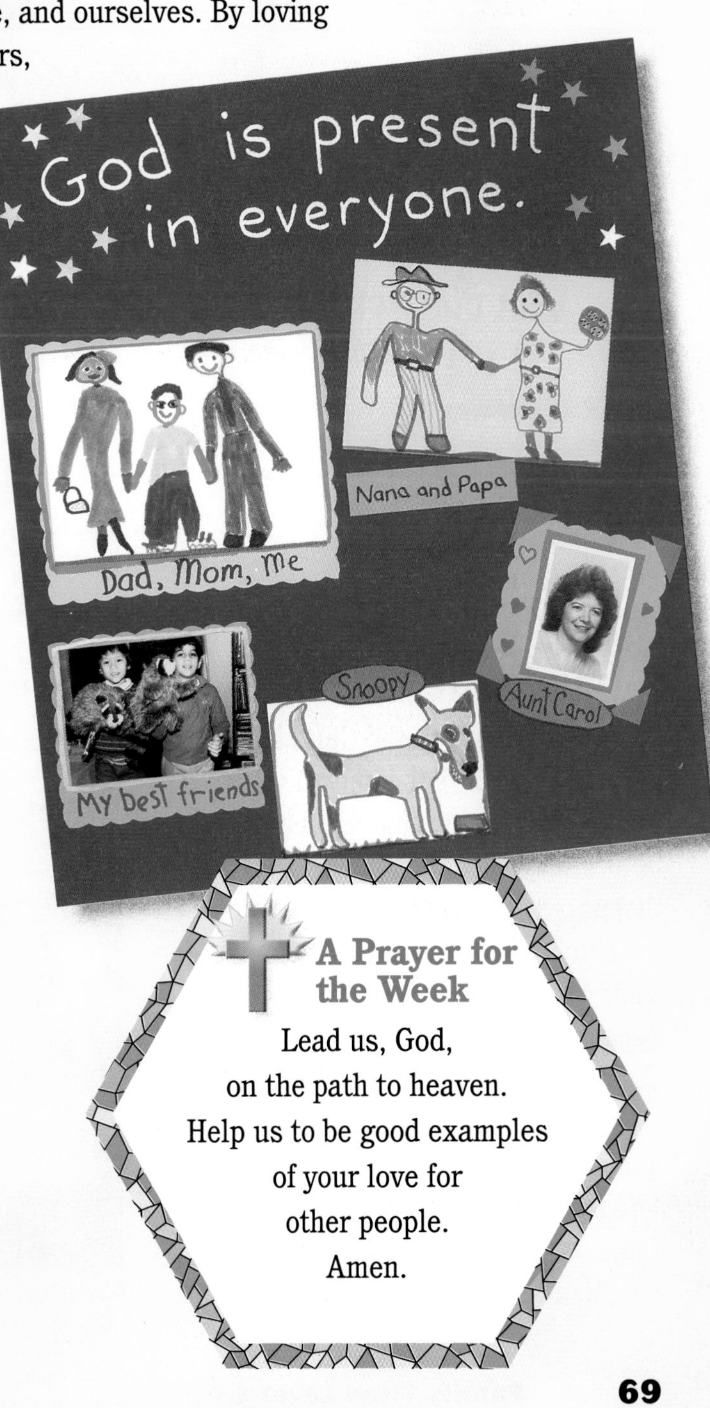

God's presence

Explain to your child that God made us and that he is present in each of us. Title a piece of construction paper "God is present in everyone." Help your child paste photos or drawings of family members and friends onto it.

Point out the good

Point out to your child something he or she said or did that was helpful or kind. Then encourage your child to point out something similar you said or did.

Deciding to do good

On a sheet of paper, write the days of the week at the top and the names of each person in your family down the left-hand margin. Ask family members to fill in one good thing they will try to do each day, such as saying a prayer for someone who is sick, or doing a chore.

A Prayer for the Week

Lead us, God,
on the path to heaven.
Help us to be good examples
of your love for
other people.
Amen.

FAMILY TIME

Something to Do . . .

On Sunday

God is present in everyone in your church community. Introduce yourselves to someone you have not yet met.

Through the Week

Think of someone who has been kind and helpful. Send the person a note to show your gratitude.

Visit Our Web Site

www.blestarewe.com

Something to Think About . . .

Why God Made Us

You shall love the Lord, your God, with all your heart, with all your being, with all your strength, and with all your mind, and your neighbor as yourself.

Luke 10:27

It is important to remember that God is good and that we are also good because we are made in the image and likeness of God. To be holy is to be like God. God made us to love and serve him. God made us to be happy with him forever in heaven.

It would be unfair, however, just to speak of how good and holy we are, because sin is also part of our lives. Despite our basic goodness we don't always live up to our calling to bring God's love to others. When this happens, we can ask for God's forgiveness.

Something to Know About . . .

Our Heritage

Throughout history the Church has declared certain good and holy people saints. Most saints had ordinary lives before they became famous. They were dismissed or thought unusual by others for much of their lives. It was only after their deaths that their good works became known. Then the Church began the process which led to canonization.

All the saints had one thing in common. They lived out the Great Commandment found in the Gospel of Luke, by loving God and loving their neighbor as themselves.

A tenth-century Byzantine ivory triptych of saints

7 God Made Us to Be Good and Holy

Children, let us love one another.

Based on 1 John 4:7

Share

Everything has a purpose.
Circle the things that you would use in a playhouse.
Why did you choose each thing?

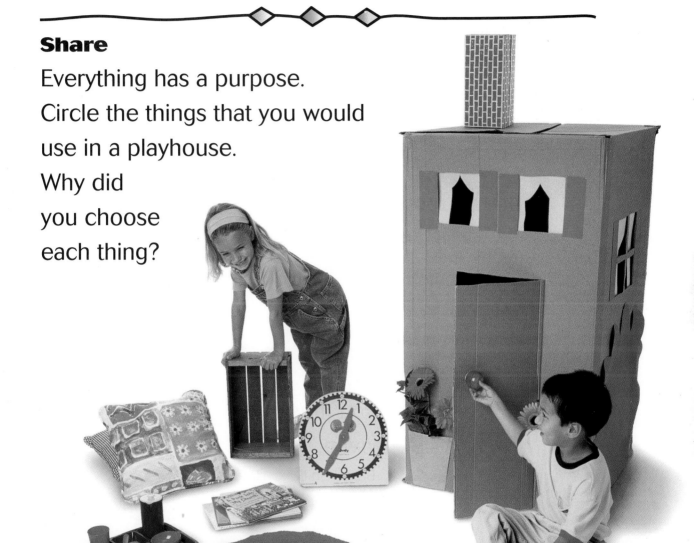

Draw one more thing to put in a playhouse.

Why God Made Us

Jesus went from town to town teaching the people. One day, a man who knew God's law asked Jesus two questions.

Man: Why did God make me? What must I do to go to heaven?

Jesus (smiling): What is written in the Bible?

Man: Love God with your whole heart. Love others as you love yourself.

Jesus: You are right. That is why God made you. That is what you must do to go to heaven.

Based on Luke 10:25–28

God Made Us Good

Jesus tells us the way to **heaven**. We should love God and other people. We should see God's goodness in everyone.

God is good and holy. God created us to be like him. When we love God more than anything, we are **holy**. When we love others and ourselves we are holy. When we act in good ways, we are holy.

Our Church Teaches

Someday every living thing will die. But death is not the end. God created us to be happy with him forever. If we love God and others, we will live forever. We will be happy forever with Jesus, Mary, and the angels. We will be with all the good and holy people who ever lived. This will be the happiness of heaven.

We Believe

God made us to know, love, and serve him. God made us to be happy with him forever in heaven.

Faith Words

heaven
Heaven is happiness with God forever.

holy
To be holy is to be like God.

How can we show love for God and others?

Respond

The Holy Young Man

Peter could not think as fast as other people. He talked very slowly. He walked with a limp. Some people made fun of Peter. But Peter always smiled back.

Peter liked people. He wanted to help them. That is why he liked his job at the grocery store. Peter put food in bags. Then he helped carry them out to the car.

While Peter worked, he listened to people's problems. He told them God loved them. He helped them feel better.

When Peter died, people were very sad. "He was a holy young man," they said. "We were lucky to know him."

 What did people learn from Peter?

Activity

Play the game about loving God and other people. Find your way to Jesus.

1. You need a penny and a game marker.
2. Toss the penny.
3. Move 1 space for heads or 2 for tails.

Start
You prayed.
1
Go 1 more space.
2
You shared.
3
Go 1 more space.
4
You cared.
5
Go 1 more space.
6
You helped.
7
Go 1 more space.
8
You thanked God.
9
Go 1 more space.
Toss heads.
10
Go to Jesus.
Jesus

How can we celebrate being holy?

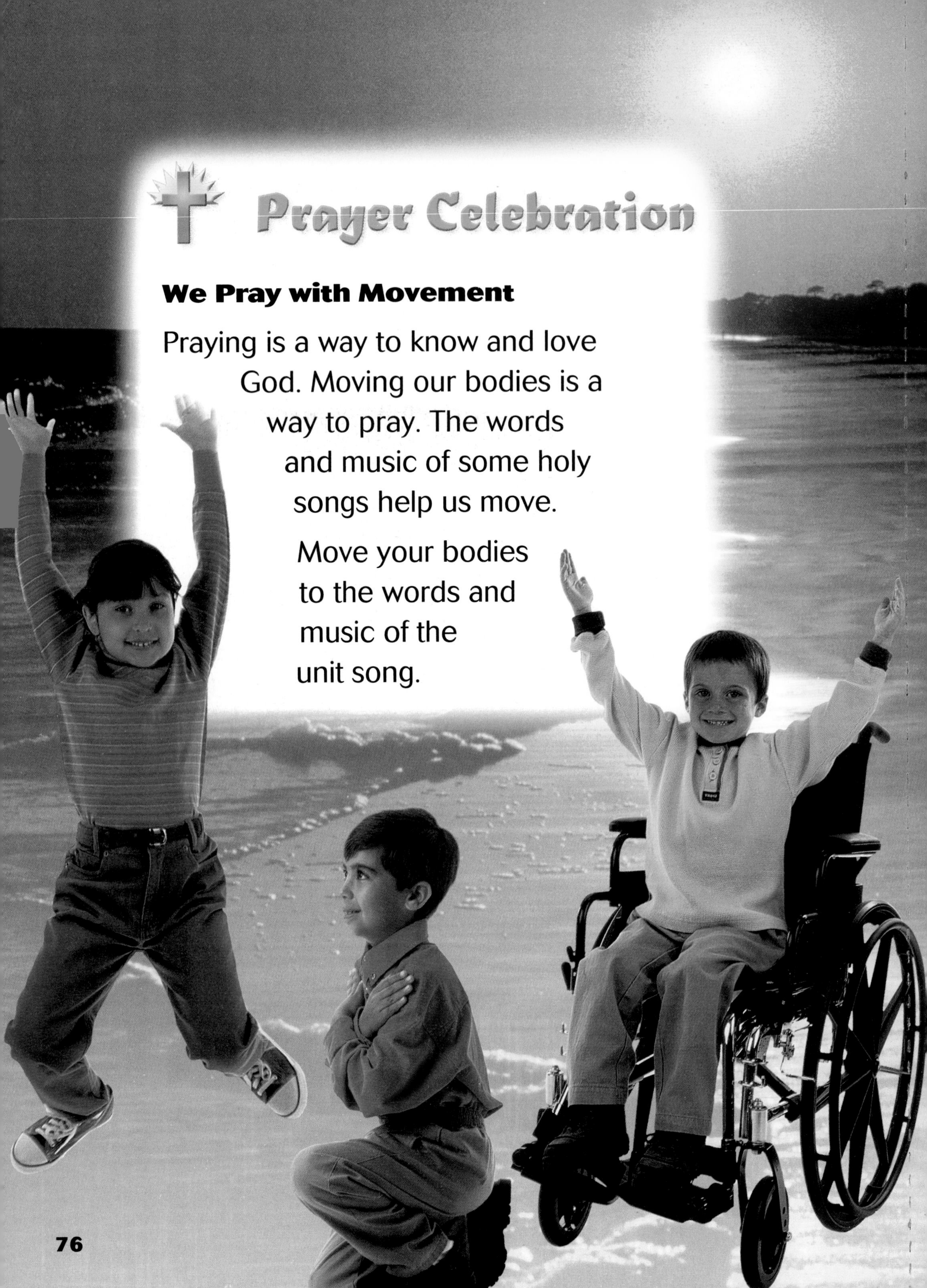

Prayer Celebration

We Pray with Movement

Praying is a way to know and love God. Moving our bodies is a way to pray. The words and music of some holy songs help us move.

Move your bodies to the words and music of the unit song.

A choice of things to do at home

We Give Thanks to God

God gives us so much to be thankful for. Children will identify some of God's special gifts to us, and realize why we pray with the words "our Father." They will learn about prayers of thanksgiving, and that God's name is holy.

A time for thanks

Together, write about a time when you and your child were thankful for something, and end your writing with a prayer of thanks to God.

Thanksgiving

Did you or your child ever make a *cornucopia* (the horn-shaped basket that has fruit in it)? A cornucopia represents the bounty that we receive from the earth. With your child, form and tape a piece of construction paper in the shape of a cornucopia. Then fill the cornucopia with fruit and vegetable shapes cut out of paper. Write something that you and your child are thankful for on each shape.

Speak to me

God wants us to speak with him every day. This week, pray with your family about things that are going on in your lives, such as taking care of a sick pet, finding a new job, or making up with a friend. Make your prayer specific to your concerns.

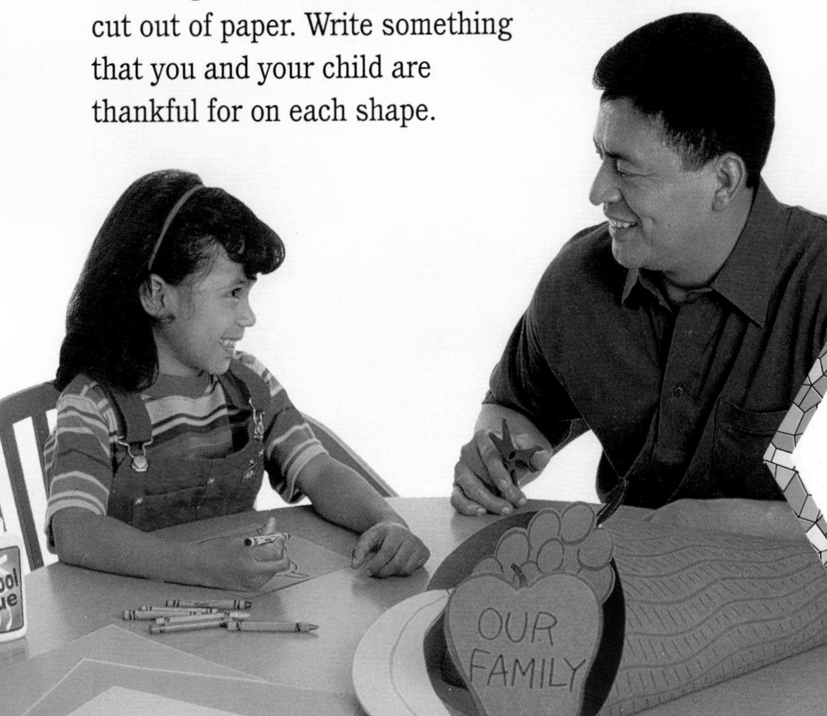

A Prayer for the Week

Thank you for our family, Lord. When we see how our family loves us, we begin to understand how much you, our Father, love us. Amen.

FAMILY TIME

Something to Do . . .

On Sunday

The word *Eucharist* means "thanks," and the Mass is a prayer of thanksgiving. Have a thankful heart when you come to the liturgy this Sunday.

Through the Week

Remember to thank God for everything he gives you and your family.

Visit Our Web Site

www.blestarewe.com

Something to Think About . . .

Expressing Thanks

He fell at the feet of Jesus and thanked him.
Luke 17:16

When Jesus cured ten lepers, only one returned to thank him. All ten had asked Jesus for help. Jesus asked the one who thanked him where the other nine were and wondered aloud why only one of them returned to thank him.

It is common in families that the work people do for others is taken for granted. Do you ever thank the one who cooks, or the one who takes out the garbage? Do you thank your child for being helpful? Thanking one another is a way of thanking God for giving us the family members who help us every day.

Something to Know About . . .

Our Heritage in Music

A well-known hymn of thanksgiving is "Now Thank We All Our God." The lyrics, based on Sirach 50:20–24, were originally written in German by Martin Rinkart under the title of "Nun danket alle Gott." The hymn probably first appeared in 1636. The hymn's composer, Johann Crüger, led the choir at St. Nicholas (Lutheran) Church in Berlin during the seventeenth century. He composed some of the finest hymn tunes of all times. Catherine Winkworth published the English translation of the hymn in 1858.

8 We Give Thanks to God

Thank you, God, for your goodness.
We bless your name.

Based on Psalm 100:4

Share

Aunt Pat helped Nick and Jenny bake cupcakes. She said they could put on the frosting. Nick and Jenny surprised Aunt Pat.

Color the letters on the cupcakes. You will find out their surprise.

Why does God give us gifts?

God Is a Good Father

One day, Jesus told some people about God.

Jesus: God is like a good father. Imagine that you are a child. You are hungry. You ask your father for a loaf of bread. Will a good father give you a stone?

People: No!

Jesus: What will a good father give you?

People: A loaf of bread.

Jesus: That's right. Now pretend that you ask your father for a fish. Will a good father give you a snake?

People: No!

Jesus: What will a good father give you?

People: A fish.

Jesus: That's right. A good father knows how to give his children what they need. So too, God knows everything we need. God gives good gifts to everyone.

Based on Matthew 7:9–11

Our Father

Jesus told the people that God is like a good father. God knows what everyone needs. God takes care of everyone. In the **Lord's Prayer**, Jesus teaches us to call God "our Father." God is the loving Father of all people.

Our Church Teaches

As Christians, we thank God for being our good Father. We pray as Jesus taught us. We say, "Our Father, who art in heaven, **hallowed** be thy name." We tell God that his name is holy.

We Believe

God loves everyone in the world. When we pray, we call God "our Father." The name of God is holy.

Faith Words

Lord's Prayer
The Lord's Prayer is the prayer that Jesus gave us. One time we pray the Lord's Prayer is during Mass.

hallowed
To be hallowed means to be holy.

How do we show thanks for God's gifts?

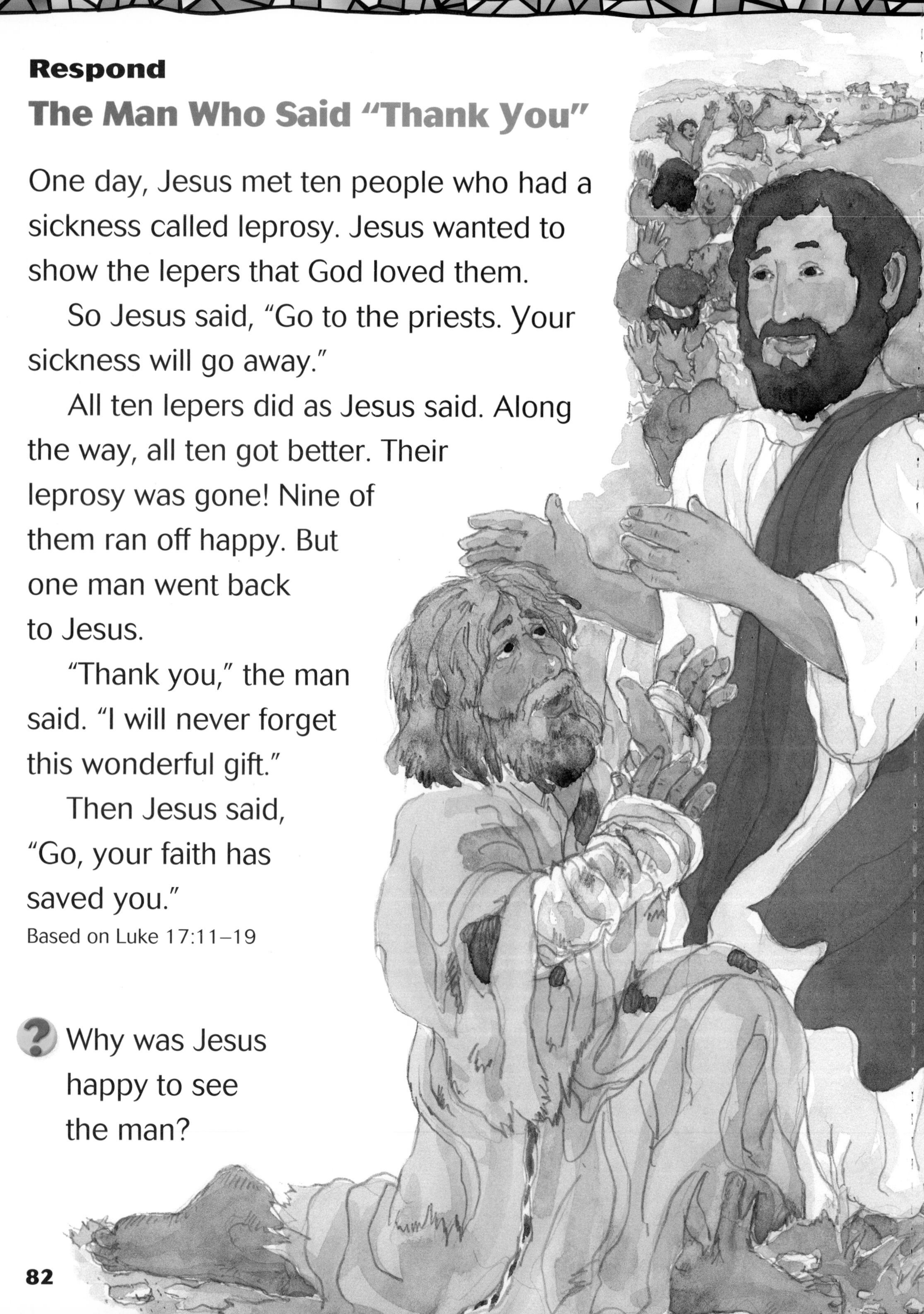

Respond

The Man Who Said "Thank You"

One day, Jesus met ten people who had a sickness called leprosy. Jesus wanted to show the lepers that God loved them.

So Jesus said, "Go to the priests. Your sickness will go away."

All ten lepers did as Jesus said. Along the way, all ten got better. Their leprosy was gone! Nine of them ran off happy. But one man went back to Jesus.

"Thank you," the man said. "I will never forget this wonderful gift."

Then Jesus said, "Go, your faith has saved you."

Based on Luke 17:11–19

Why was Jesus happy to see the man?

Activities

1. Trace the letters to complete the prayer.

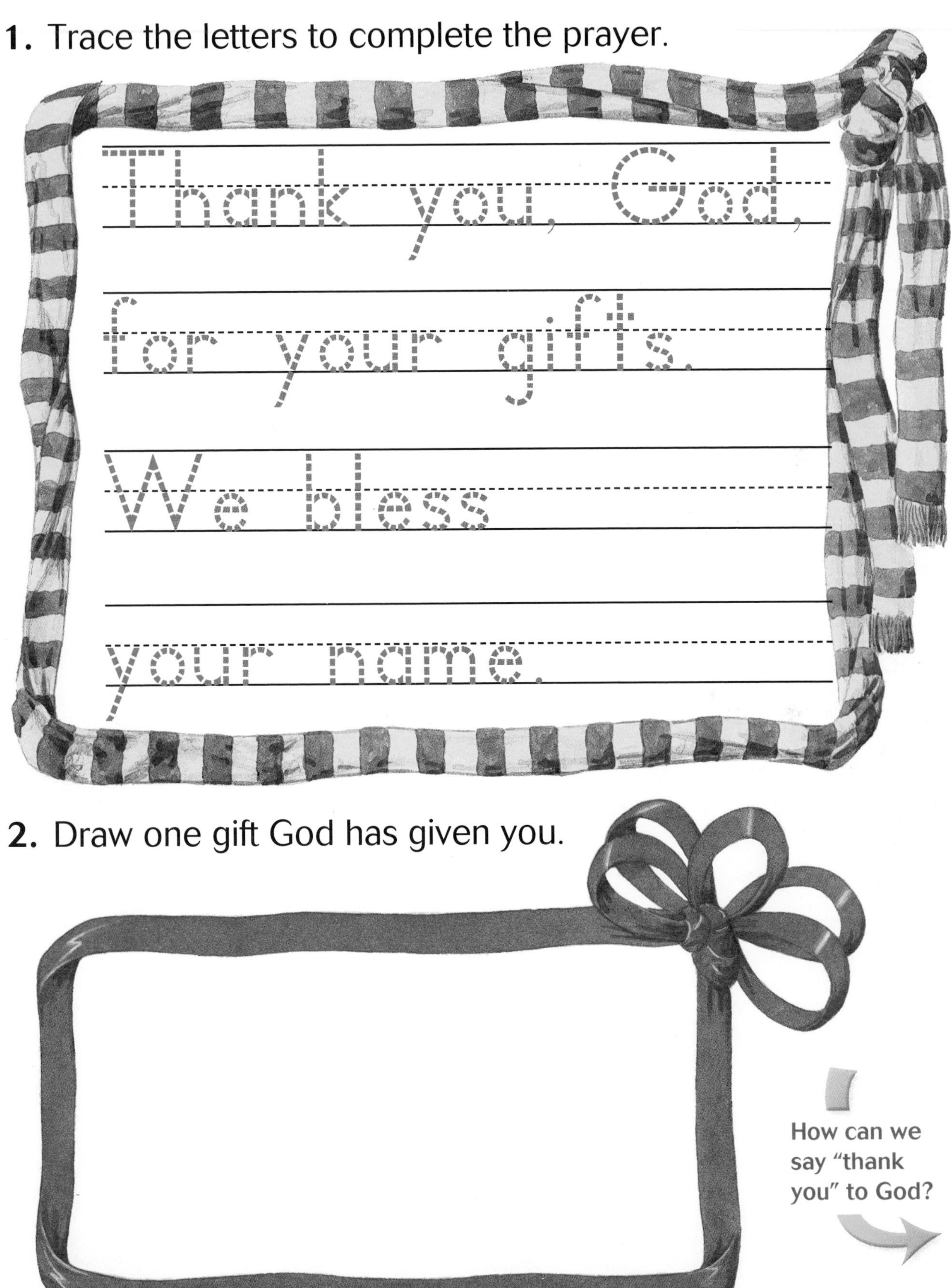

Thank you, God,
for your gifts.
We bless
your name.

2. Draw one gift God has given you.

How can we say "thank you" to God?

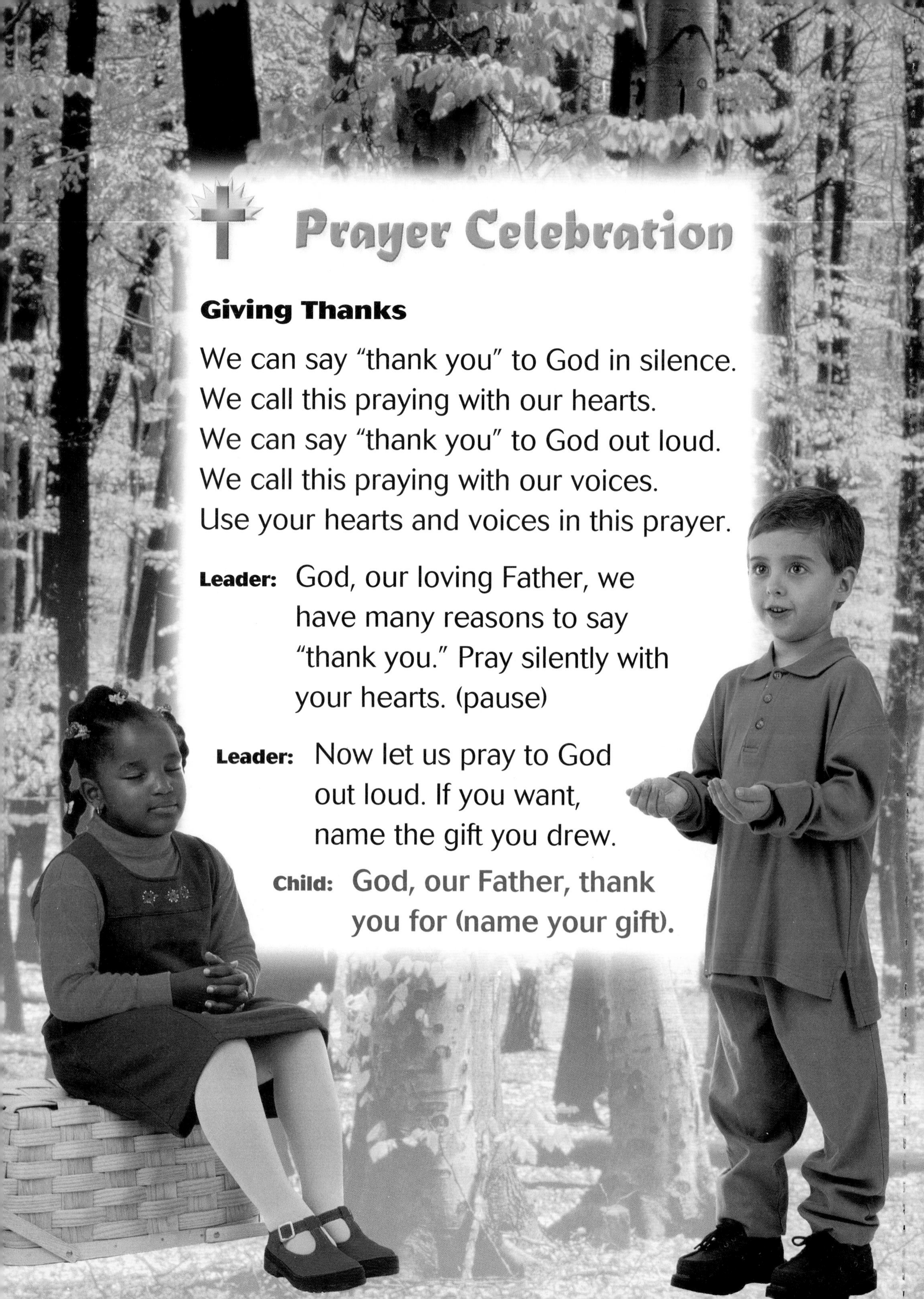

Prayer Celebration

Giving Thanks

We can say "thank you" to God in silence.
We call this praying with our hearts.
We can say "thank you" to God out loud.
We call this praying with our voices.
Use your hearts and voices in this prayer.

Leader: God, our loving Father, we have many reasons to say "thank you." Pray silently with your hearts. (pause)

Leader: Now let us pray to God out loud. If you want, name the gift you drew.

Child: God, our Father, thank you for (name your gift).

Pretty Flowers All in a Row

Lisa's church has flower gardens all around it. Some women in the parish buy and plant the flowers. The women ask Lisa's class to help take care of the gardens.

Each week the children water the plants. They pull out the weeds. They pick up papers that blow into the gardens.

Sometimes the children pick the flowers. They help the women put the flowers into vases. They carry the vases into the church and put them near the altar.

People in Lisa's parish like to see the flowers at Mass. Lisa's class feels proud that they help make their church beautiful.

Why do the people like the flower gardens?

Think About It

Why do you think God created so many different kinds of flowers?

Cross out the wrong answer.

to make our Earth beautiful

to make us happy

to feed the elephants

Learn About It

God loves the Earth very much. He created many things to make it beautiful. God created mountains, rivers, lakes, trees, and animals. These things make God happy. They make us happy, too. God wants us to take care of his creation.

Do Something About It

Do you have any flowers growing in your house or in your yard? Plan how you will help take care of them. Think of a way to share their beauty with others. **Draw a picture of your favorite flower.**

UNIT 2

Organizer

Look at the words on the bow.

Write the word that completes each sentence.

Baptism holy thanks Father

God is our loving

______________________.

____

is a wonderful gift.

God made us to be good and

______________________.

We give

____

to God.

UNIT 2

Review

A **Write the correct word on each line.**

1. Who is our loving Father and Creator?

2. Who does God make like himself?

3. What does God's creation show us?

4. Who is a special helper from God?

UNIT 2

Review

B Circle the correct words to complete the sentences.

1. Jesus invites us to belong to the ____.

   soccer team **Catholic Church**

2. Baptism is a celebration of ____.

   welcome **a birthday**

3. Followers of Jesus are called ____.

   students **Christians**

4. Another name for Jesus is ____.

   Christ **Father**

C Draw lines to the words that complete the sentences.

1. Jesus teaches us to call God our	•	• **people.**
2. God is the loving Father of all	•	• **Lord's Prayer.**
3. The prayer that Jesus gave us is called the	•	• **Father.**
4. The word holy means	•	• **hallowed.**

UNIT 2 Review

D Write the number of the correct word on each blank line. The first one is done for you.

1. God made us to 3, ____, and ____ him.

2. God made us to be ____ with him in ____.

3. To be ____ is to be like God.

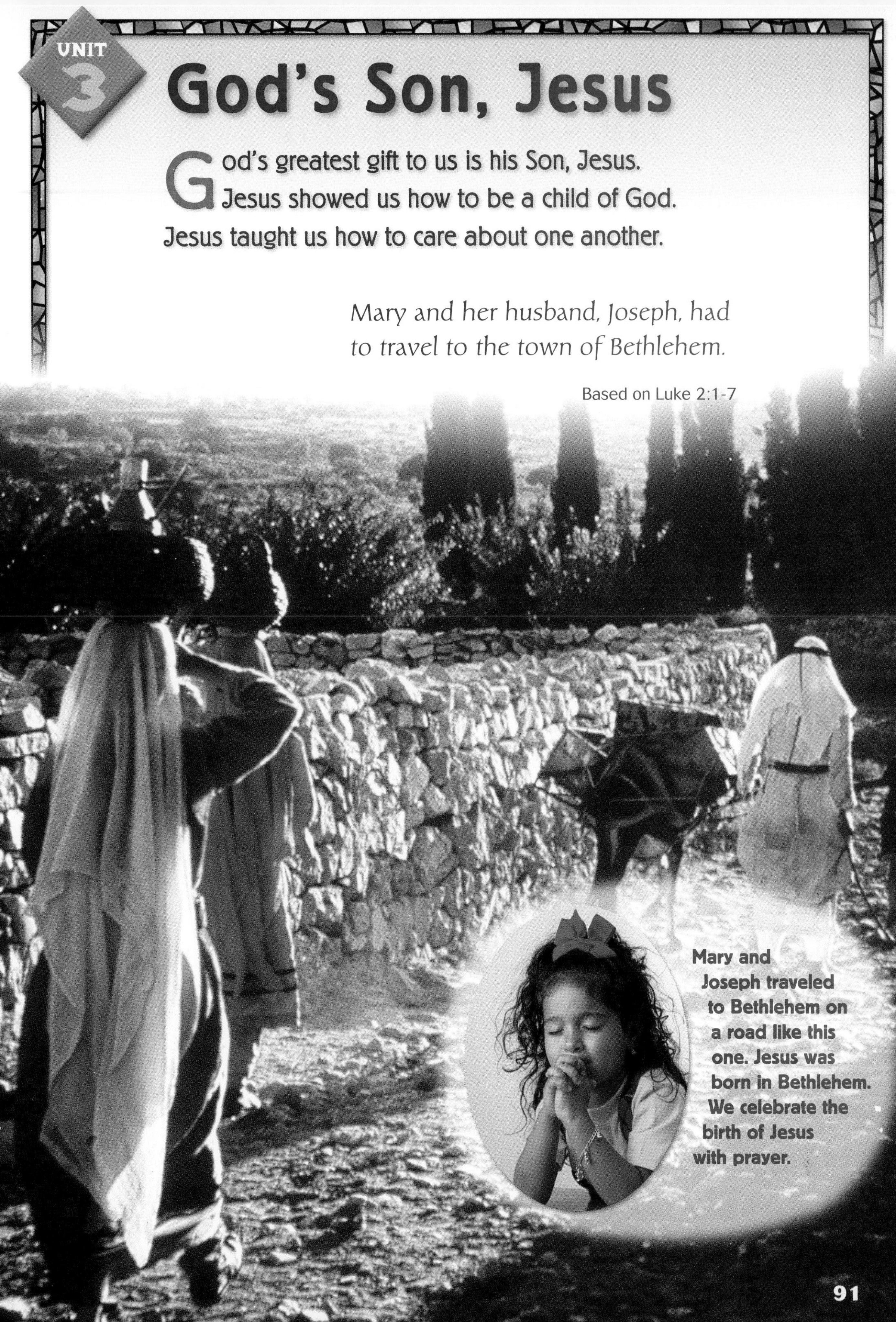

UNIT 3

God's Son, Jesus

God's greatest gift to us is his Son, Jesus. Jesus showed us how to be a child of God. Jesus taught us how to care about one another.

Mary and her husband, Joseph, had to travel to the town of Bethlehem.

Based on Luke 2:1-7

Mary and Joseph traveled to Bethlehem on a road like this one. Jesus was born in Bethlehem. We celebrate the birth of Jesus with prayer.

UNIT
3
SONG

He Came Down

Traditional from Cameroon
Transcribed and Arranged by John L. Bell

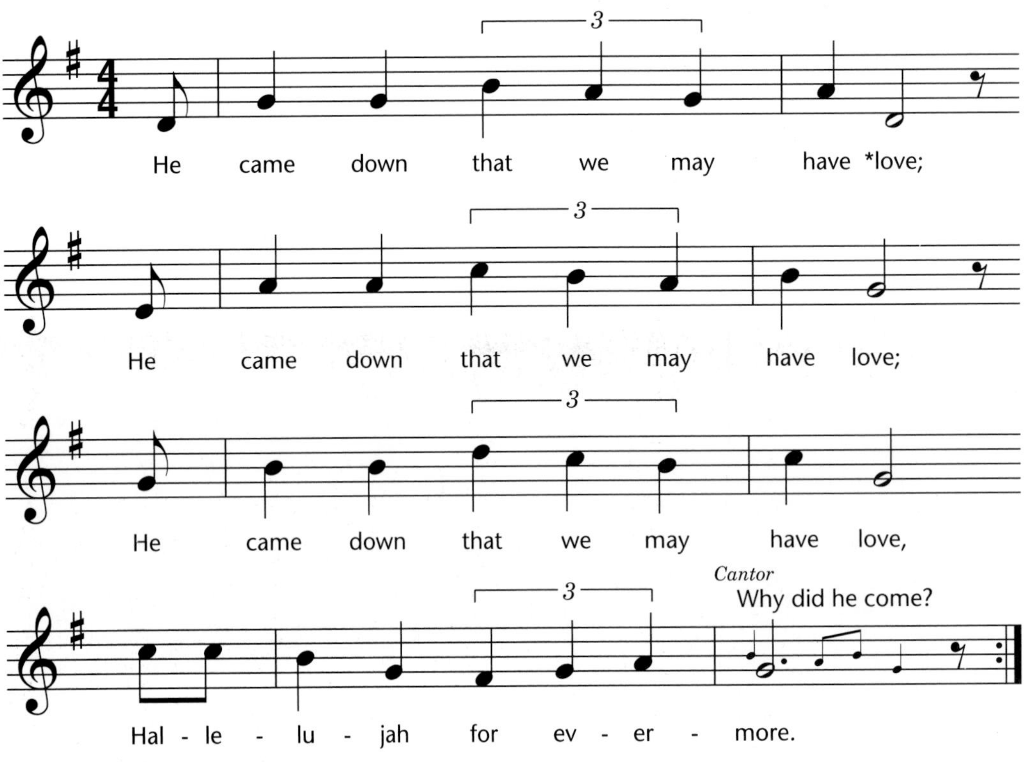
He came down that we may have *love;
He came down that we may have love;
He came down that we may have love,
Cantor
Why did he come?
Hal - le - lu - jah for ev - er - more.

*Substitute peace, joy, hope, life, *etc.*

Getting ready for Chapter 9

A choice of things to do at home

Jesus Is God's Son

In this chapter the children will hear the Gospel story of the Annunciation. The apostle Luke tells us that the angel Gabriel announced to Mary the good news that she would be the mother of God's Son, Jesus.

Sensing memories

Together, leaf through a family photo album. Invite your child to pause at favorite pictures and use the senses of sight, hearing, taste, smell, and touch to describe the occasion. Talk about the good news found in each photo.

Dinnertime news

Arrange candles on the dinner table. Take turns sharing the good news of the day. Each time someone tells good news, light a candle.

A "Good News" collage

Using old magazines, together find and cut out pictures that show "good news." Arrange them on construction paper or butcher paper, making a collage. When it is finished, let your child explain why each picture was chosen.

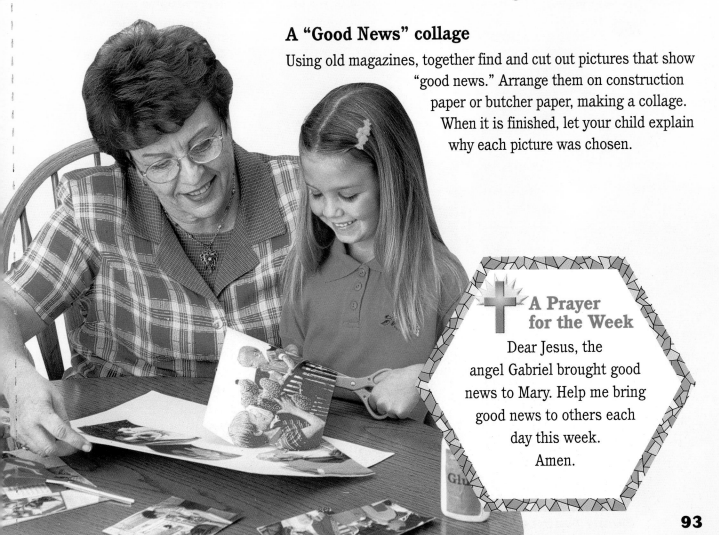

A Prayer for the Week

Dear Jesus, the angel Gabriel brought good news to Mary. Help me bring good news to others each day this week. Amen.

FAMILY TIME

Something to Do . . .

On Sunday

Look around your church for artwork depicting angels. Then listen to the words of the liturgy and the hymns for references to angels.

Through the Week

Whenever your family gathers, have each member tell about bringing good news to someone during the day.

Visit Our Web Site

www.blestarewe.com

Something to Think About . . .

Mary's Good News

The child to be born will be called holy,
the Son of God.
Luke 1:35

In the Gospel story of the Annunciation, the angel Gabriel brings good news to Mary and to all of us. God's Son is about to come to us as a savior and as a model for living.

Mary understands that this news means that she is called to commit herself as a mother to this very special baby, and that this commitment may be difficult at times. Still, Mary says "Yes" to God, and at that moment the salvation of the world begins. We are called to bring the good news of Jesus Christ to others in all that we say and do. We pray for God's help to live this commitment in spite of any difficulties.

Something to Know About . . . Our Heritage in Art

The Annunciation is one of the most frequently depicted Scripture stories by famous "old master" artists. One of the greatest is by the Italian Renaissance master Fra Angelico (Brother Angel).

Brother Angel did many pictures, known as frescoes, on the walls of monks' rooms in his monastery in Florence, Italy. The Annunciation, however, he reserved for a very special place at the top of a staircase. The painting can still be seen in that same spot, just as it was hundreds of years ago.

9 Jesus Is God's Son

We praise you, O God.
Your love for us is wonderful.

Based on Psalm 136:1–4

Share

Good news makes people happy.
Look at each picture.
Tell the good news that you
think each person hears.

Draw yourself hearing good news.

What good news did God send?

The Good News

A long time ago, God sent an angel to **Mary**. The angel had good news for Mary. He told Mary that God wanted her to be the mother of a special baby. God wanted her to name the baby **Jesus**. This special baby would be the Son of God. Mary said, "Yes, I will do whatever God wants."

Based on Luke 1:26–38

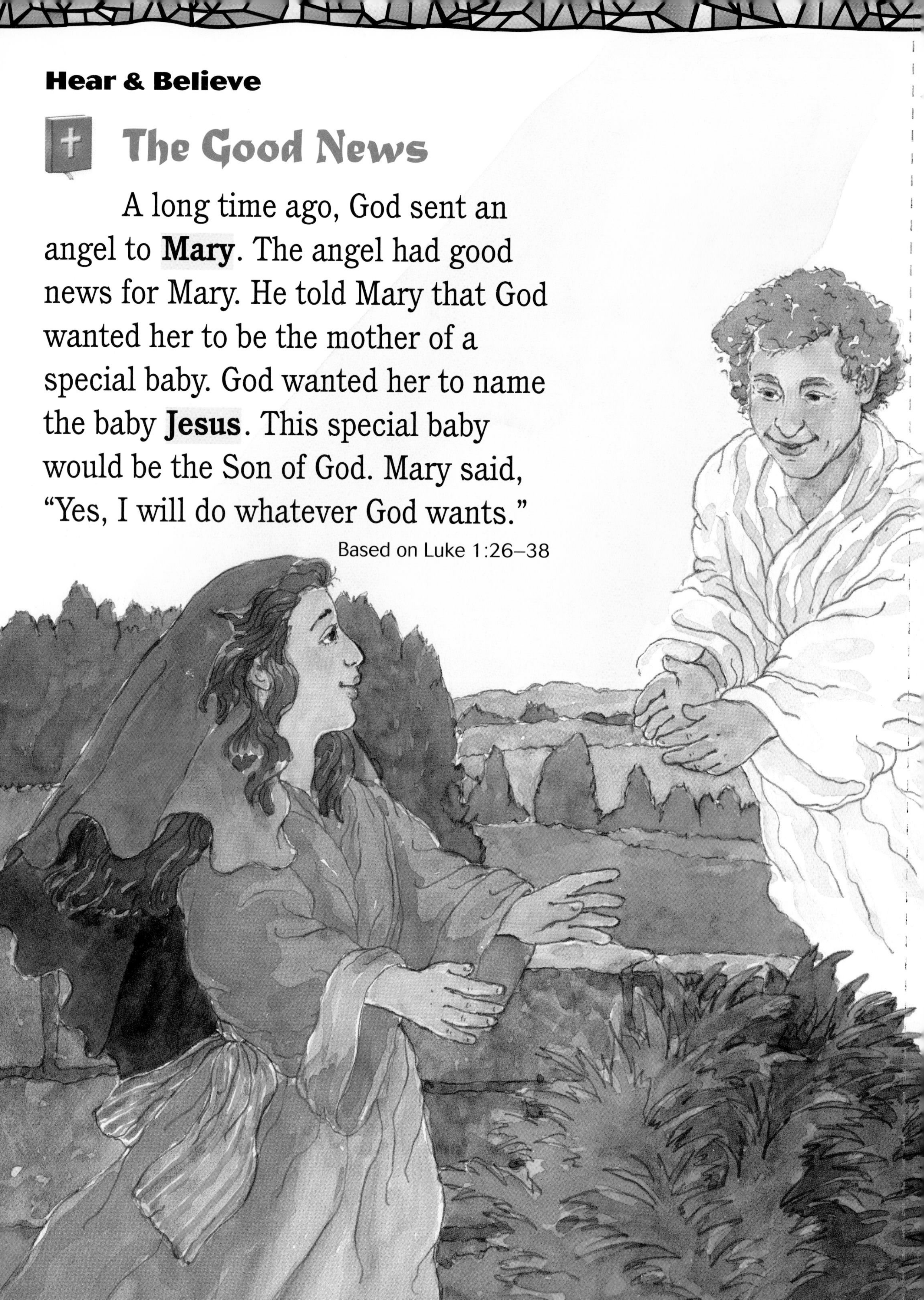

Jesus Is Born

It was almost time for Mary's baby to be born. Mary and her husband, Joseph, had to travel to the town of Bethlehem. But there was no room for them in the inn. So baby Jesus was born in a stable.

Based on Luke 2:1–7

We Believe

God asked Mary to be the mother of his Son, Jesus. Jesus is God's most special gift to us.

Our Church Teaches

God loves us very much. God sent his own Son, Jesus, to be our Savior. Jesus became one of us. He shared his life with us and is always with us.

Faith Words

Mary
Mary is the mother of Jesus.

Jesus
Jesus is the Son of God.

How can we share the good news about Jesus?

Respond

Telling the Good News

David likes it when his dad reads to him. He loves to hear Bible stories about Jesus. One day David's dad read the story about the birth of Jesus.

Later David went to his friend Mike's house to play. He told his friend the good news about Jesus.

? What do you think David told his friend?

Activities

1. Learn to sign the words
   "I bring you good news."
   Then share good news about
   Jesus with others.

2. Color the spaces that have an X in them.
   Whose name do you see?

How can we celebrate the good news about Jesus?

Prayer Celebration

An Echo Prayer

Did you ever hear an echo?
You can pray an echo prayer.
Just repeat the words you hear.

Leader: Jesus, we believe you are the Son of God.

All: **Jesus, we believe you are the Son of God.**

Leader: Jesus, we believe you are always with us.

All: **Jesus, we believe you are always with us.**

Leader: Jesus, we believe you love us very much.

All: **Jesus, we believe you love us very much.**

Getting ready for Chapter 10

A choice of things to do at home

We Celebrate the Gift of Eucharist

In this chapter the children will come to recognize that the words of the Eucharistic Prayer at Mass describe the Last Supper that Jesus shared with his disciples on the night before he died. Children will learn about our Catholic belief that Jesus is present in the Eucharist as a sign of God's love for us. They will also practice genuflecting and bowing as signs of respect for the Blessed Sacrament.

Please and thank you

A sense of respect for God can begin with a sense of respect for others. Encourage your child to say "please" and "thank you" at the appropriate times, and remember to say them yourself as a model for your child.

A celebration is coming

Make plans together for the next big family celebration. Who will be invited? How will your home be decorated? Will any special foods be part of the celebration? Will certain members of the family be expected to perform special tasks?

The exact words

Select one of your child's favorite storybooks to read together. Choose a quiet time and place. Your child may wish to read familiar parts of the story, or recite them from memory. Notice how important it is to your child that the words are just right.

A Prayer for the Week

Give us thankful hearts, O Lord, and joyful hearts as well, so that we can celebrate the gift of your Son, Jesus. Amen.

FAMILY TIME

Something to Do . . .

On Sunday

Point out the tabernacle. Demonstrate how we genuflect and bow in church to show respect for the Blessed Sacrament.

Through the Week

Remember that Jesus is present in the Eucharist and in each person. Show love for others as Jesus did.

Visit Our Web Site

www.blestarewe.com

Something to Think About . . .

Recalling the Last Supper

Take this, all of you, and eat it: this is my body which will be given up for you.

Eucharistic Prayer 1

In the Liturgy of the Eucharist the followers of Jesus recall the night he shared a special meal with his disciples. The Last Supper was much more than a meal. It was the promise that Jesus would remain with his Church until the end of time. The words of consecration not only recall the Last Supper, but make the sacrifice of Jesus present to us in our own time. At the words of consecration, the bread and wine become the Body and Blood of Christ.

Something to Know About . . . Our Heritage

The word *tabernacle* means “tent,” or more generically “dwelling place.” We find the word used in the Bible to describe the special tent in which the ark of the covenant with the tablets of the law was kept while the Hebrew people were in the desert. When Solomon built the Temple in Jerusalem, the ark was housed in the Holy of Holies. The place of the ark was considered the presence of God on earth.

In Catholic churches the tabernacle is the place where we reserve the Eucharist for those who cannot attend Mass with the community. Traditionally Catholics have the practice of “visiting” the Blessed Sacrament in the tabernacle, to pray and remember that Jesus is always present.

King David bringing the Ark of the Covenant into Jerusalem, shown in an illuminated manuscript by an unknown 14th–century artist

10 We Celebrate the Gift of Eucharist

When you eat this bread and drink from this cup of wine, remember me.

Based on Luke 22:19–20

Share

Special meals can be fun.
There is good food.
There are people we like.

Plan a special meal for your family.
Circle the foods you want at this meal.

Draw another food you would like to eat at this meal.

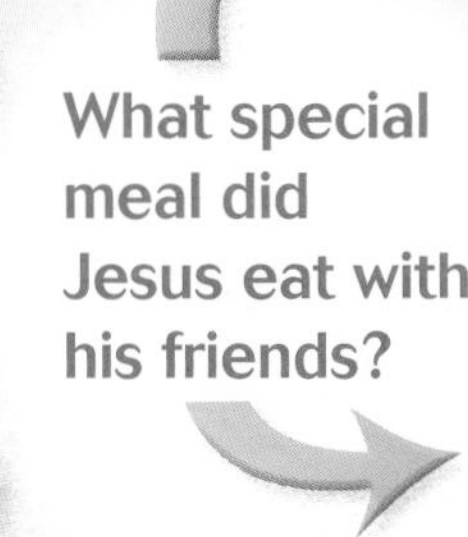

What special meal did Jesus eat with his friends?

Hear & Believe

A Special Meal

On the night before he died, Jesus ate a special meal with his friends. We call this meal the **Last Supper**. Here is what Jesus said and did.

Jesus took bread from the table. He gave God thanks and praise. Then he broke the bread. He gave it to his friends and said, "Take this and eat it. This bread is my body."

When supper was ended, Jesus took a cup of wine. He thanked God. He gave the cup to his friends and said, "Take this and drink from it. This is the cup of my blood."

Based on Eucharistic Prayer I for Children

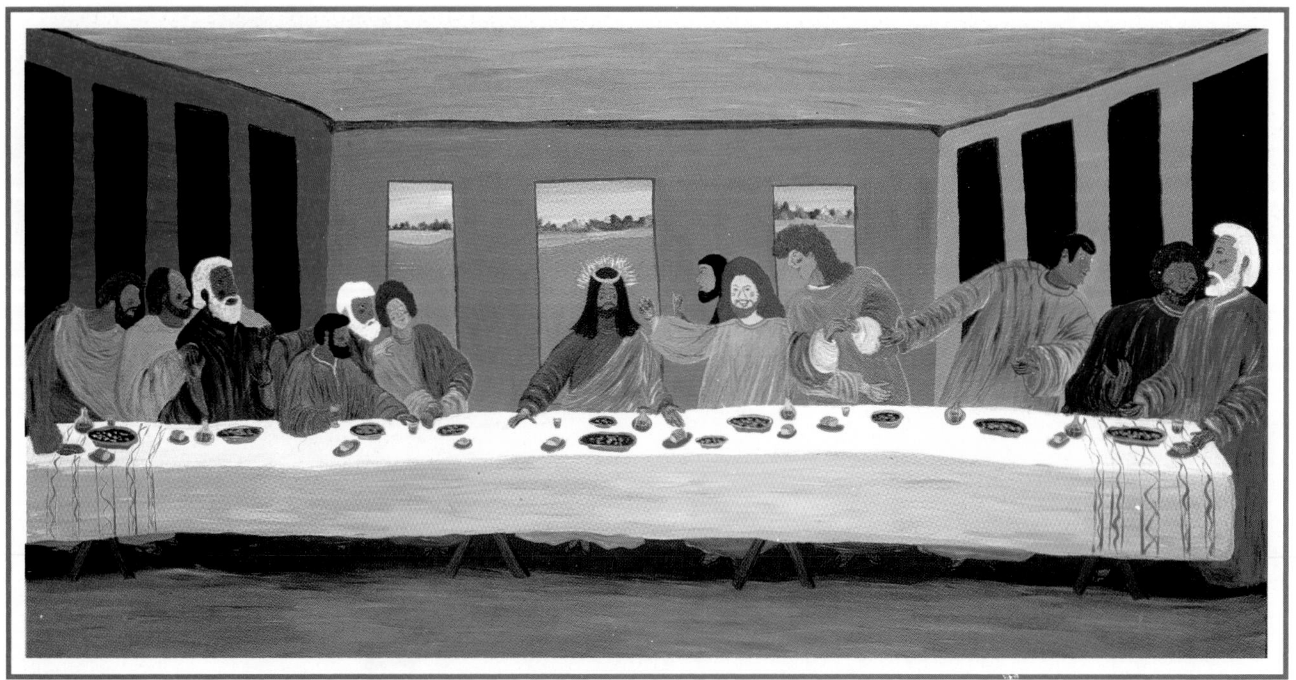

Jesus Is with Us

At the Last Supper, Jesus gave us the **Eucharist**. We believe Jesus is present in the bread and wine. At Mass we thank God for the gift of Jesus' Body and Blood.

Our Church Teaches

Jesus is present in the Eucharist. After Mass the priest puts the Eucharist in a special place called the **tabernacle**. The Eucharist is taken to people who are ill and cannot come to Mass. Some people pray before the tabernacle during the week because they know Jesus is present.

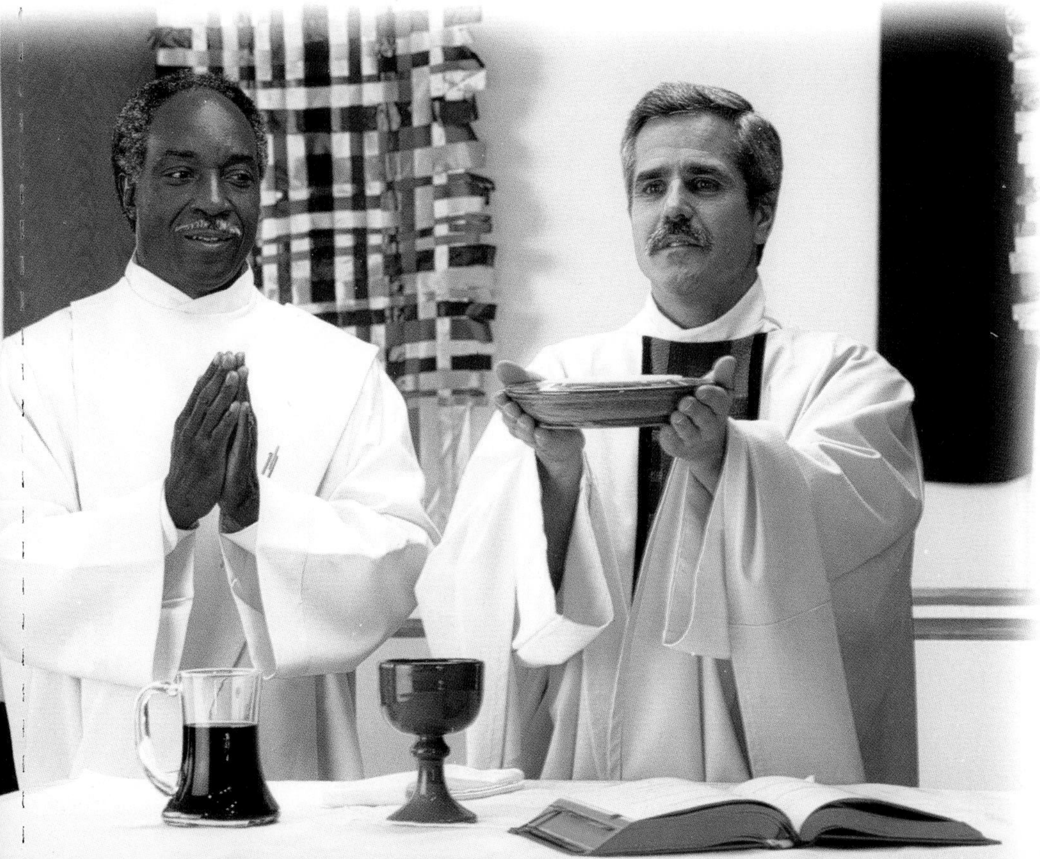

We Believe

Jesus is present in the Eucharist. The Eucharist is a sign of Jesus' love for us.

Faith Words

Last Supper
The Last Supper is the special meal that Jesus shared with his friends.

Eucharist
The Eucharist is a special meal that Jesus shares with us today. We receive the Body and Blood of Christ.

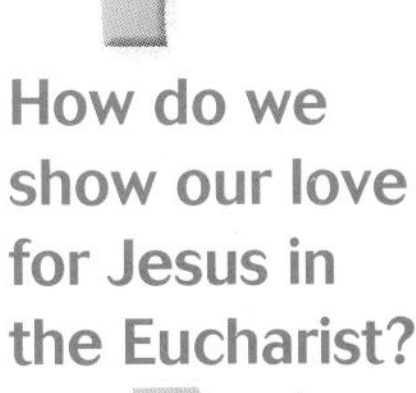

How do we show our love for Jesus in the Eucharist?

Respond

Saint Katharine Drexel

As a child, Katharine went to Mass with her family. She knew that the bread and wine are changed into the Body and Blood of Christ. Katharine learned that the Eucharist in the tabernacle is called the Blessed Sacrament.

Katharine's parents helped people in need. Katharine wanted to help, too.

When she grew up, Katharine helped Native Americans and African Americans. She paid to have schools built for them. Katharine started a community called the Sisters of the Blessed Sacrament. She and the sisters taught others about the Eucharist. They shared the good news about Jesus.

? How did Katharine show her love for Jesus?

Activities

1. These objects help us remember Jesus.

Connect the dots. What do you see?

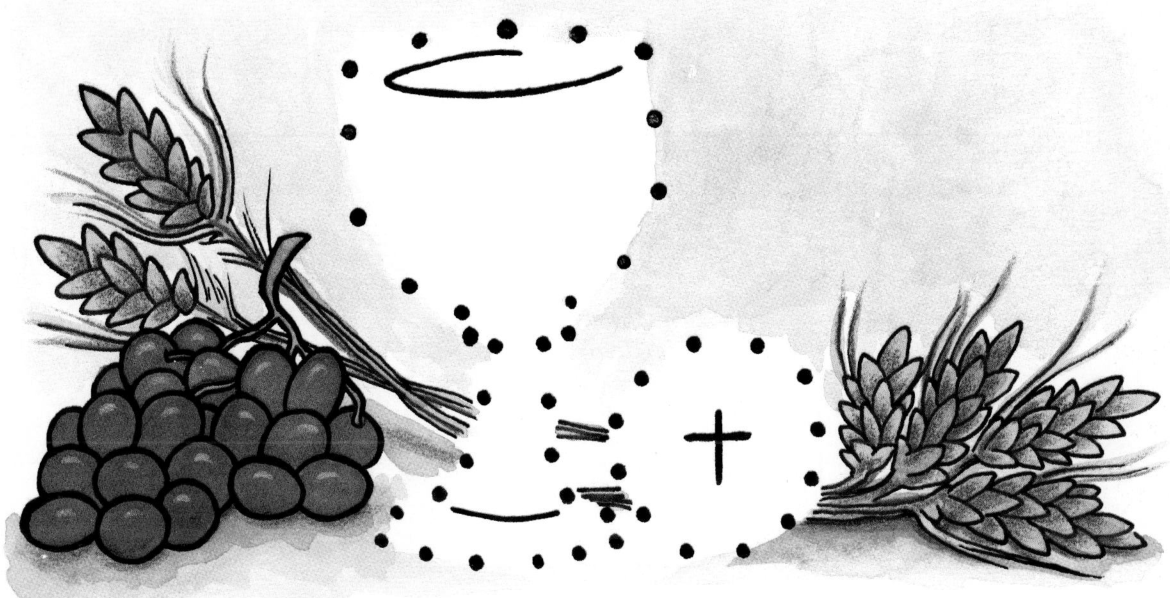

2. Do you remember what Jesus said at the Last Supper?

Finish the sentences.

This is my

____

______________________________________.

This is the cup of my

____

______________________________________.

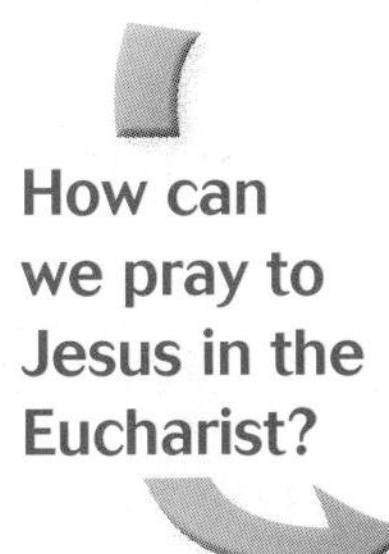

How can we pray to Jesus in the Eucharist?

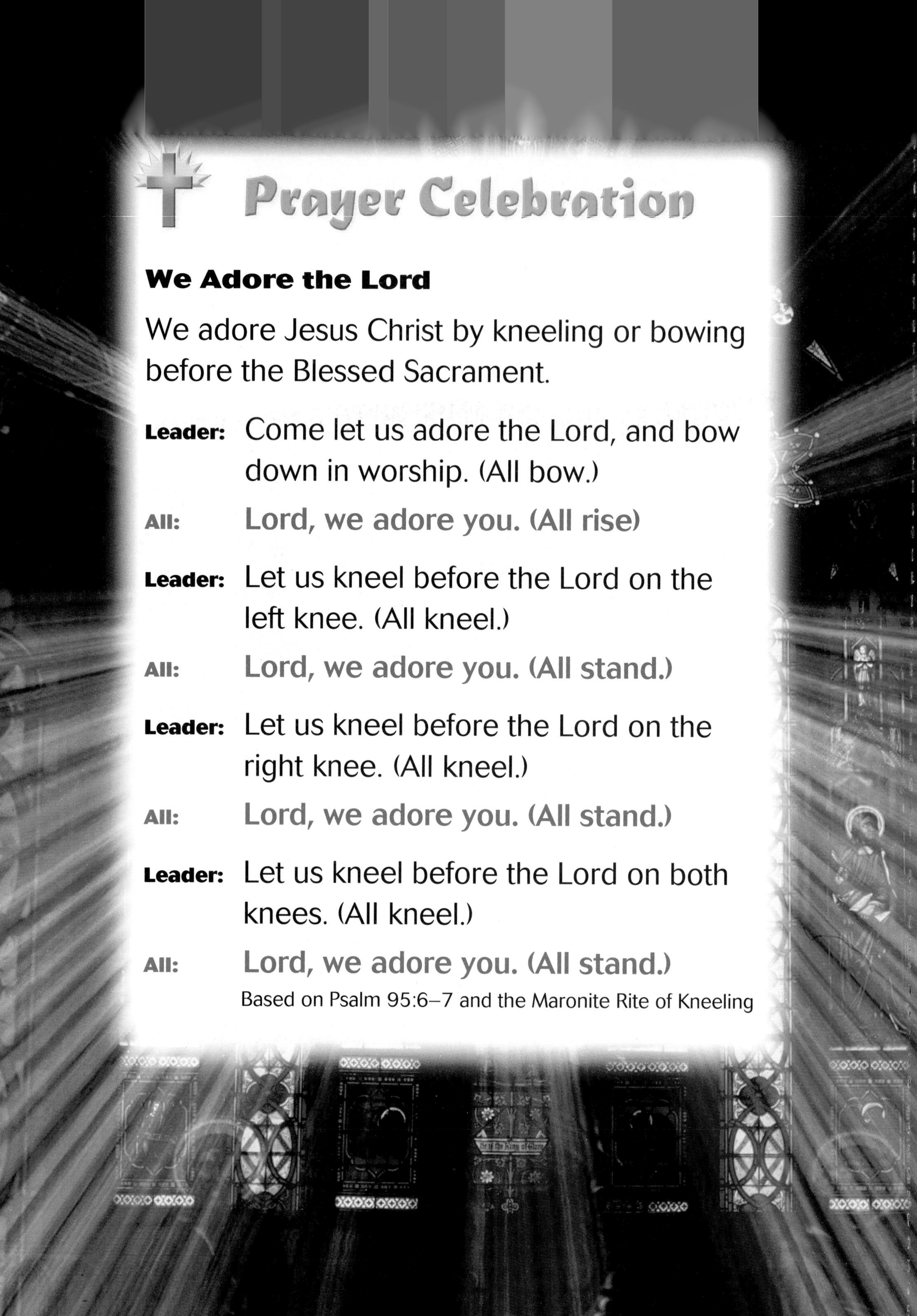

Prayer Celebration

We Adore the Lord

We adore Jesus Christ by kneeling or bowing before the Blessed Sacrament.

Leader: Come let us adore the Lord, and bow down in worship. (All bow.)

All: **Lord, we adore you. (All rise)**

Leader: Let us kneel before the Lord on the left knee. (All kneel.)

All: **Lord, we adore you. (All stand.)**

Leader: Let us kneel before the Lord on the right knee. (All kneel.)

All: **Lord, we adore you. (All stand.)**

Leader: Let us kneel before the Lord on both knees. (All kneel.)

All: **Lord, we adore you. (All stand.)**

Based on Psalm 95:6–7 and the Maronite Rite of Kneeling

A choice of things to do at home

Jesus Teaches Us About Forgiveness

In this chapter, children will learn that God's laws help them follow Jesus and make loving choices. The children will come to understand the importance of saying they are sorry when they have chosen to do wrong things. They will learn that God is always ready to forgive them.

Read all about it

Read *Where the Wild Things Are* by Maurice Sendak (HarperCollins) with your child. Discuss the ending of the book as it relates to forgiveness and reconciliation.

Being responsible

Although we have not personally caused war, poverty, injustice, and hunger, all Christians are responsible for working toward solving the suffering caused by these social sins. Your family can do something to bring about healing and reconciliation, such as putting money you would have spent on a video rental in the poor box at church, or donating food to a food pantry.

Praying for forgiveness

Together, talk about a time when you or your child did something hurtful to another person. Make up a prayer with your child that asks for God's forgiveness.

A Prayer for the Week

You call us
to forgiveness and
reconciliation in our family,
Lord. Help us heal the
hurts of one another in
the days ahead.
Amen.

FAMILY TIME

Something to Do . . .

On Sunday

Spend a few moments before Mass thinking about how you failed to be loving people. Pray, "Lord, have mercy," with reverence.

Through the Week

Show others the importance of forgiveness by being ready to forgive them if they hurt you.

Visit Our Web Site

www.blestarewe.com

Something to Think About . . .

God's Forgiveness

For the Son of Man has come to seek and to save what was lost.

Luke 19:10

Jesus taught people God's laws: Love God with your whole mind, heart, and soul, and love your neighbor as yourself. Jesus also taught that God wants people to be sorry for doing wrong, and that God will always forgive. In the Gospel story, Zacchaeus is sorry for his sins, and he promises to help others. Jesus forgives Zacchaeus. When we fail to live according to our beliefs, God's love and forgiveness is there for us. Each day provides opportunities to follow God's laws, and it is up to us to see these opportunities, and respond with love.

Something to Know About . . . Our Heritage in Bible Times

The Gospel story about Zacchaeus tells how he climbed up a sycamore tree to see Jesus over a crowd of people. The view from the sycamore tree enabled Zacchaeus, a short man, to see Jesus clearly.

Jericho, where the story takes place, is agriculturally rich and full of tree groves. The sycamore is a type of fig tree, called the mulberry fig, with edible fruit. This tree is not the same as the American sycamore. Zacchaeus found the Jericho tree convenient for climbing because of its low, spreading branches. Today, many families in Jericho still eat the figs from the sycamore tree.

11 Jesus Teaches Us about Forgiveness

Forgive me, O God, for I have done wrong.

Based on Luke 18:13

Share

Sometimes we do what is right.

Sometimes we do what is wrong.

Look at these pictures.

Draw a ☺ if the action is right.

Draw a ☹ if the action is wrong.

What does Jesus teach us to do?

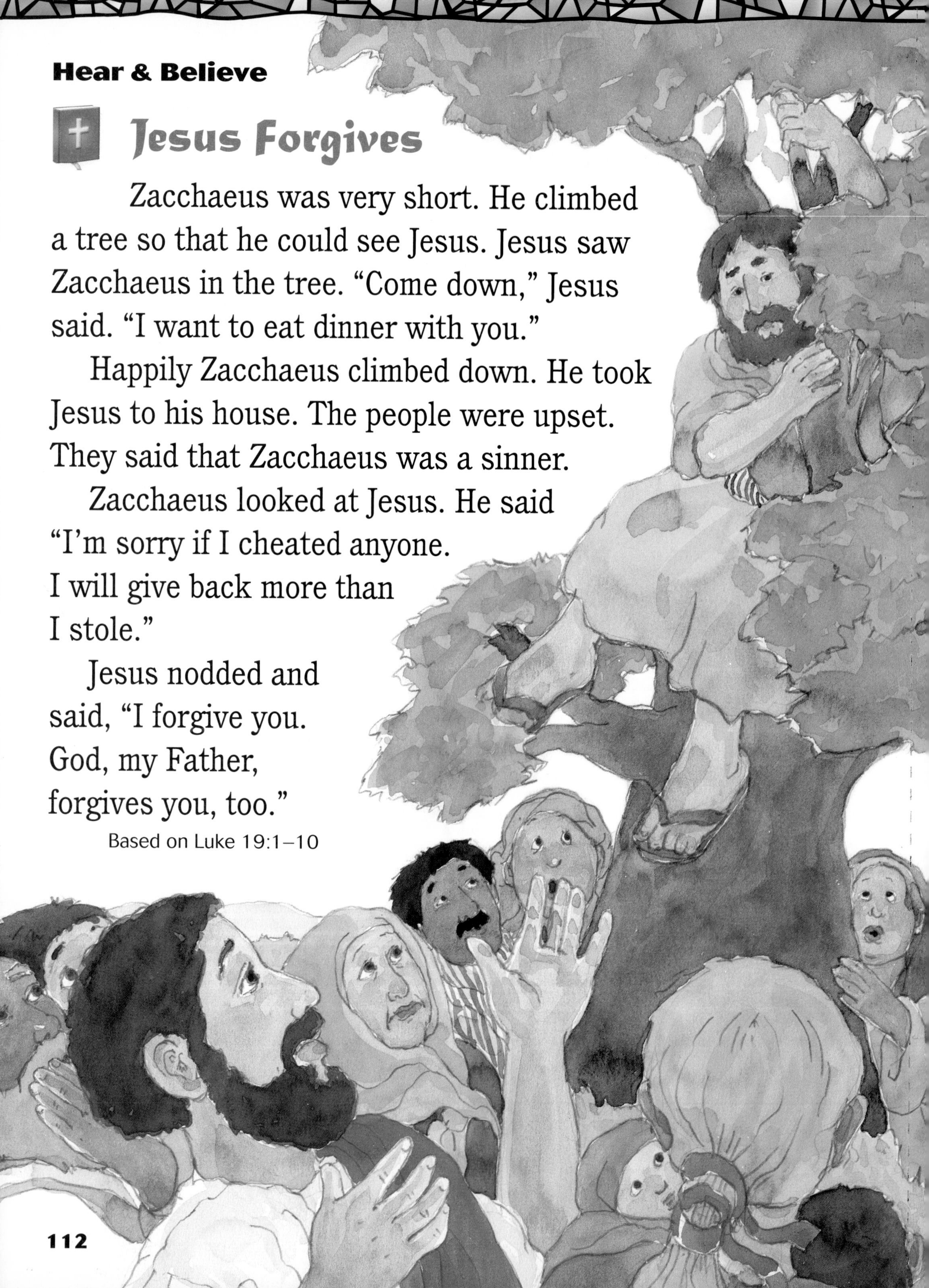

Hear & Believe

Jesus Forgives

Zacchaeus was very short. He climbed a tree so that he could see Jesus. Jesus saw Zacchaeus in the tree. "Come down," Jesus said. "I want to eat dinner with you."

Happily Zacchaeus climbed down. He took Jesus to his house. The people were upset. They said that Zacchaeus was a sinner.

Zacchaeus looked at Jesus. He said "I'm sorry if I cheated anyone. I will give back more than I stole."

Jesus nodded and said, "I forgive you. God, my Father, forgives you, too."

Based on Luke 19:1–10

What Jesus Wants

Zacchaeus was a selfish man. But he was sorry and began to help others. Jesus loved Zacchaeus and forgave him. Jesus wants us to love God and others. When we do not act in a loving way, God wants us to be sorry. God will always **forgive** us.

We Believe

God loves us and is always ready to forgive us. We must show our love for God.

Our Church Teaches

Jesus wants us to obey God's laws. The laws of God help us to choose what is right. Sometimes we choose to do what is wrong. This is called **sin**. We turn away from God when we sin. Sin also hurts our friendship with other people. God never stops loving us. He is always ready to forgive us.

Faith Words

forgive
Forgive means "to excuse or to pardon."

sin
Sin is choosing to do something we know is wrong.

How can we be forgiven?

Respond

A Forgiveness Story

Ricky played his video game over and over again. His mom told him to stop and to do his homework. Ricky was angry and said something mean to his mom. So she sent him to his room.

Ricky lay on his bed. He heard his parents talking. He heard his little sisters playing. He wanted to be with them. But soon Ricky fell asleep.

When Ricky awoke, he saw a bowl of hot soup on his table. Next to the soup was a note from his mom.

? How did Ricky know that his mom forgave him?

Activities

1. Write the answers on the lines.

   If you hurt someone, what can you say?

   ____

   ______________________________.

   Someone is sorry for hurting you. What can you say?

   ____

   ______________________________.

2. Color the spaces marked with a † green.

   Color the other spaces as you like.

   What words do you see?

How can we celebrate God's forgiveness?

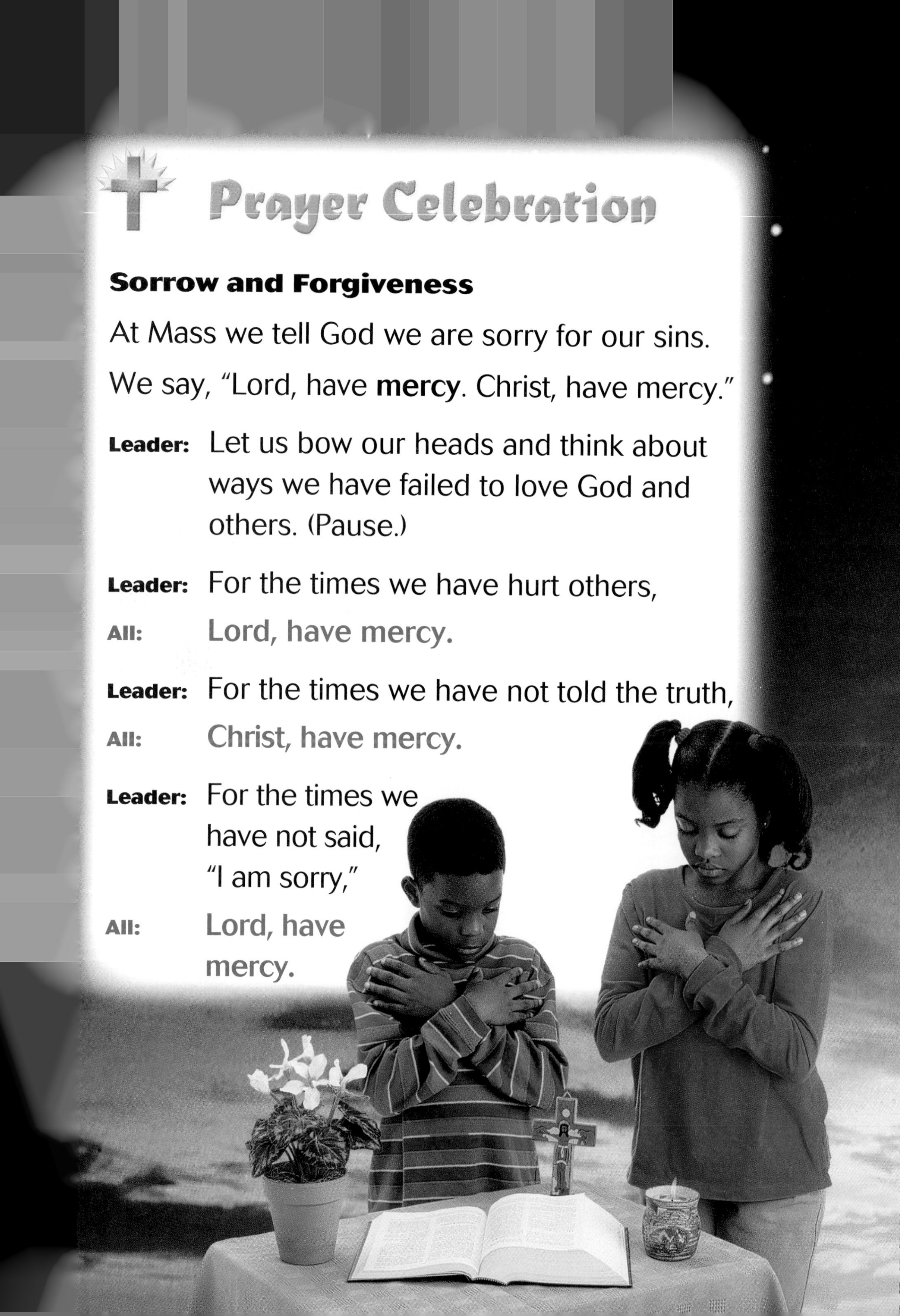

Prayer Celebration

Sorrow and Forgiveness

At Mass we tell God we are sorry for our sins. We say, "Lord, have **mercy**. Christ, have mercy."

Leader: Let us bow our heads and think about ways we have failed to love God and others. (Pause.)

Leader: For the times we have hurt others,

All: **Lord, have mercy.**

Leader: For the times we have not told the truth,

All: **Christ, have mercy.**

Leader: For the times we have not said, "I am sorry,"

All: **Lord, have mercy.**

Getting ready for Chapter 12

A choice of things to do at home

We Pray with God's Word

Children will learn that Jesus prayed with his heart, his voice, and his mind. They will realize that meditation helps them get closer to Jesus, and that they can pray by using their imagination. By putting themselves into a Gospel story, they can imagine what they would see, hear, say, think, and feel.

Just relax

Relaxing is the first step in praying with a Gospel story. Practice relaxing with your child. Begin by sitting comfortably in a quiet place. Next, close your eyes. Then breathe naturally and observe your breathing. If you begin to focus on something else, bring your attention back to your breathing.

Silence please!

With your child, listen for things in your home that make noise. Notice when it seems quiet. Talk about how you feel when it's quiet. Becoming quiet and listening are steps in praying with God's word.

If you were there

Together, read your child's favorite story. Discuss what it would be like to be in the story. Your child can look at the pictures and talk about what happens.

A Prayer for the Week

Bless our family this week, dear God, with your presence. Help us listen for your voice when we pray with your word. Amen.

FAMILY TIME

Something to Do . . .

On Sunday

Listen carefully to the Gospel story during Mass. Imagine what it would be like to be in the story.

Through the Week

Pray with God's word by meditating on a favorite Gospel story. Imagine what you would see, hear, say, think, and feel.

Visit Our Web Site

www.blestarewe.com

Something to Think About . . .

Praying With a Gospel Story

Amen, I say to you, whoever does not accept the kingdom of God like a child will not enter it.

Mark 10:15

In the Gospel story, Jesus' disciples discourage parents from bringing their children to him. Jesus rebukes his disciples and encourages the children to come to him. He embraces the children and blesses them.

Imagine if you were a parent in this Gospel story. What would you want Jesus to say to your child? What would you want your child to say to Jesus? How would you feel about Jesus blessing your child?

Meditation helps us come closer to Jesus. Using the four steps (relax, look and listen, imagine, and think) will help you and your child pray with God's word.

Something to Know About . . .

Our Heritage in Prayer

Ignatius Loyola, born in Spain in 1491, became the founder of the Jesuits. While studying his own spiritual life, Ignatius took notes on his experiences with prayer, suffering, and conversion of heart. His writings became known as the *Spiritual Exercises*. The exercises include Ignatius's approach to meditation. His method involves asking God for a special grace, reflecting on a Gospel scene by using one's imagination and senses, putting oneself into the scene, and applying the Gospel message to one's own life. Ignatius believed that everyone could learn to pray in this way. The *Spiritual Exercises* became Ignatius's greatest single contribution to Western spirituality.

12 We Pray with God's Word

Lord, teach us how to pray.

Based on Luke 11:1

Share

People pray in many ways. Think about how you pray. How do you talk to and listen to God?

Mark an X in each picture that shows how you pray.

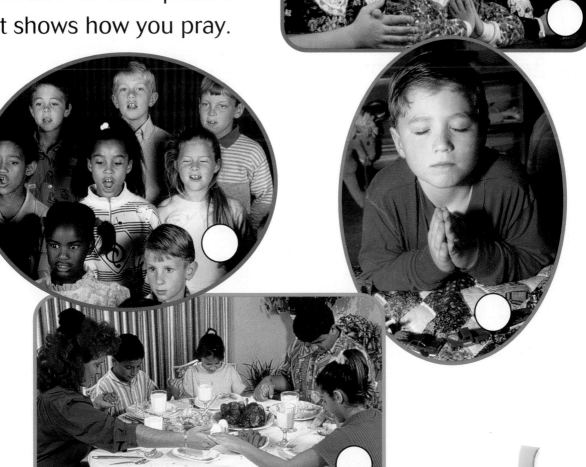

Circle your favorite way to pray.

How did Jesus pray?

Hear & Believe

The Prayer of Jesus

The Bible tells us how Jesus prayed. He prayed with his heart and voice. He prayed with his mind.

Jesus prayed with his family in the **Temple**. Jesus prayed alone in the desert. Sometimes he prayed on a mountain. Sometimes he prayed in a boat.

After the Last Supper, Jesus sang **psalms** with his friends. Then he went into a garden to pray.

The Temple in Jerusalem

A Bible land desert

A Bible land mountain

Praying Like Jesus

We can learn to pray like Jesus. We can pray aloud with our voices. We can pray silently with our hearts and minds. We can pray alone or with other people. We can pray anywhere and any time.

We Believe

Thinking about God's word is a good way to pray. It helps us get closer to Jesus.

Our Church Teaches

We can pray with **Gospel** stories from the Bible. The Gospels are the Good News of Jesus. They tell us how to show our love for God and other people. We grow closer to Jesus when we pray with the Gospels.

Faith Words

psalms
Psalms are prayers that people often sing. The Book of Psalms is in the Bible.

Gospel
The Gospel is the Good News of Jesus. There are four Gospels in the Bible.

The Sea of Galilee

The Garden of Gethsemane

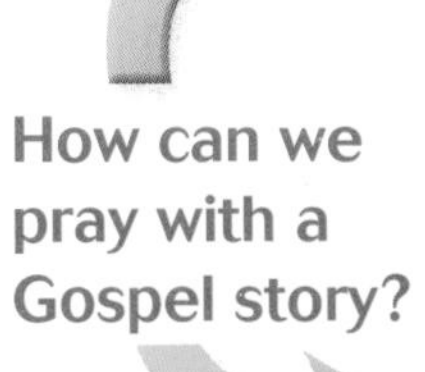

How can we pray with a Gospel story?

Respond

Praying with God's Word

There are four steps in praying with a Gospel story.

Relax | Look and Listen | Imagine | Think

Relax Close your eyes. Become quiet. Ask God to fill your heart and mind.

Look and Listen Look at the picture of Jesus and the children. Listen to the Bible story.

Jesus Blesses the Children

Jesus had been teaching all day. He was tired and sat down to rest.

Many parents started to bring their children to Jesus. They wanted Jesus to bless the children. But Jesus' friends told the people not to bother Jesus.

When Jesus saw this, he said, "Don't stop them. Let the children come closer. I love little children." Then Jesus placed his hands on the children. He gave them his blessing.

Based on Mark 10:13–16

Imagine Put yourself in the story. Imagine that your parents are taking you to see Jesus. He is on a hillside with his friends. Jesus is sitting under a tree.

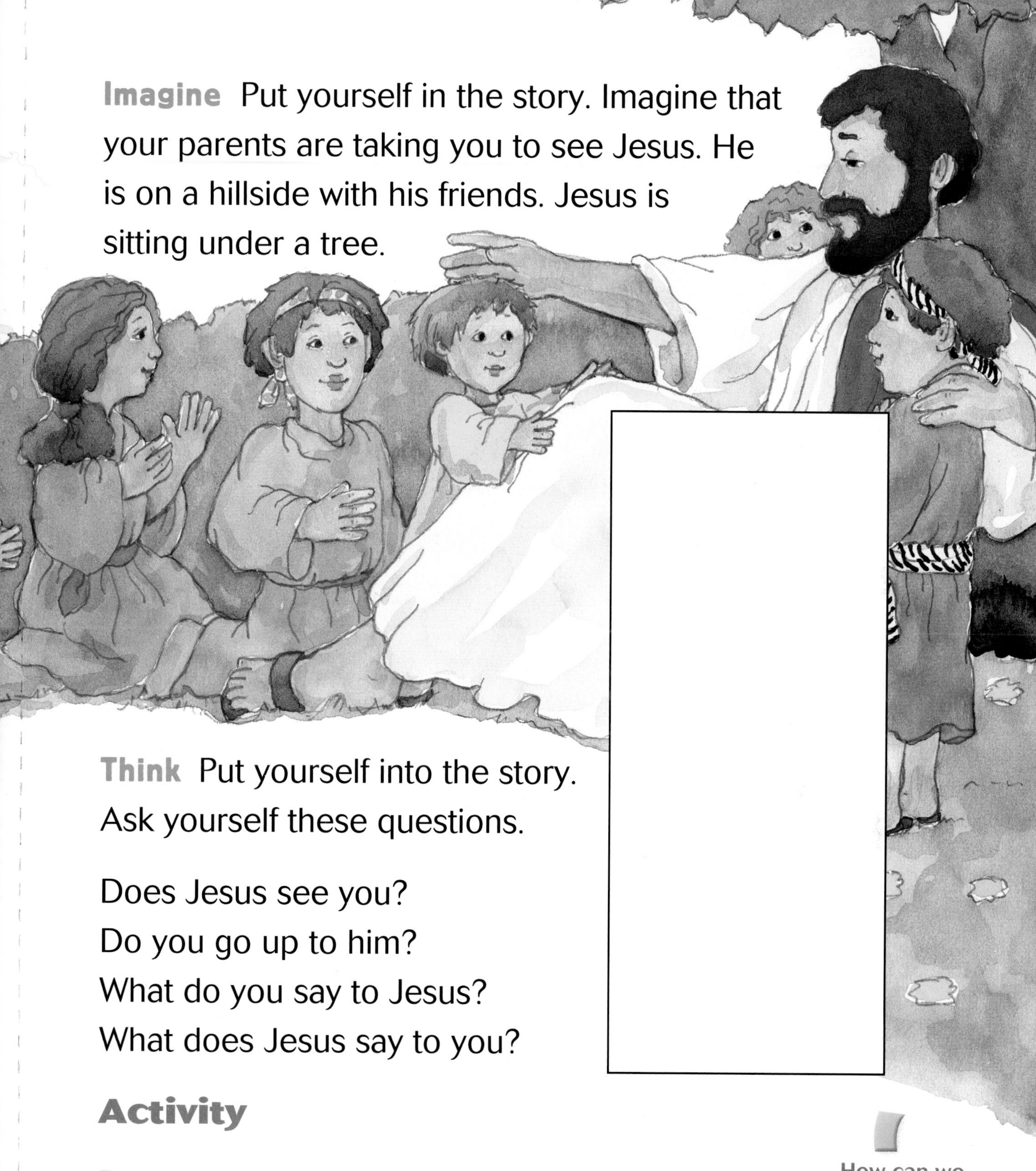

Think Put yourself into the story. Ask yourself these questions.

Does Jesus see you?
Do you go up to him?
What do you say to Jesus?
What does Jesus say to you?

Activity

Draw yourself in the picture with Jesus and the children.

How can we celebrate Jesus' love for us?

Prayer Celebration

An Acting Prayer

You can pray by acting out a Bible story. Putting on a play helps you to think about the story. You can imagine what the people said and did.

Act out the story of Jesus blessing the children.

Grandparents' Day

What is something you learned from a grandparent or older relative?

This year Lucy's parish celebrated Grandparents' Day. The children invited their grandparents to a party in the church hall. Lucy shared her grandmother with a friend. Her friend's grandparents live too far away, in Cuba.

Lucy's favorite part of the party was called "Remember when . . ." The grandparents told about things they remembered from childhood. They also taught the children to play games of long ago. Lucy's favorite games were pick-up-sticks, marbles, and hopscotch.

Lucy is very proud of her grandmother. She learned to respect the other children's grandparents, too. She learned that older people are fun to be with.

Think About It

We respect people by making them feel special. How did the children in Lucy's parish show respect for grandparents?

Use a ✔ to show your answers.

- [ ] by inviting them to a party
- [ ] by listening to their stories
- [ ] by asking them for money
- [ ] by playing their games

Learn About It

Jesus loved and respected his family and friends. He obeyed Mary and Joseph. Jesus liked being with his friends. He visited them when they were sick. He fed them when they were hungry. Jesus teaches us to love and respect our family and friends.

Do Something About It

We love and respect others in many ways. Find a way to make someone in your family and a friend feel special.

Write their names on the badges.

UNIT 3

Organizer

Read the names of the chapters.
Think about the pictures.
Draw a line to show what you learned in each chapter.

1. Jesus Is God's Son •

2. We Celebrate the Gift of Eucharist •

3. Jesus Teaches Us About Forgiveness •

4. We Pray with God's Word •

UNIT 3

Review

A Circle the word that completes each sentence.

1. Jesus is God's __.	Son	book
2. The mother of Jesus is __.	Anne	Mary
3. Jesus was born in __.	Bethlehem	Nazareth
4. Jesus is God's special __.	gift	angel

B Draw a line to the words that complete each sentence.

1. Jesus ate a special meal with his friends called •	• "This is my Blood."
2. Jesus took the bread and said, •	• the tabernacle.
3.Jesus took the cup of wine and said, •	• "This is my Body."
4. At the Last Supper, Jesus gave us •	• the Last Supper.
5. The Eucharist is kept in a container called •	• the Eucharist.

UNIT 3

Review

C **Look at the words in the box. Write the best word to complete each sentence.**

loving
wrong
mercy
forgive
laws

1. Jesus wants us to obey God's

_______________.

2. Sin is choosing to do what we know is

_______________.

3. God never stops _______________ us.

4. God is always ready to _______________ us.

5. We ask God to forgive us when we say "Lord have

_______________."

UNIT 3

Review

D Circle the correct answer.

1. Jesus prayed with his family in the Temple. **Yes** **No**
2. Thinking about computer games is a good way to pray. **Yes** **No**
3. Psalms are prayers that we can sing. **Yes** **No**
4. The Gospel is the good news of Jesus. **Yes** **No**
5. There are two Gospels in the Bible. **Yes** **No**

E Draw yourself praying with a Gospel story.

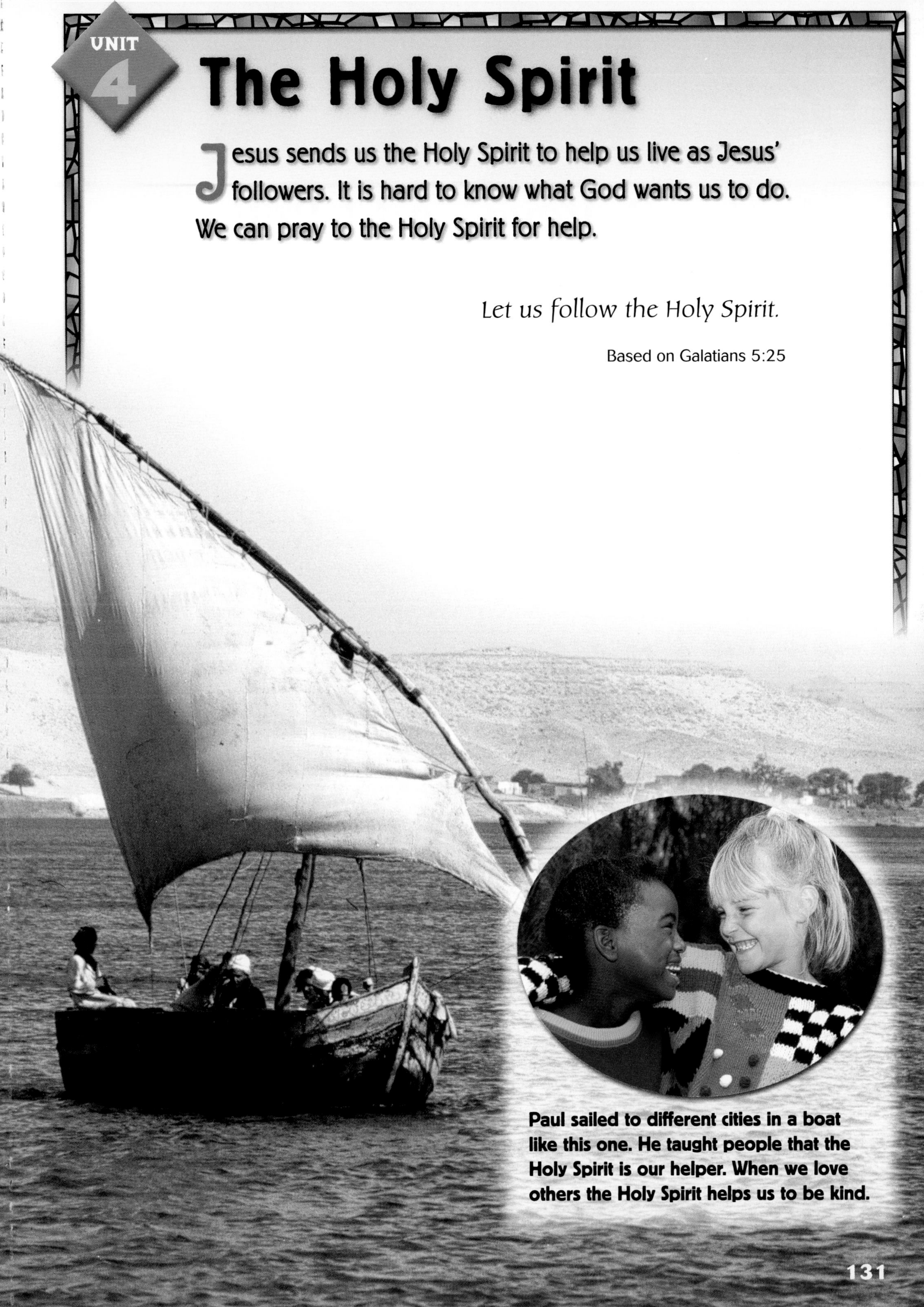

UNIT 4

The Holy Spirit

Jesus sends us the Holy Spirit to help us live as Jesus' followers. It is hard to know what God wants us to do. We can pray to the Holy Spirit for help.

Let us follow the Holy Spirit.

Based on Galatians 5:25

Paul sailed to different cities in a boat like this one. He taught people that the Holy Spirit is our helper. When we love others the Holy Spirit helps us to be kind.

UNIT
4
SONG

If You Believe and I Believe

Traditional from Zimbabwe
Adaptation of English traditional as taught by Tarasai
Arranged by John L. Bell

If you be-lieve and I be-lieve And we to-geth - er pray,

The Ho - ly Spir - it must come down And set God's peo - ple free,

And set God's peo - ple free, And set God's peo - ple free;

The Ho - ly Spir - it must come down And

set God's peo - ple free.

Getting ready for Chapter 13

FAMILY TIME

A choice of things to do at home

Jesus Sends Us the Holy Spirit

It is the Spirit that fills the Church with God's presence and guides its members in living out the Gospel message. In this chapter the children will come to understand that the Holy Spirit is the gift of God's love. They will realize that the Holy Spirit helps us understand Jesus' teaching, and discover ways the Holy Spirit helps us love God and others.

Welcome to our home.

Welcome to our home

The Holy Spirit strengthens us to share our love with others. This can be done through a spirit of hospitality. Invite another family to your home this week for dinner and/or dessert. In preparation, discuss with your child the importance of hospitality, and together make a welcome sign for the family you invite.

Family spirit

Work with your child on a project that will benefit the entire family. The project might be an activity like yard work, or cleaning out a closet or some drawers. The goal is to work together and experience a spirit of cooperation. Common projects build togetherness and lessen the burden on any one family member.

That's us

Ask your child to look through family pictures with you to find a photograph that captures the spirit of your family. It might be a picture of a birthday party, a holiday, or a favorite activity. Other members of the family might pick out their favorite photos, and explain why they show the spirit of your family.

A Prayer for the Week

Come, Holy Spirit, fill our hearts with your grace. Bring our family together in a spirit of peace and love. Help us be signs of your presence to all we meet.
Amen.

FAMILY TIME

Something to Do . . .

On Sunday

One image of the Holy Spirit is the dove. Look for images of the Holy Spirit when you are at Mass.

Through the Week

The Spirit is God's gift of love to us. Be a bearer of the Spirit to others at work, at home, or in school this week.

Visit Our Web Site

www.blestarewe.com

Something to Think About . . .

Jesus Promises the Holy Spirit

The advocate, the holy Spirit that the Father will send in my name—he will teach you everything and remind you of all that I told you.
John 14:26

When it was time for Jesus to leave the world, his disciples did not want him to go. In the Gospel, Jesus explains that he must leave, but promises that he will ask God, the Father, to give the disciples the Holy Spirit to be with them always. Jesus tells the disciples that the Holy Spirit will guide and help them, teaching them everything and reminding them of his words. He says he is leaving them peace so that they should not be worried or afraid.

The Holy Spirit helps each of us as well, by bringing us peace. The Holy Spirit is God's special gift of love.

Something to Know About . . . Our Heritage in Symbols

The image of the dove representing the Holy Spirit goes back to the origins of the Church, and the image of the dove in Scripture goes back to the story of Noah. As a sign of the union of the Holy Spirit and Jesus, receptacles for the Eucharist were made in the shapes of doves, and hung in churches since the early Middle Ages. The Eucharist that was to be taken to the sick was in a container suspended by chains. The container was shaped like a dove and made of a precious metal, usually gold or silver. Later the dove was made of different materials, including gilded leather. The dove became the outer vessel holding the smaller container, or pyx, with the Blessed Sacrament inside.

13 Jesus Sends Us the Holy Spirit

The Spirit of God's love lives within me.

Based on Romans 5:5

Share

Your family loves you very much.
Your family helps you in many ways.
But your family needs helpers to care for you and help you to grow.

Tell how each person helps you.

Write about a person who helps you.

____

____

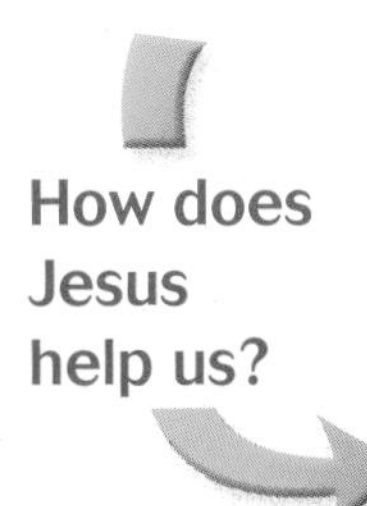

How does Jesus help us?

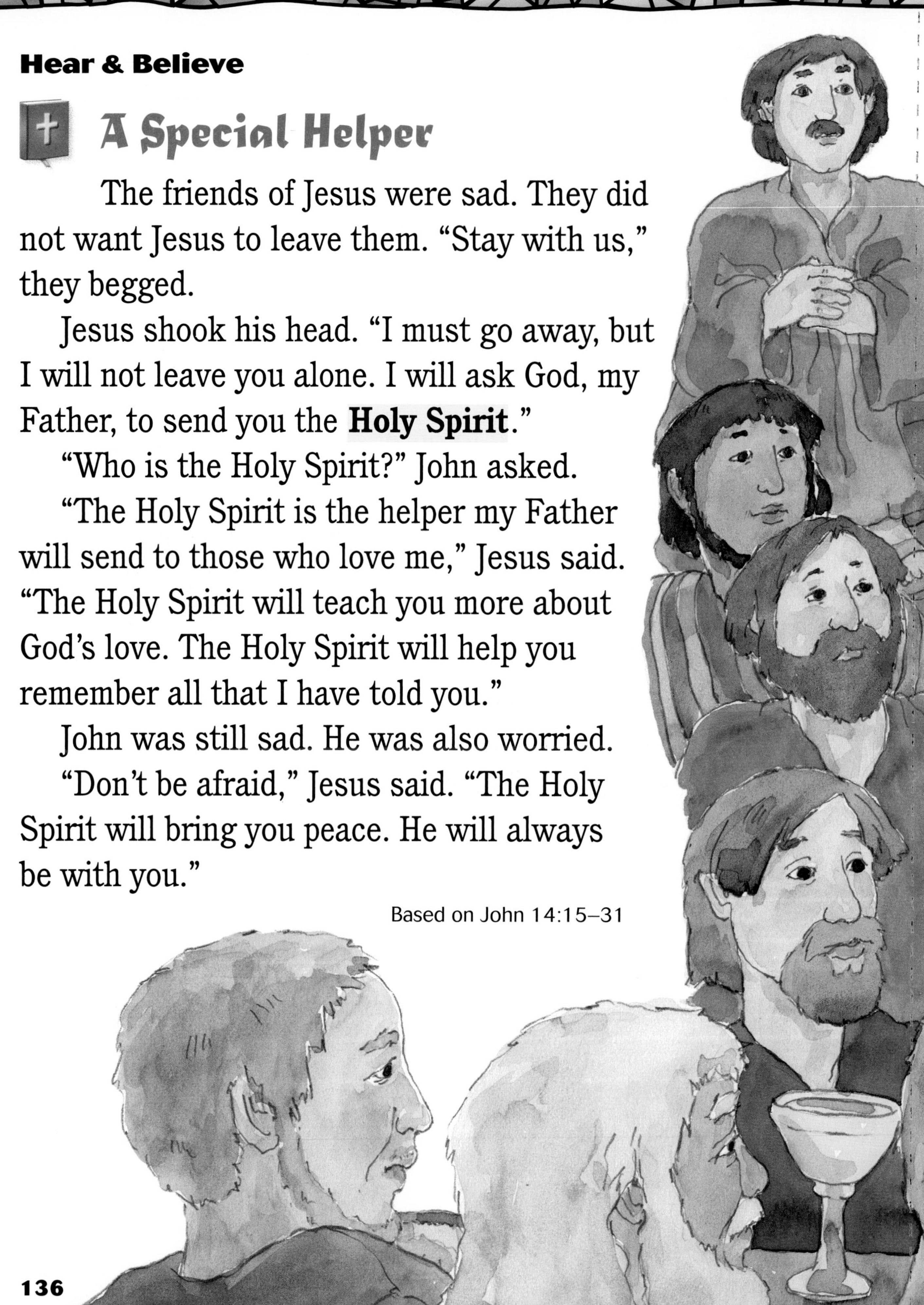

Hear & Believe

A Special Helper

The friends of Jesus were sad. They did not want Jesus to leave them. "Stay with us," they begged.

Jesus shook his head. "I must go away, but I will not leave you alone. I will ask God, my Father, to send you the **Holy Spirit**."

"Who is the Holy Spirit?" John asked.

"The Holy Spirit is the helper my Father will send to those who love me," Jesus said. "The Holy Spirit will teach you more about God's love. The Holy Spirit will help you remember all that I have told you."

John was still sad. He was also worried.

"Don't be afraid," Jesus said. "The Holy Spirit will bring you peace. He will always be with you."

Based on John 14:15–31

Jesus' Promise

Jesus promised his friends that he would not leave them alone. He promised to send the Holy Spirit to be their helper. The Holy Spirit is our helper, too. The Holy Spirit helps us grow in God's love. He helps us love others. The Holy Spirit brings us peace.

Our Church Teaches

The Holy Spirit is God's special gift of love to us. The Holy Spirit is always with us. The Holy Spirit leads us and guides us.

We Believe

God's Holy Spirit is always with us. This Spirit helps us grow in God's love.

Faith Words

Holy Spirit
The Holy Spirit is the Spirit of God. This Spirit helps us follow Jesus.

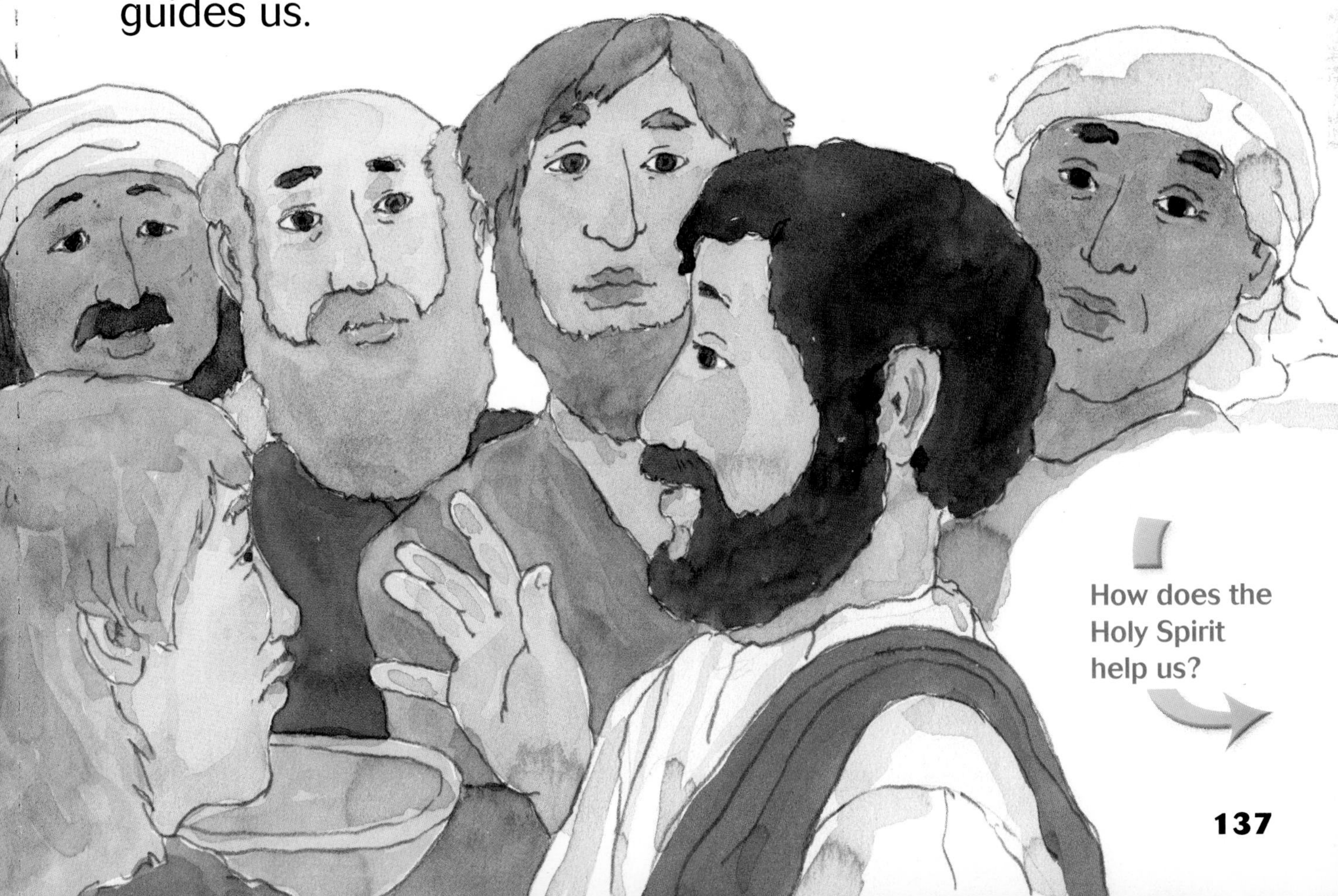

How does the Holy Spirit help us?

Respond

Terry's Problem

One morning, Terry and some other children were waiting for the school bus. Something very scary happened. Two older boys pushed a first grade boy into the street. The older boys thought it was funny and laughed.

When Terry got to school, she told her teacher what happened. Terry was afraid of what the other children might say.

That night, Terry's mother said that she did the right thing. Her mother said that her teacher would know how to handle the problem.

At bedtime Terry's mother taught her this prayer. "Holy Spirit, help me always do what is right."

Why did Terry's mother teach her this prayer?

Activities

1. Color the border around this prayer.

Holy Spirit, help me always do what is right.

2. Circle the choice the Holy Spirit helps these children make.

Kim's friend wants her to steal a candy bar.

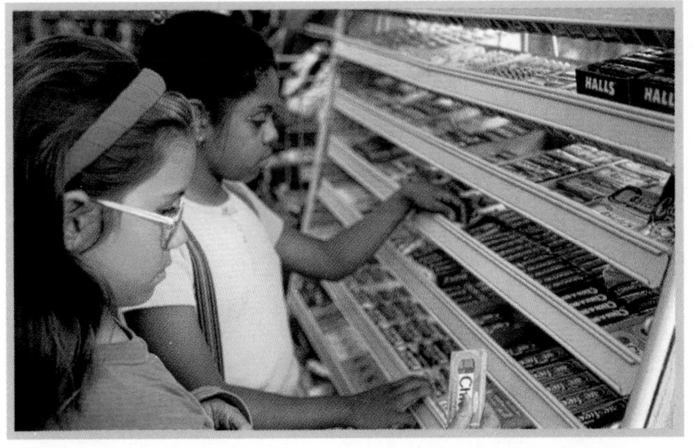

steal **be honest**

A neighbor tries to start a fight with Tony.

make peace **fight**

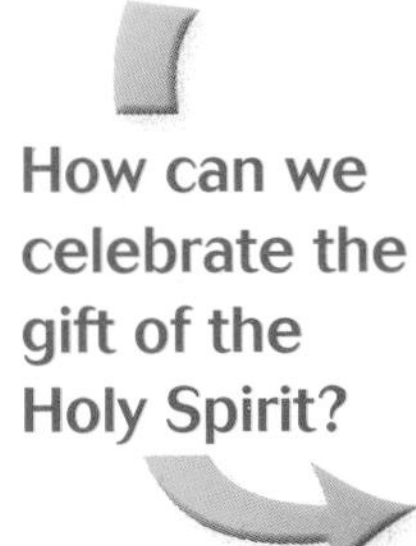
How can we celebrate the gift of the Holy Spirit?

Prayer Celebration

Glory Be

We praise God as Father, Son, and Holy Spirit when we make the Sign of the Cross. Let us now praise God by praying the Glory Be to the Father.

Glory be to the Father,
and to the Son,
and to the Holy Spirit.
As it was in the beginning,
is now, and will be forever.
Amen.

Getting ready for Chapter 14

A choice of things to do at home

We Celebrate the Gift of the Holy Spirit

Through the sacraments of Baptism and Confirmation, we are initiated into the life of the Church. In this chapter, children will realize that they receive God's gift of the Holy Spirit in Baptism and Confirmation. They will learn that the pouring of water in Baptism means being born in the Holy Spirit and that the oil used in Confirmation is the seal of the Holy Spirit.

Family celebration

Locate your child's baptismal certificate. Together, find the date on which your child was baptized by water and the Holy Spirit. With your family, plan a special celebration of that event. Include your child's godparents in your celebration.

Gifts given, gifts received

The extent of God's gifts of Jesus and the Holy Spirit cannot be fully grasped, but we do understand the idea of a gift freely given out of love. Together, recall a favorite gift your child received and another one your child gave. Talk about how gifts can be expressions of love.

Acts of kindness

Often the best gift is not a material object but an act of kindness. With your child, choose a way your family can share its time and effort by doing something for another family or for the community. Remember that praying for others is also a gift.

A Prayer for the Week

Spirit of God, you are
our source of joy, energy, and
celebration. Stay with our family,
we pray, and help us remember
how blest we are to
have one another.
Amen.

FAMILY TIME

Something to Do . . .

On Sunday

Look at the baptismal font in your church. Remind your family that the Holy Spirit first came to them at Baptism.

Through the Week

Share times when family members felt that the Holy Spirit helped them make good choices.

Visit Our Web Site

www.blestarewe.com

Something to Think About . . .

The Spirit in the Sacraments

Be sealed with the Gift of the Holy Spirit.
Rite of Confirmation

Baptism, Eucharist, and Confirmation were all part of one celebration of initiation in the early Church. Over the years they became separate and conferred at different times. Confirmation completes Baptism as our birth and growth in the Holy Spirit. The Eucharist is our nourishment as we grow in the Spirit.

In the Rite of Confirmation, the bishop makes a sign of the cross with chrism oil on the forehead of the one being confirmed. This seals the person with the gift of the Holy Spirit. At Confirmation our faith becomes stronger. We become more like Christ. Our lives should always reflect the goodness of Christ.

Something to Know About . . . Our Heritage

Each year during Holy Week, there is a solemn ritual at the cathedral church. During the ritual, the holy oils used in the parishes throughout the coming year are consecrated by the bishop at the Chrism Mass. These oils are the oil of chrism, a mixture of olive oil and fragrant balm used in Baptism, Confirmation, and Holy Orders; the oil of catechumens used to anoint adults preparing for Baptism; and the oil of the sick, used in the sacrament of the Anointing of the Sick. Parish representatives return to their churches with the consecrated oils, to be used in the celebration of sacraments throughout the year.

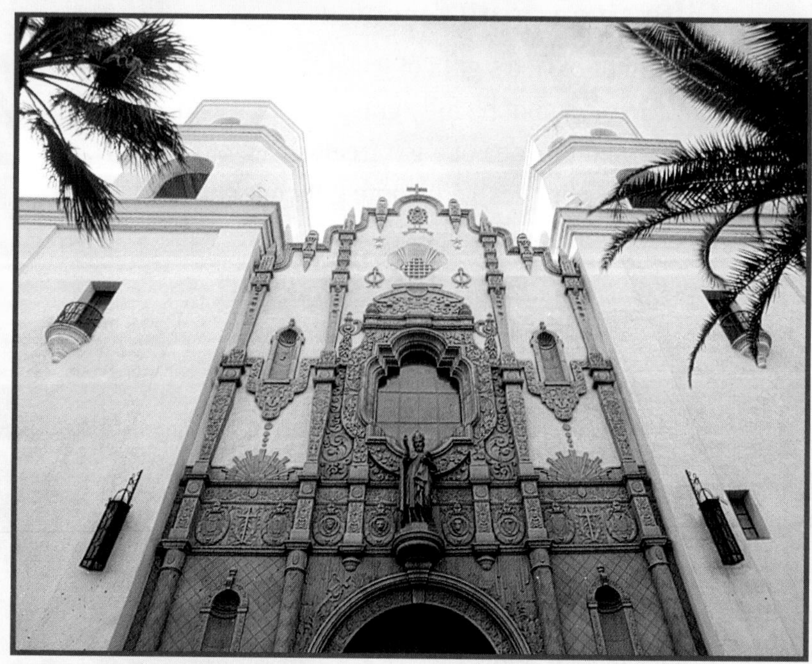

St. Augustine's Cathedral in Tuscon, Arizona

14 We Celebrate the Gift of the Holy Spirit

O God, help us and guide us.
Send us your Holy Spirit.

Based on the Rite of Confirmation

Share

Water and oil are used in many ways. Circle the sign for water or oil under each picture.

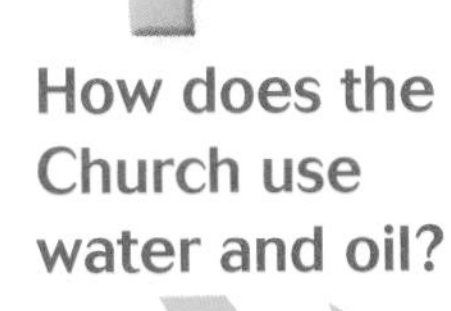

How does the Church use water and oil?

The Gift of the Holy Spirit

We receive the gift of the Holy Spirit in the **sacraments**. The Church celebrates sacraments as signs of Christ's love and presence.

In Baptism the priest or deacon blesses water before he pours it on the person. He prays, "Father, by the power of the Holy Spirit, we ask you now to bless this water. May it wash away our sins and give us new life in Jesus."

Based on the Rite of Baptism for Children

In **Confirmation** the bishop uses holy oil to make the sign of the cross on the forehead of the person. He says, "Be sealed with the gift of the Holy Spirit." That means, "Be filled with God's Spirit."

Based on the Rite of Confirmation

The Holy Spirit Comes to Us

The Holy Spirit gives us new life in the sacraments. The waters of Baptism wash us clean of all sin. The Holy Spirit fills us with God's love. The holy oil of Confirmation is a symbol that our faith in Christ is stronger. The Holy Spirit guides us to make good choices.

We Believe

We receive the gift of the Holy Spirit in the sacraments. The Holy Spirit helps us live as followers of Jesus.

Our Church Teaches

In Baptism we are born to new life in the Holy Spirit. The Holy Spirit helps us to be more like Jesus. This Spirit helps us live as good Catholics.

In Confirmation the Holy Spirit makes our faith stronger. The holy oil is a sign that the Holy Spirit is working in us.

Faith Words

sacraments
Sacraments are special signs of Christ's love and presence.

Confirmation
Confirmation is the sacrament in which the Holy Spirit makes our faith in Jesus Christ stronger.

How can we use our gift of the Holy Spirit?

Respond

Life in the Holy Spirit

Nicodemus went secretly to Jesus at night. "What must I do to become a member of God's family?" he asked Jesus.

Jesus said, "You must be born of water and the Spirit."

"How can this happen?" Nicodemus asked.

Jesus explained. "If you believe in me, the Holy Spirit will bring you God's own life. This life lasts forever."

"What is this life like?" Nicodemus asked.

Jesus explained, "Instead of living in darkness, you will live in the light. Instead of doing bad things, you will do what is true and good."

Based on John 3:1–21

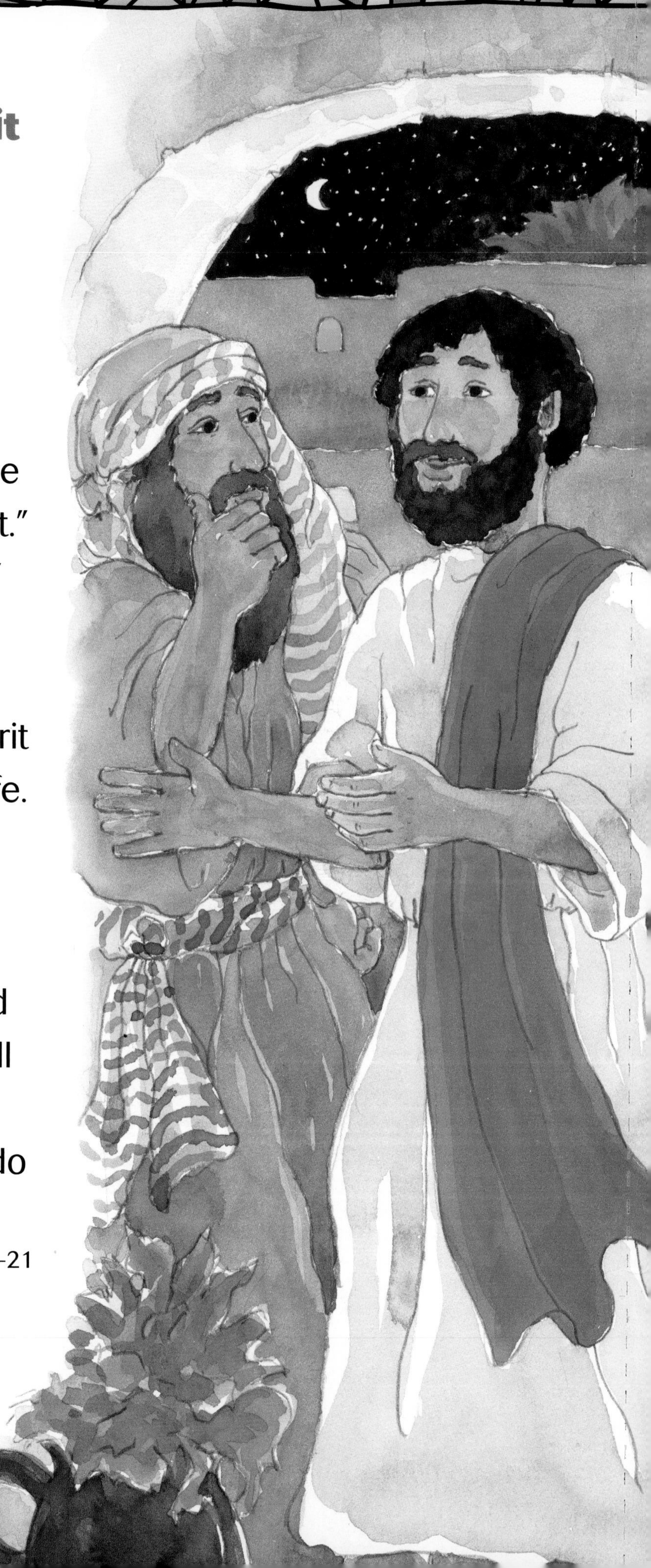

? What do you think Nicodemus did next?

Activity

Look at the pictures about making good choices. In each pair of sentences, find the good choice. Draw a line under it.

Lisa watches TV.

Lisa takes out the garbage.

Tim keeps playing with the truck.

Tim lets Bruce play with the truck.

Rosa tries to sing and pray.

Rosa plays with her toys.

How can we celebrate our new life in the Holy Spirit?

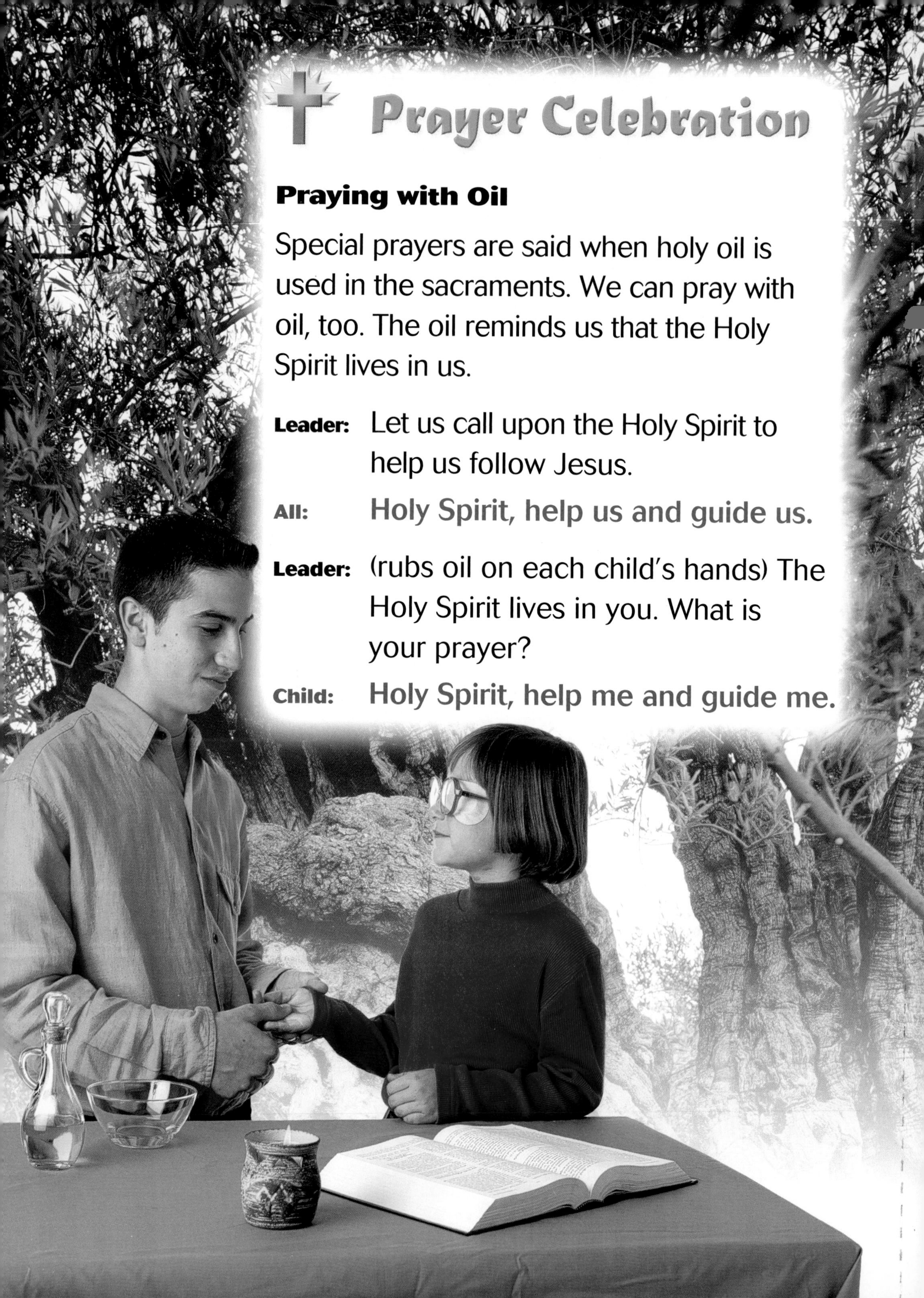

Prayer Celebration

Praying with Oil

Special prayers are said when holy oil is used in the sacraments. We can pray with oil, too. The oil reminds us that the Holy Spirit lives in us.

Leader: Let us call upon the Holy Spirit to help us follow Jesus.

All: **Holy Spirit, help us and guide us.**

Leader: (rubs oil on each child's hands) The Holy Spirit lives in you. What is your prayer?

Child: **Holy Spirit, help me and guide me.**

Getting ready for Chapter 15

A choice of things to do at home

The Holy Spirit Is Our Helper

In this chapter, children will come to understand that the Holy Spirit helps us to follow Jesus. The Holy Spirit helps us learn good habits so that we can become more like Jesus. Children will learn how the Holy Spirit helps Christians show love for others.

Seeds of virtue

The family has been called the seedbed of virtue because it is in the family that children learn the skills and good habits necessary for a mature Christian life. This week, purchase an envelope of seeds and label them with the names of good habits you would like for your child. Plant the seeds and watch them grow.

You've got mail

Have family members write notes of praise to one another about the good habits they see being used for others.

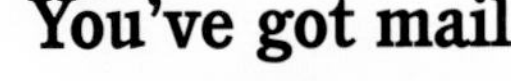

Read all about it

With your child, look for examples of people in the news who are showing their love for others. Point out and discuss stories in the local paper or on local television that feature the good being done in your community.

A Prayer for the Week

Loving God, you send us your Spirit to help us follow Jesus. We promise to use our good habits to help others. Amen.

FAMILY TIME

Something to Do . . .

On Sunday

Ask the Holy Spirit, during the Prayer of the Faithful, to help you develop habits that will make you more loving.

Through the Week

Make a special effort to acknowledge each other's good habits.

Visit Our Web Site

www.blestarewe.com

Something to Think About . . .

Fruits of the Holy Spirit

The fruit of the Spirit is love, joy, peace, patience, kindness, generosity, faithfulness, gentleness, self-control. Against such there is no law.

Galatians 5:22–23

For Christians, Jesus is the model of how to live and the Holy Spirit is our source of courage. Christ gave us the Holy Spirit to be our helper and guide.

In Paul's letter to the first Christians in Galatia, he refers to the fruits of the Holy Spirit. He says that these fruits, or qualities, will be ours if we follow the Spirit. When we act with these fruits, we exhibit our good habits and show our love for others. By using these good habits, we are living like Jesus and following God's law to love our neighbors as ourselves.

Something to Know About . . .

Our Heritage in Theology

Thomas Aquinas, who lived in the thirteenth century, became known as one of the best thinkers in history. He greatly influenced theological thought in the Western Church. Aquinas developed a theology of the Holy Spirit based on his understanding of the gifts in Isaiah 11:2–3 and the fruits in Galatians 5:22–23. He taught not only that we should use the Spirit's power and gifts in our lives, but that we should truly enjoy and feel close to the Holy Spirit, just as we do with a dear friend.

Aquinas believed that the Spirit's peace and joy make us content and that these fruits transform our hearts, changing fear and anxiety into security and the desire to give to others.

15 The Holy Spirit Is Our Helper

Let us follow the Holy Spirit.

Based on Galatians 5:25

Share

Some things we do are habits. We brush our teeth every day. We say "please" when we want something. Some people bite their nails.

Habits can be good or bad. Write a **G** in the box before Nick and Jenny's good habits. Write a **B** in the box before Nick and Jenny's bad habits.

☐ Jenny puts her toys away before bedtime.

☐ Nick always leaves his jacket on the floor.

☐ Nick says "thank you" when he gets a gift.

☐ Jenny prays to God each day.

☐ Jenny slams the door every morning.

How does the Holy Spirit help us learn good habits?

A Letter from Paul

Paul became a follower of Jesus Christ. He wrote this letter to a group of the first Christians.

My Dear People,

Jesus Christ loves you. He wants you to love others the way you love yourselves. Sometimes it will be hard to be kind and helpful. But Christ gave you the Holy Spirit to be your helper and guide.

If you follow the Spirit, the **fruits of the Holy Spirit** will be yours. You will act with love, joy, and peace. You will be patient, gentle, and kind. You will have self-control.

Based on Galatians 5:14–25

Kindness

JOY

Love

The Holy Spirit Helps Us

Paul's letter is about loving others. Jesus knew that it would not always be easy to love. That is why Jesus gave us the Holy Spirit. When we love others, the Holy Spirit helps us to be joyful, peaceful, patient, gentle, and kind. He helps us to use self-control.

We Believe

The Holy Spirit helps us follow Jesus. The Spirit helps us learn good habits of showing love for others.

Our Church Teaches

When we practice **good habits**, we share the fruits of the Holy Spirit with others. These fruits are signs that the Holy Spirit is acting in our lives. When we do kind acts again and again, kindness becomes a habit. Our kindness teaches others about the kindness of God.

Faith Words

fruits of the Holy Spirit
The fruits of the Holy Spirit are signs of the Holy Spirit's action in our lives.

good habits
Good habits are ways of acting for the good of others.

Peace Patience Gentleness

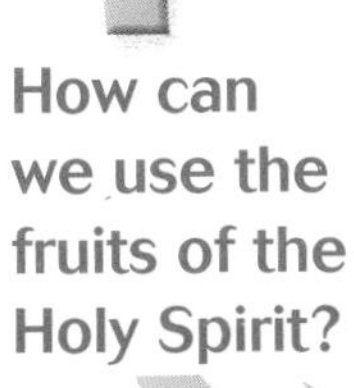

How can we use the fruits of the Holy Spirit?

Respond

Tony's Saturday Habit

Tony is fun to play with. He shares his toys. He helps younger children learn new games. He stops fights by saying funny things. Everyone feels good when Tony is around.

But, Tony has a Saturday habit. He watches TV for three hours. All his friends want him to come out and play. But Tony says, "I can't. I need to watch my shows."

What do you think about Tony's habit?

peace

patience

self–
control

gentleness

kindness

Activities

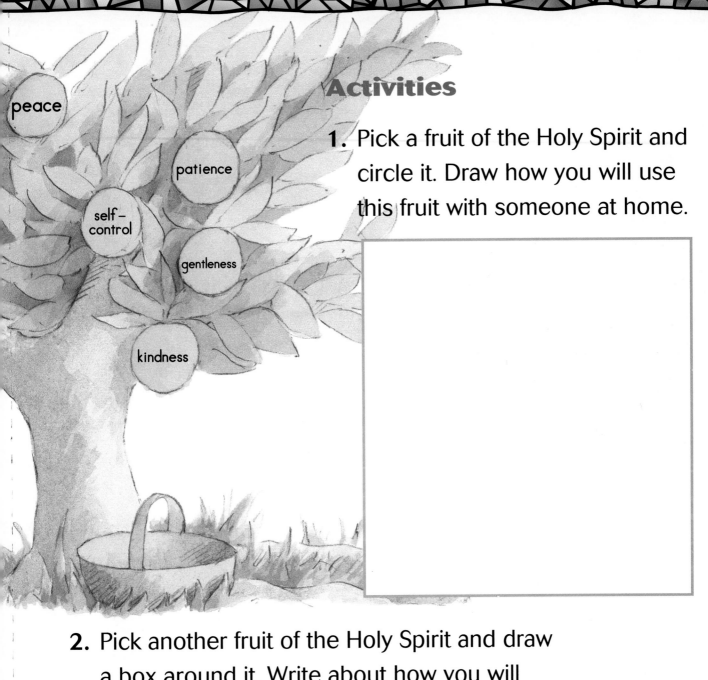

1. Pick a fruit of the Holy Spirit and circle it. Draw how you will use this fruit with someone at home.

2. Pick another fruit of the Holy Spirit and draw a box around it. Write about how you will use this fruit in school.

How can we celebrate the fruits of the Holy Spirit?

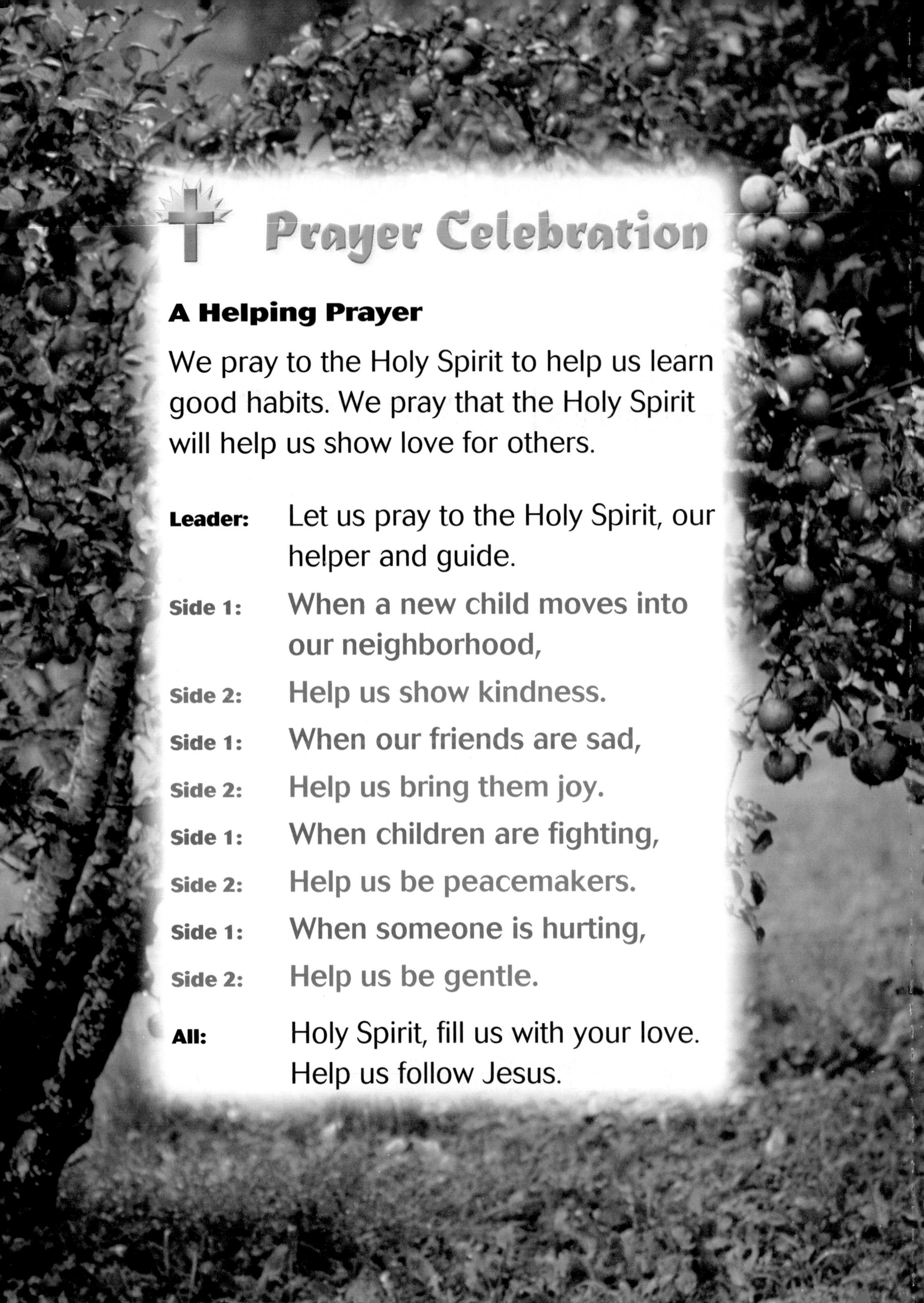

Prayer Celebration

A Helping Prayer

We pray to the Holy Spirit to help us learn good habits. We pray that the Holy Spirit will help us show love for others.

Leader: Let us pray to the Holy Spirit, our helper and guide.

Side 1: When a new child moves into our neighborhood,

Side 2: Help us show kindness.

Side 1: When our friends are sad,

Side 2: Help us bring them joy.

Side 1: When children are fighting,

Side 2: Help us be peacemakers.

Side 1: When someone is hurting,

Side 2: Help us be gentle.

All: Holy Spirit, fill us with your love. Help us follow Jesus.

Getting ready for Chapter 16

A choice of things to do at home

The Holy Spirit Helps Us Pray

In this chapter, children will realize that it is the Holy Spirit who helps us pray and who helps us ask God for qualities we need to follow Jesus. The Holy Spirit brings us peace, joy, love, grace, and courage. Children will discover how the Church prays to the Holy Spirit, and will participate in a Holy Spirit prayer celebration.

Prayer box

Decorate a small, empty box with symbols of the Holy Spirit, such as doves and flames of fire. Leave blank pieces of paper next to the box. Invite your family to write prayers of petition on the papers and place them in the prayer box. When your family is together, read the petitions and pray for each other's requests.

United in prayer

Is there another family in your parish or neighborhood who would be willing to be a prayer partner for your family? Ask this family to pray for members of your family each day and you pray for theirs.

Table prayer

One night this week, ask the members of your family to say the names of people they want to remember in prayer. Before your evening meal, have one person say, "For (name of person)." Then the others at the table respond, "We pray to the Lord."

A Prayer for the Week

Holy Spirit, we
ask you to help our family
remember the teachings of
Jesus and to follow
his example.
Amen.

FAMILY TIME

Something to Do . . .

On Sunday

Listen for the times during the Mass when the priest and people pray to the Holy Spirit. Talk about these prayers on your way home from church.

Through the Week

Pray to the Holy Spirit to help you bring love, joy, and peace to others.

Visit Our Web Site

www.blestarewe.com

Something to Think About . . .

Prayers of Petition

With all prayer and supplication, pray at every opportunity in the Spirit.
Ephesians 6:18

Children are naturally spiritual. They do not seem to have some of the barriers to belief that adults do, and they are often very comfortable with prayer. Our faith is a gift from God. Our ability to pray is also a gift from God through the Holy Spirit. In order to pray with your child, simply allow the Holy Spirit to lead you. In prayers called petitions, the Holy Spirit helps us ask God for what we need to follow Jesus. When composing prayers of petition, remember to request the Holy Spirit's help.

Something to Know About . . . Our Heritage in Liturgy

Prayers to the Holy Spirit reveal the Spirit's role in the liturgical life of the Church. During the Eucharistic Prayer at Mass, we petition God to send the Holy Spirit as Sanctifier to change the bread and wine and to change us, so that we too, become holy and united in the Body of Christ.

The principal prayers of the sacraments reveal more about the Holy Spirit's role. In Baptism, we pray to the Holy Spirit for new life. In Confirmation, we ask the Spirit to be our Helper and Guide. In Reconciliation, we ask the Holy Spirit as Comforter to forgive our sins. Through the Holy Spirit, we are given the graces to lead a Christian life.

16 The Holy Spirit Helps Us Pray

Come, Holy Spirit,
fill our hearts with your love.

Based on the Pentecost Sequence

Share

We all need teachers.
Teachers help us learn new words.
Teachers show us how to do new things.

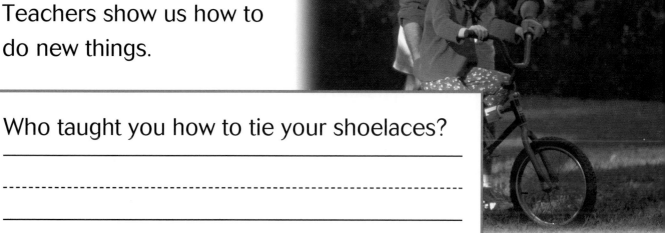

Who taught you how to tie your shoelaces?

Who taught you how to write your name?

Who taught you how to ride a bike?

Who taught you about Jesus?

Who teaches us how to pray?

Hear & Believe

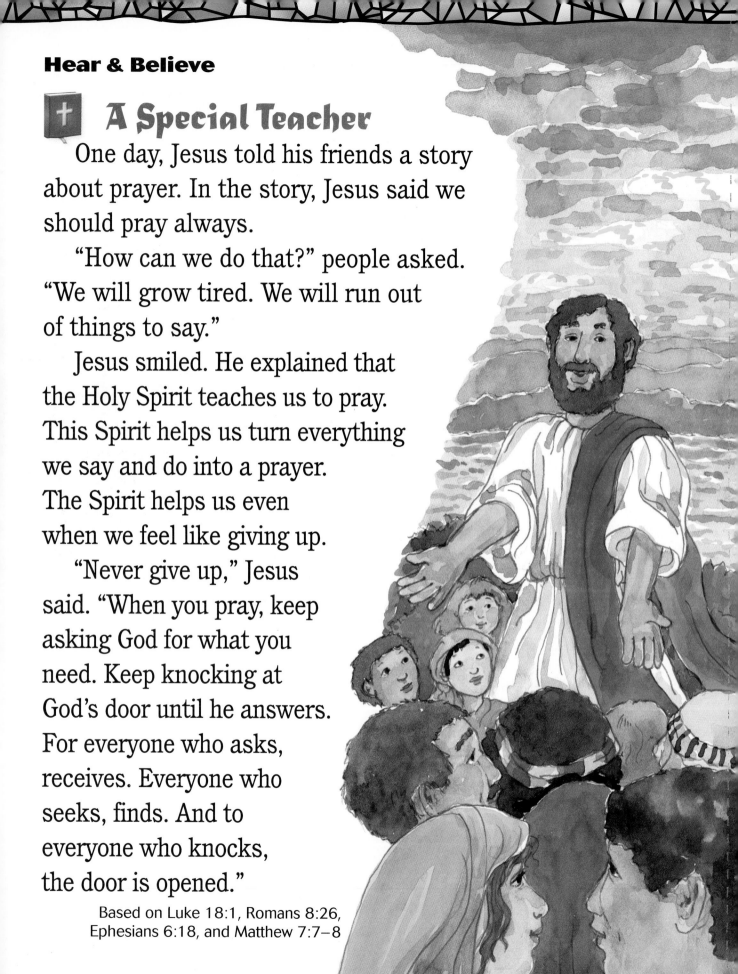

A Special Teacher

One day, Jesus told his friends a story about prayer. In the story, Jesus said we should pray always.

"How can we do that?" people asked. "We will grow tired. We will run out of things to say."

Jesus smiled. He explained that the Holy Spirit teaches us to pray. This Spirit helps us turn everything we say and do into a prayer. The Spirit helps us even when we feel like giving up.

"Never give up," Jesus said. "When you pray, keep asking God for what you need. Keep knocking at God's door until he answers. For everyone who asks, receives. Everyone who seeks, finds. And to everyone who knocks, the door is opened."

Based on Luke 18:1, Romans 8:26, Ephesians 6:18, and Matthew 7:7–8

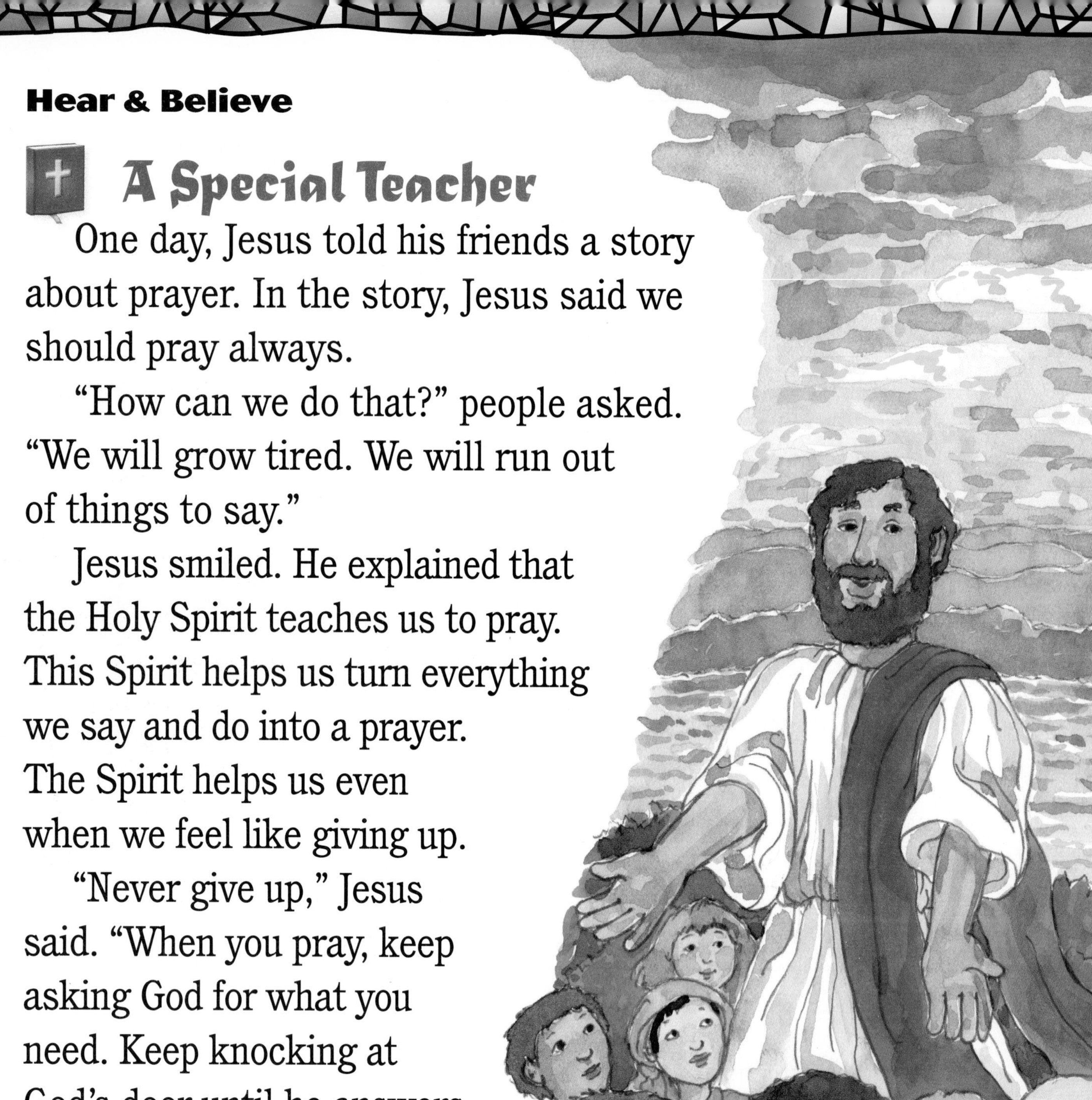

Ways the Holy Spirit Helps Us

The Holy Spirit teaches us to pray. He helps us pray for what we need. We call these prayers **petitions**. Even our actions can become prayers. Helping a person shows our love for God. Our kind act becomes a prayer.

Our Church Teaches

At Mass we pray to the Holy Spirit many times. He helps us listen and respond to the Bible readings. The Holy Spirit changes the bread and wine into the Body and Blood of Christ. He makes us one with our church community. The Holy Spirit helps us bring love, joy, and peace to others.

We Believe

There are many ways to pray. In each kind of prayer, the Holy Spirit acts.

Faith Words

petitions
Petitions are asking prayers. We ask God to give us the things we need.

How does the Church honor the Holy Spirit?

Respond

The Holy Parade

Lucia and her grandfather are on the church steps. She hears joyful music from a band. Then she sees the marchers coming down the street.

The men and boys wear colorful shirts and vests. The women and girls wear long dresses. Each group carries a bright banner.

Lucia asks, "Why are they marching?"

"It is a holy parade, or procession," her grandfather replies. "Every year, we honor the Holy Spirit in a special way. At Mass today, we will thank God for the gift of the Holy Spirit."

Why are the people having a holy parade?

Activity

Write a petition to the Holy Spirit.
Ask the Holy Spirit to help you.
Then sign your name.

Come, Holy Spirit,

____

fill me with ______________________________.

____

Help me to ______________________________

____

______________________________.

My name is

____

______________________________.

LOVE gentleness self-control peace JOY kindness patience

How can we celebrate the Holy Spirit?

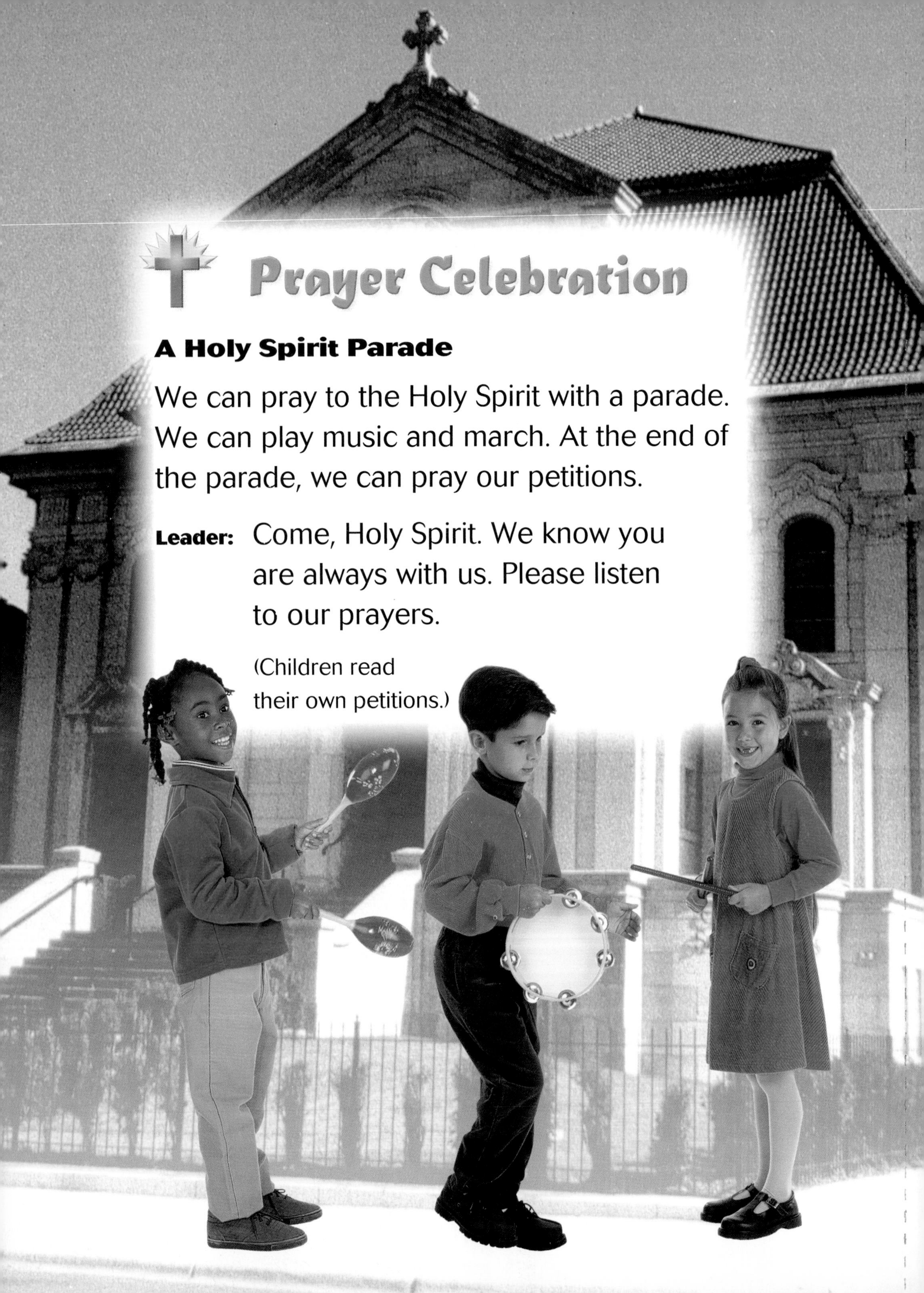

Prayer Celebration

A Holy Spirit Parade

We can pray to the Holy Spirit with a parade. We can play music and march. At the end of the parade, we can pray our petitions.

Leader: Come, Holy Spirit. We know you are always with us. Please listen to our prayers.

(Children read their own petitions.)

Gift Boxes

Andy lives in a city where there are many poor children. Some live in shelters. Many eat their meals in soup kitchens.

The children in Andy's parish were asked to help the poor children. Andy and the other young children decorated empty shoeboxes. The older children had a bake sale to raise some money. The teenagers used the money to buy toys, books, and snacks. The children filled more than 300 gift boxes.

One Sunday, Andy went with a group of parents and children to deliver the gifts. Andy saw smiles on the faces of the poor children. He thought to himself, "It's more fun to give than to receive."

What did Andy mean by those words?

Think About It

Why is it important to help poor people?

Circle the two best reasons.

People will like us.

God wants us to share.

The poor need our help.

We will feel important.

Learn About It

Jesus teaches us to care for the poor. He tells us that poor people are our brothers and sisters. They do not have to be in our family. They do not have to be in our parish. This is one important lesson the children in Andy's parish learned. They also learned that they can help many children by working together.

Do Something About It

Do you know about any poor children in your community? Find out what they need. Plan how you can get these things. Ask some grown-ups to help you. **Add to the list things you would like to give a poor child.**

UNIT 4 Organizer

We celebrate the gift of the Holy Spirit.
The Holy Spirit is our helper.
Jesus sends us the Holy Spirit.
The Holy Spirit helps us pray.

Read the sentences on the posters.

1. Find the poster that tells who the Holy Spirit is. Color the border yellow.
2. Find the poster that tells who Jesus sends us. Color the border red.
3. Find the poster that tells how the Holy Spirit helps us. Color the border green.
4. Find the poster that tells what we celebrate. Color the border blue.

UNIT 4

Review

A **Choose a word from the box to finish each sentence.**

peace	love	Jesus	helper	us

1. ______________ promised to send the Holy Spirit.

2. The Holy Spirit is our ______________.

3. The Holy Spirit teaches us about God's ______________.

4. Jesus said that the Holy Spirit brings ______________.

5. The Holy Spirit is always with ______________.

UNIT 4

Review

B Circle the best word to complete each sentence.

1. We are born to new life in Jesus at __. **Baptism** **birth**
2. The Holy Spirit comes to us in the __. **saints** **sacraments**
3. The Holy Spirit helps us follow __. **Joseph** **Jesus**
4. Jesus told Nicodemus that God's life lasts __. **forever** **ten years**

C Draw a line to the word that completes each sentence.

1. The Holy Spirit is our helper and	•	• **habits.**
2. The Holy Spirit helps us learn good	•	• **guide.**
3. Good habits are ways of acting for the good of	•	• **love.**
4. The fruits of the Holy Spirit help us show our	•	• **others.**

Unit 4 Review

D Write a prayer of petition to the Holy Spirit. Use some of the words in the box.

Holy Spirit	love	to	peace
gentle	come	us	bring
others	help	be	Jesus
follow	joy	me	kind

My Prayer to the Holy Spirit

UNIT 5

Jesus' Church of Followers

The Catholic Church throughout the world helps people in need. These people are our brothers and sisters. As baptized Christians, we are called to love and serve others.

Go into the whole world. Share the good news about Jesus with everyone.

Based on Mark 16:15

Early Christians traveled this road to faraway countries. They helped people learn about Jesus. These children are helping by sending clothes to needy people around the world.

UNIT 5 SONG

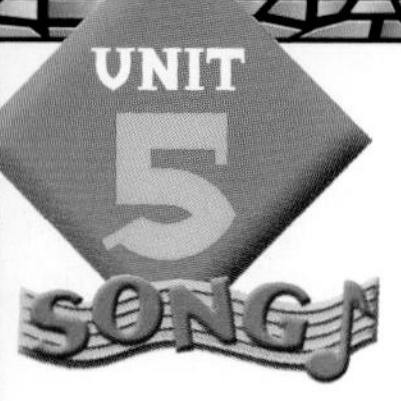

Laudate Dominum

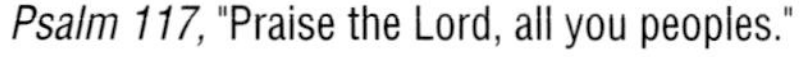

Psalm 117, "Praise the Lord, all you peoples."

om - nes gen - tes, al - le - lu - ia. al - le - lu - ia.

Music by Jacques Berthier

OSTINATO REFRAIN

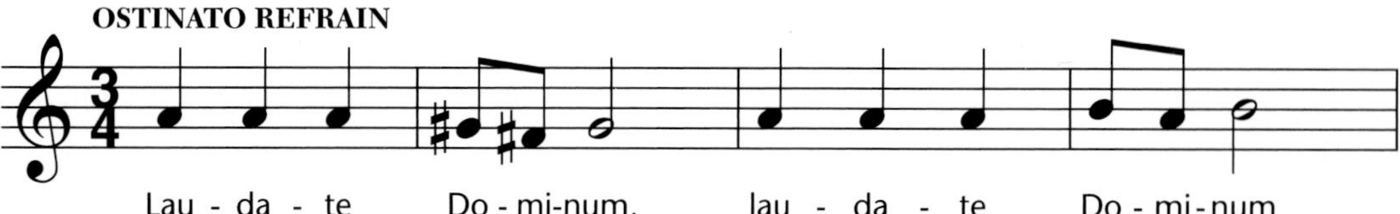

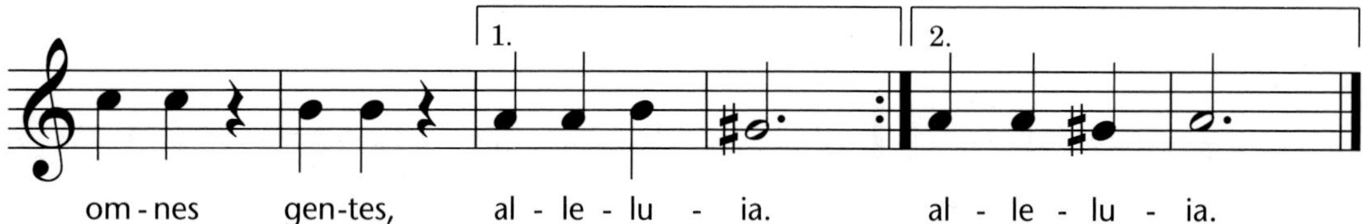

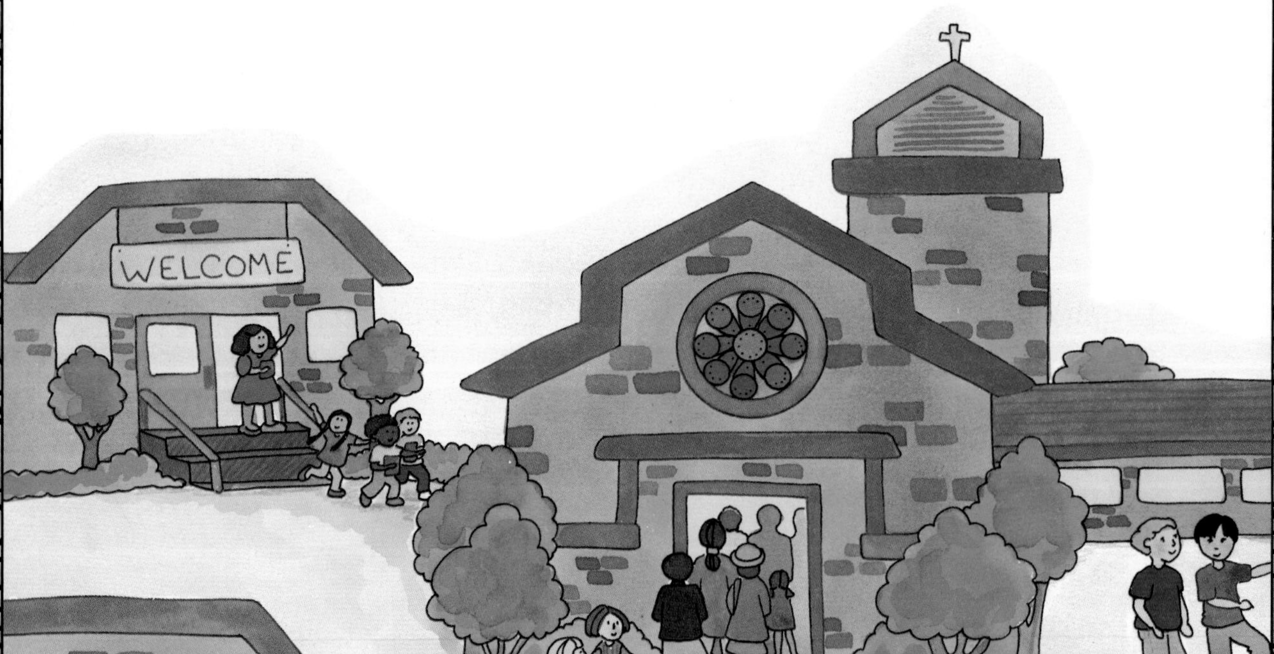

Getting ready for Chapter 17

A choice of things to do at home

Jesus' Followers Become the Church

Most of us see the Church as a big organization that we either are born into or join. In this chapter the children will discover that Jesus invites his followers to become the Church. The children will learn that the first Christians prayed together, celebrated the Eucharist, and helped poor people. The children will also learn that *Amen* means, "Yes, I believe. It is true."

We choose you

Have a ceremony of commitment to your family. Light a candle, pray a favorite prayer, and tell your children that you are pledging your love to them. Let all family members know that they are respected and cherished.

Family traditions

Tell your children stories about relatives who were role models for the way your family prays, celebrates, and helps others. If you have letters or photos about these traditions, share them with your children.

We follow Jesus

With your child, make a poster that represents how your family responds to Jesus' invitation to belong to the Church. Help your child write the words "We Follow Jesus." Hang the poster in your kitchen.

A Prayer for the Week

Lord Jesus Christ,
We ask you to be with our family and send your Spirit to guide us as we try to follow in your footsteps.
Amen.

FAMILY TIME

Something to Do . . .

On Sunday

Point out ways that your parish church is like a home for your community.

Through the Week

Make a list of the ways your family has stayed true to the spirit of the first Christians.

Visit Our Web Site

www.blestarewe.com

Something to Think About . . .

Early Christian Role Models

They devoted themselves to the teaching of the apostles and to the communal life, to the breaking of the bread and to the prayers.

Acts 2:42

The first members of the Church loved one another and tried to act as friends to everyone. The description of the early Christian community sounds so simple and well-balanced.

Studying, eating, and praying are part of a family's life. There is also shopping, sports, paying bills, work, and travel. By simplifying our lives we can imitate the early Christians. What one thing are you willing to give up? Is it something that disrupts your family life? Trying to be more like the early Christians may help your family focus on what is truly important.

Something to Know About . . .

Our Heritage in Architecture

In Eastern Christianity the churches are usually topped with domes instead of steeples. These domes are often gilded, expressing the radiance of heaven. One of the most famous of the domed churches is the Cathedral of St. Basil in Moscow, Russia. Building began in the sixteenth century during the reign of Czar Ivan IV. Many colorful, onion-shaped domes are covered with intricate patterns. Gold is used heavily in the decoration.

17 Jesus' Followers Become the Church

Jesus' followers were filled with joy and the Holy Spirit.

Based on Acts 13:52

Share

Our friends bring joy to our lives.
We can do things with our friends.
We can share things with our friends.
We can tell our friends how we feel.

Draw something you do with a friend.

How do Christians act as friends?

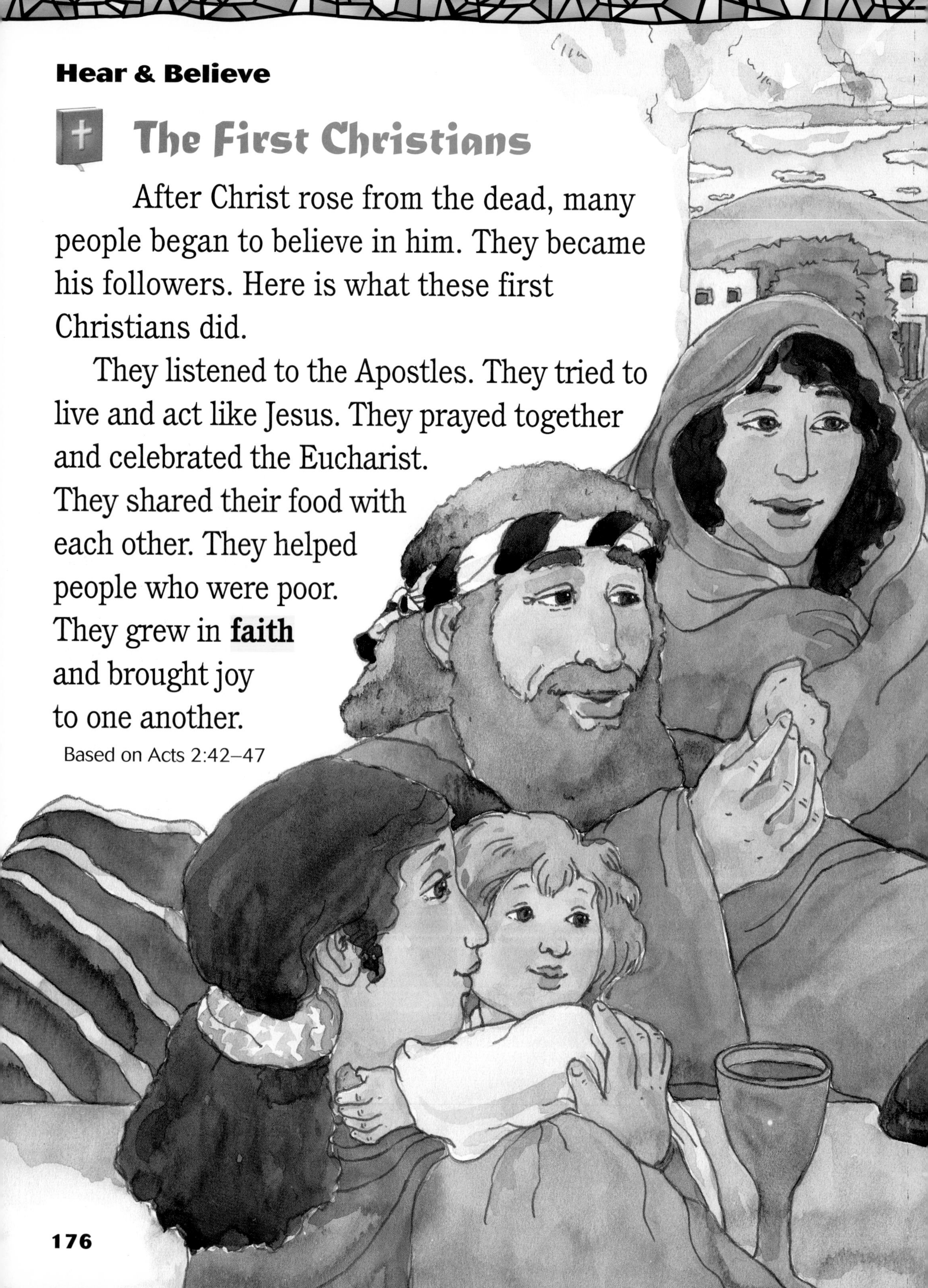

Hear & Believe

The First Christians

After Christ rose from the dead, many people began to believe in him. They became his followers. Here is what these first Christians did.

They listened to the Apostles. They tried to live and act like Jesus. They prayed together and celebrated the Eucharist. They shared their food with each other. They helped people who were poor. They grew in **faith** and brought joy to one another.

Based on Acts 2:42–47

Acting as Christians

The followers of Jesus became the first members of the Church. They loved one another and tried to act as friends to everyone. Jesus calls us, too, to be members of his Church. When we act as friends to others, we are true Christians.

We Believe

Jesus invites his followers to belong to the Church. He wants his followers to show love for others.

Our Church Teaches

Amen is a prayer often prayed by the first Christians. We pray "Amen" many times at Mass. We pray "Amen" at the end of prayers we say each day. Amen means "Yes, I believe. It is true."

Faith Words

faith
Faith is belief and trust in God.

Amen
Amen means "Yes, I believe. It is true." We often say "Amen" at the end of prayers.

How can we act like the first Christians?

Respond

Saint Paul's Parish

The people of Saint Paul's parish try to act like the first Christians. Here are some ways they are friends to others.

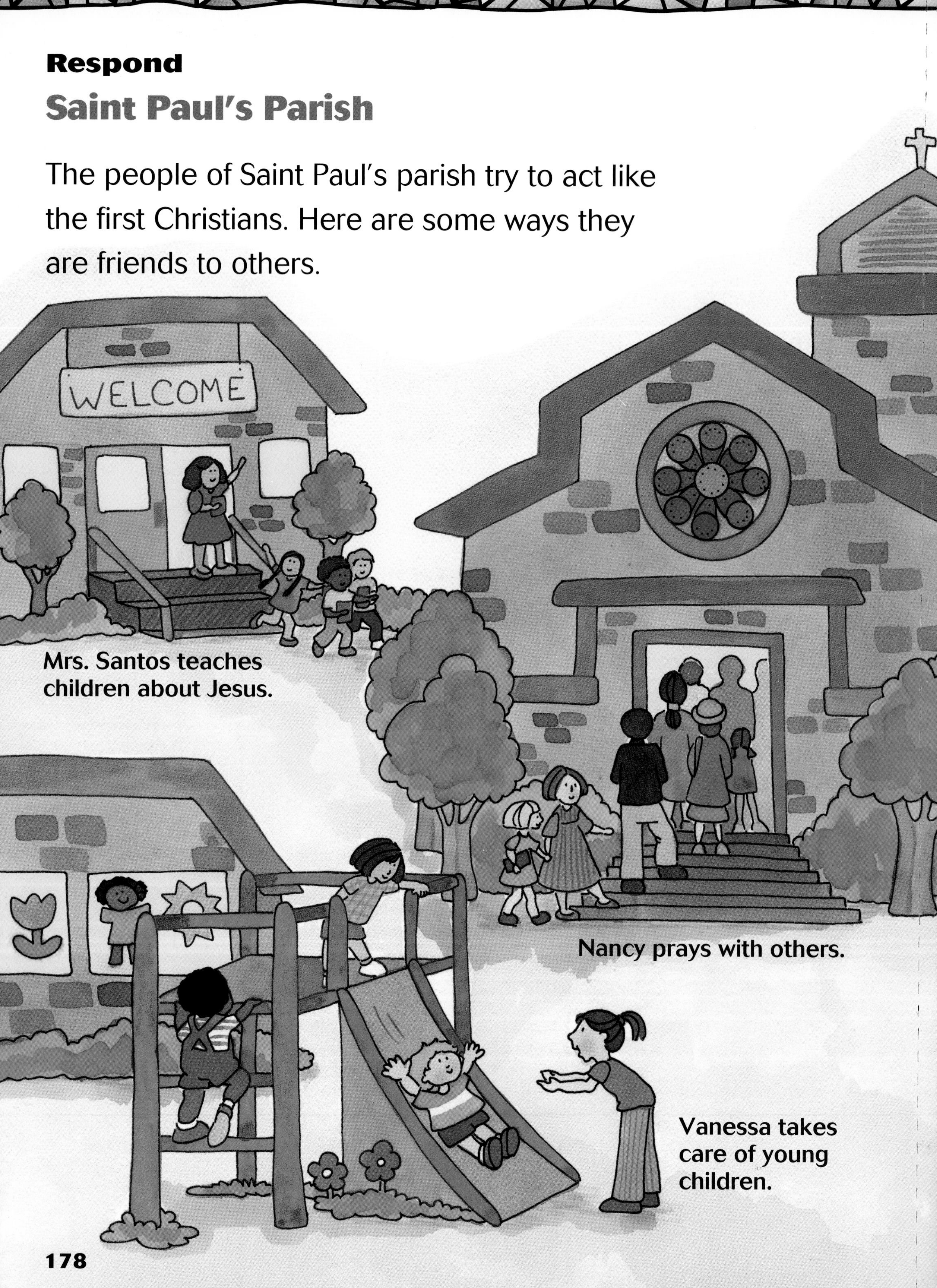

Mrs. Santos teaches children about Jesus.

Nancy prays with others.

Vanessa takes care of young children.

Activity

There are six words hidden in this church window.

These words tell how Christians try to act.

Find the words and circle them.

Mrs. Carr helps people who are poor.

Ryan listens to a friend.

Mr. Smith drives senior citizens to lunch.

How can we pray "Amen"?

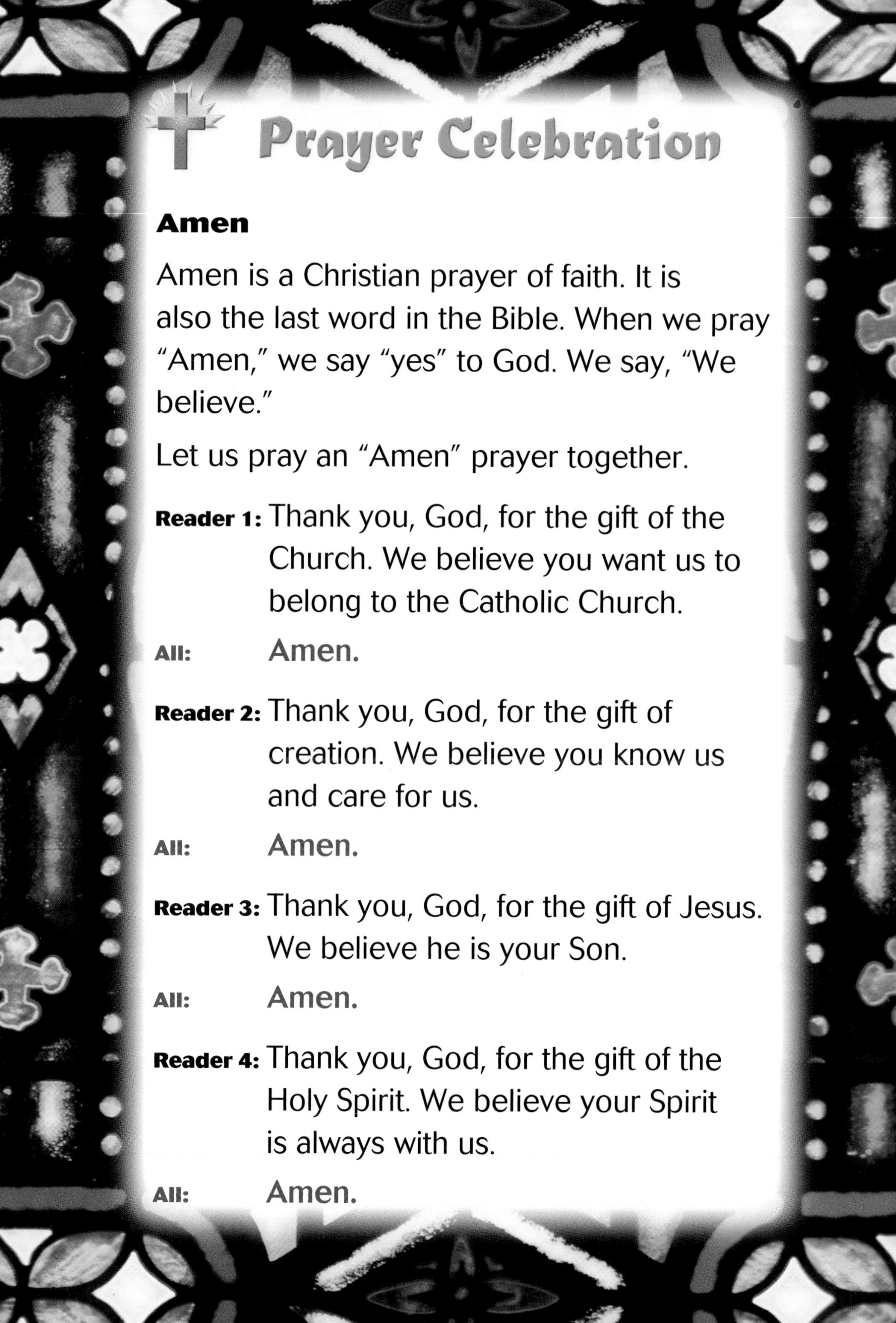

Prayer Celebration

Amen

Amen is a Christian prayer of faith. It is also the last word in the Bible. When we pray "Amen," we say "yes" to God. We say, "We believe."

Let us pray an "Amen" prayer together.

Reader 1: Thank you, God, for the gift of the Church. We believe you want us to belong to the Catholic Church.

All: Amen.

Reader 2: Thank you, God, for the gift of creation. We believe you know us and care for us.

All: Amen.

Reader 3: Thank you, God, for the gift of Jesus. We believe he is your Son.

All: Amen.

Reader 4: Thank you, God, for the gift of the Holy Spirit. We believe your Spirit is always with us.

All: Amen.

Getting ready for Chapter 18

A choice of things to do at home

We Celebrate Pentecost

In this chapter, children will recognize the Feast of Pentecost as the birthday of the Church. They will learn that the Church is a community of people from all over the world. Children will come to realize that the Holy Spirit filled Jesus' followers with the gift of God's love.

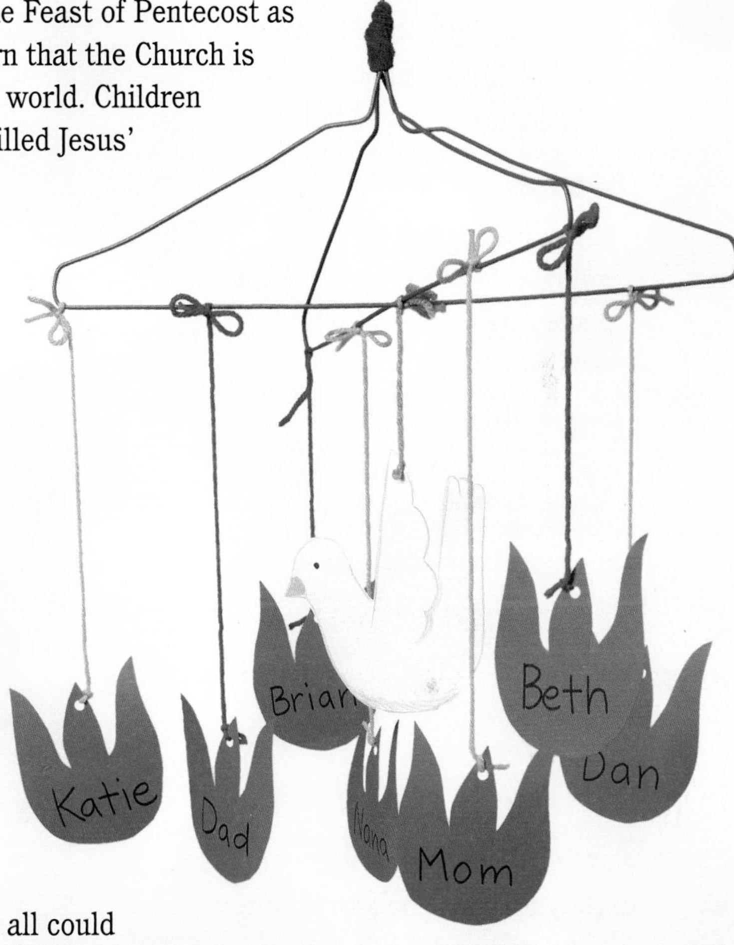

Pentecost mobile

With your child, make a Pentecost mobile out of a hanger, thread, and red and white construction paper. Cut out a white dove and red flames. Label each flame with a family member's name. Using thread, hang the dove and flames from the hanger. The dove symbolizes God's power to make us holy, and the flames represent the outpouring of the Holy Spirit.

Speaking different languages

The disciples spoke on Pentecost so that all could understand them. Have foreign-language night at your house, and say words you know in a different language. Talk about the languages your ancestors spoke.

Tongues of fire

Tongues of fire appeared over the heads of the disciples on Pentecost. Cut out pieces of red paper in the shape of flames. Put them at each place at your dinner table. Then have family members take turns holding a flame and telling how the Spirit helped them.

A Prayer for the Week

Thank you, Lord, for the gift of the Church. Help us share the love, peace, and joy of the Holy Spirit with everyone we meet.
Amen.

FAMILY TIME

Something to Do . . .

On Sunday

Look in your parish bulletin to find out how aware your parish is of the Church's needs around the world.

Through the Week

Tell one another what it means to be Catholic. If the opportunity arises, share what it means with someone outside your family.

Visit Our Web Site

www.blestarewe.com

Something to Think About . . .

Strength in Unity

When the time for Pentecost was fulfilled, they were all in one place together.
Acts 2:1

We have often heard that there is strength in unity, and it seemed to be true with the disciples on Pentecost. They were all praying together when the Holy Spirit came to them and filled them with God's love. As a result, the disciples felt strong and gained enthusiasm. They began telling everyone about Jesus.

Strength in unity is also possible in our families. If we work together to keep the Spirit alive in our homes, we will be able to go out and do our various tasks with a greater ability to model what we believe.

Something to Know About . . .

Our Heritage in Culture

The celebration of Pentecost differs around the world. In Italy it was customary to throw down rose leaves from church ceilings to symbolize the fiery tongues. In France, trumpets were blown to recall the sound of the mighty wind that came with the descent of the Holy Spirit.

Today in Eastern Catholic Churches, the Vespers of Pentecost includes a ritual of genuflection. In Russia, people carry flowers and green branches in a procession. The photo shows pilgrims journeying to the annual Pentecost festival held in El Rocio in southern Spain.

18 We Celebrate Pentecost

The Spirit of the Lord fills the whole world.

Based on Wisdom 1:7

Share

Birthdays are very special days.
Our families and friends celebrate with us.
They are glad that we belong to them.
When is your birthday?

____

Month Day

Circle the things that were part of your last birthday celebration.

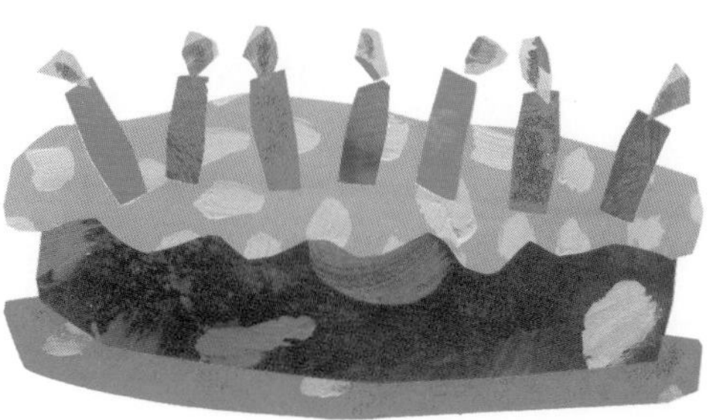

Draw another special thing that was at your birthday celebration.

When does the Church celebrate its birthday?

Hear & Believe

The Church's Birthday

A reading from the Acts of the Apostles

Fifty days after Easter, Jesus' followers were praying together. Suddenly there was a sound like a great wind blowing. The noise filled the whole house. Then flames, like tongues of fire, appeared over each person's head. The Holy Spirit filled all the people in the house with God's love. The Apostles and the others rushed outside. They began telling everyone about Jesus.

Outside there were people from many countries. These people spoke different languages. But they all understood what Jesus' followers were saying. That day the Church was born!

Based on Acts 2:1–6

Reader: The word of the Lord.

All: **Thanks be to God.**

Pentecost Sunday

We celebrate the birthday of the Church every year on **Pentecost** Sunday. We remember how Jesus' followers were filled with the Holy Spirit. We remember how the Spirit helped them teach people of all nations about Jesus.

Our Church Teaches

The Church welcomes people of all races, languages, and abilities. Today people all over the world belong to the Church. As Catholics, we try to live in **peace** with everyone.

We Believe

On Pentecost the Holy Spirit filled Jesus' followers with God's love. The Church that began on Pentecost is now all over the world.

Faith Words

Pentecost
On Pentecost we celebrate the coming of the Holy Spirit and the birthday of the Church.

peace
To be at peace means to get along with others.

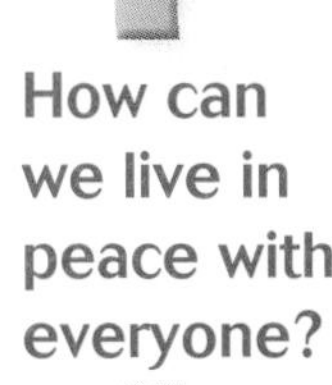

How can we live in peace with everyone?

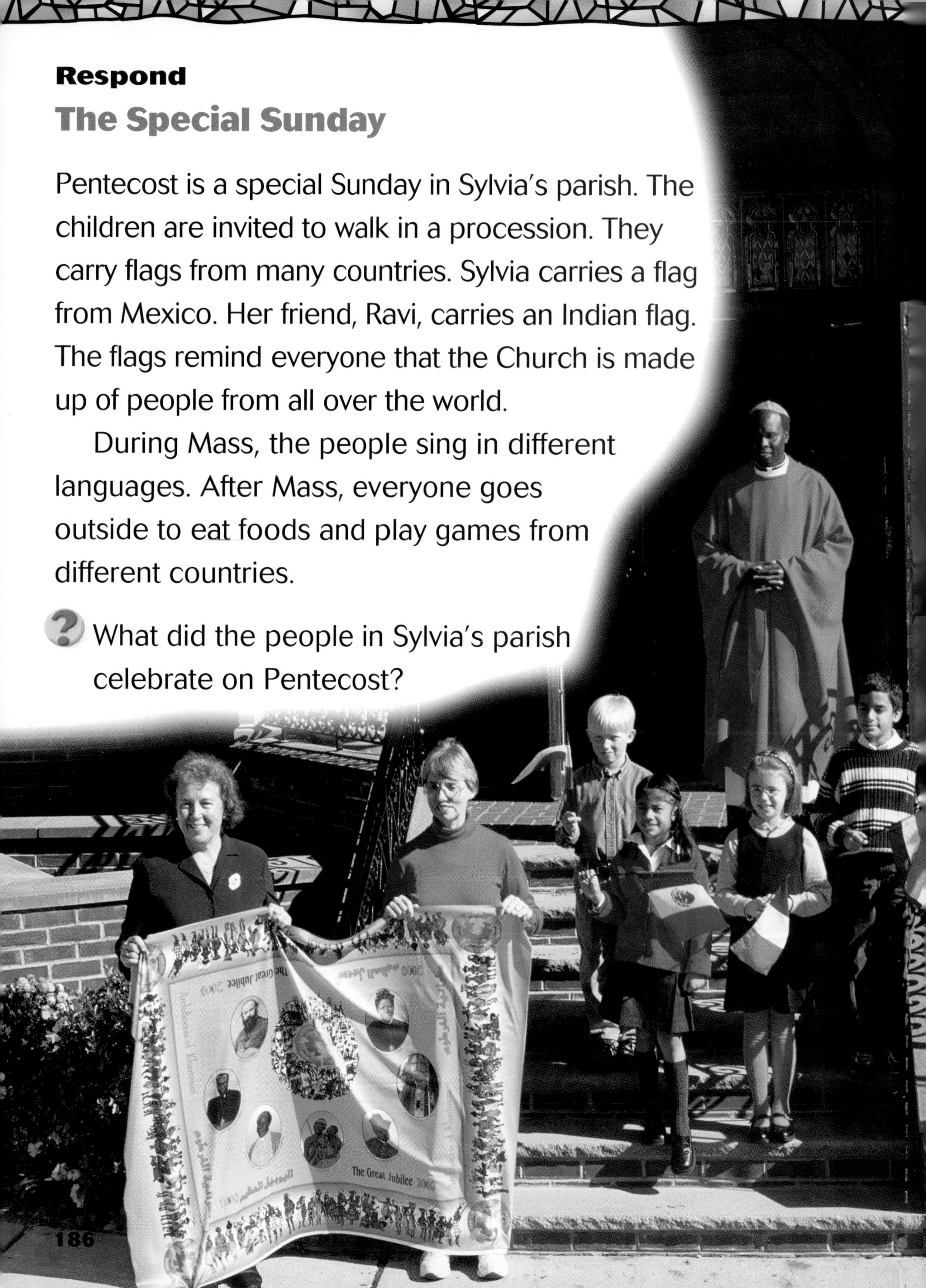

Respond

The Special Sunday

Pentecost is a special Sunday in Sylvia's parish. The children are invited to walk in a procession. They carry flags from many countries. Sylvia carries a flag from Mexico. Her friend, Ravi, carries an Indian flag. The flags remind everyone that the Church is made up of people from all over the world.

During Mass, the people sing in different languages. After Mass, everyone goes outside to eat foods and play games from different countries.

❓ What did the people in Sylvia's parish celebrate on Pentecost?

Activities

1. Many different people make up the Church. Many colors make a beautiful picture. Use this code to color the picture. What do you see?

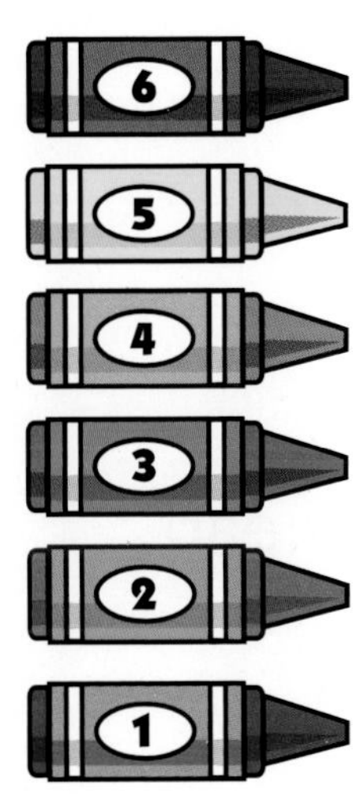

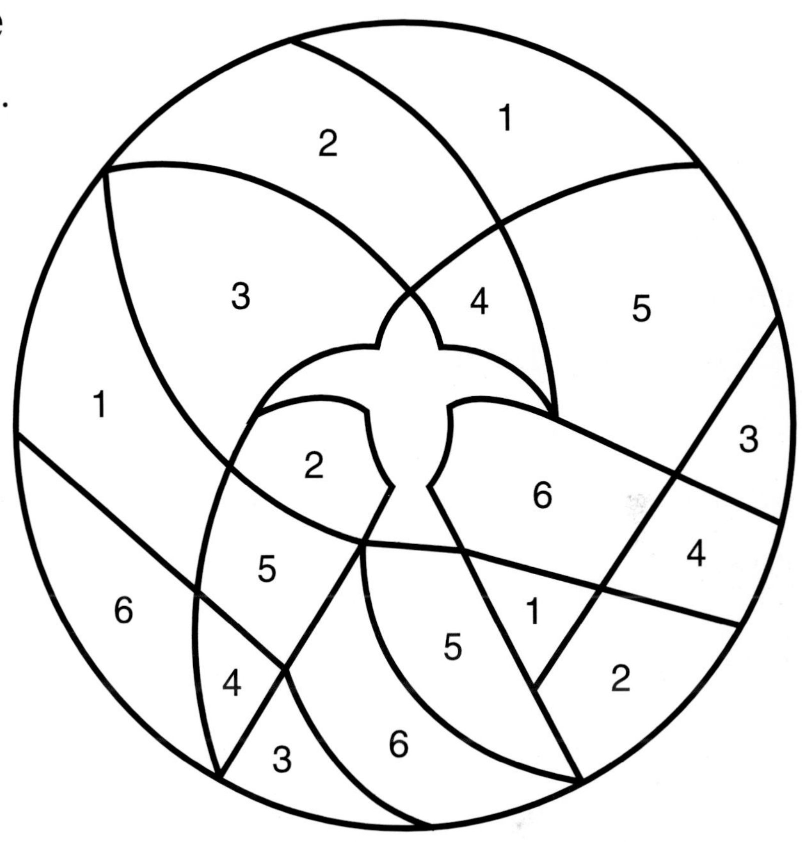

2. Circle the words that tell ways to keep peace.

You are playing a game with a friend.

cheat **play fair**

A friend calls you names.

forgive **act mad**

There is one toy, but three people.

take it **share it**

A family member needs you.

help **watch TV**

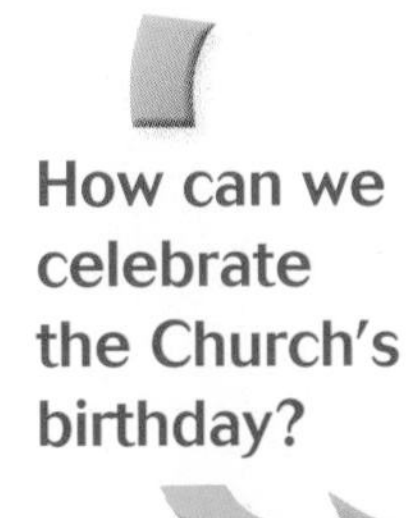

How can we celebrate the Church's birthday?

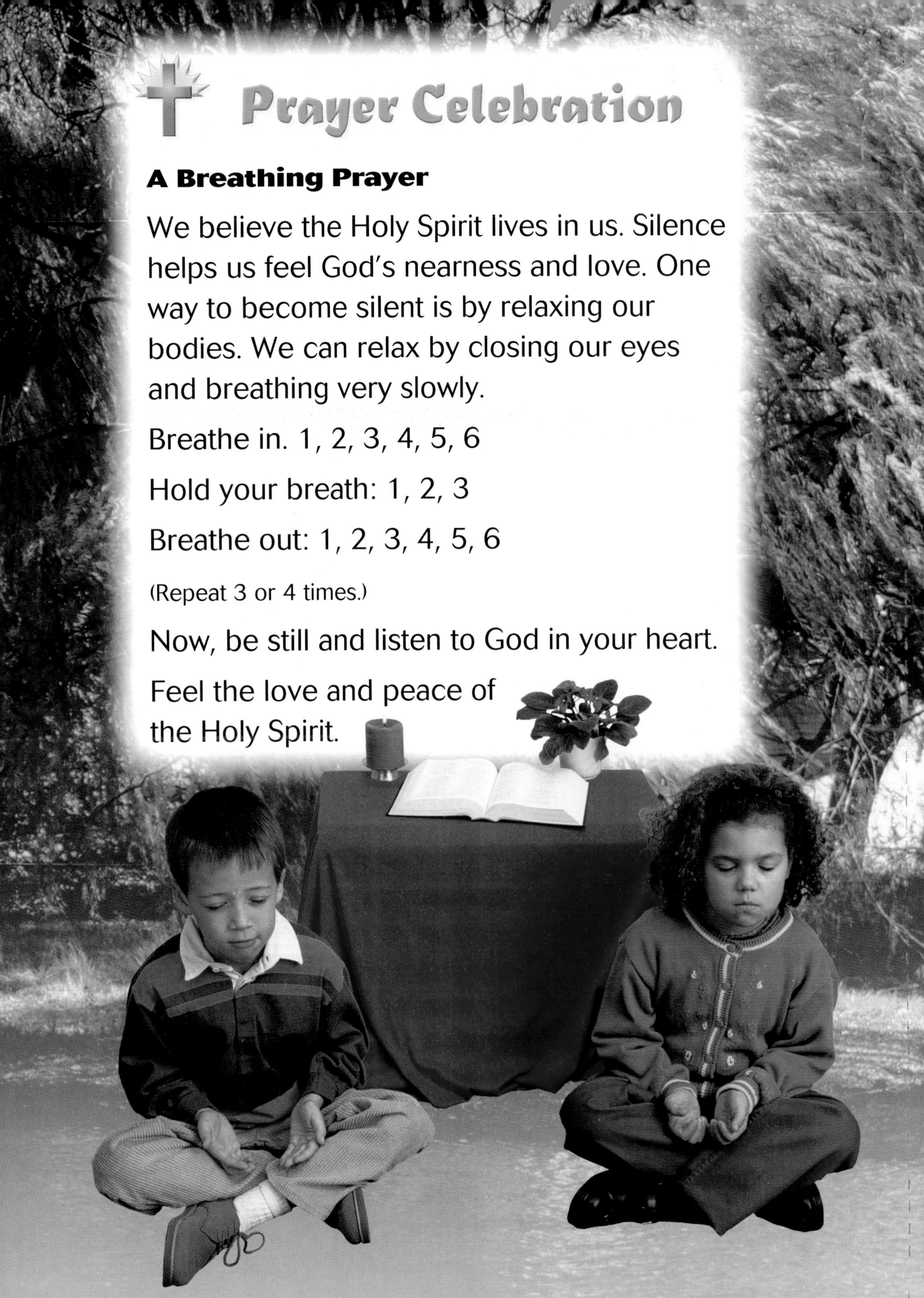

Prayer Celebration

A Breathing Prayer

We believe the Holy Spirit lives in us. Silence helps us feel God's nearness and love. One way to become silent is by relaxing our bodies. We can relax by closing our eyes and breathing very slowly.

Breathe in. 1, 2, 3, 4, 5, 6

Hold your breath: 1, 2, 3

Breathe out: 1, 2, 3, 4, 5, 6

(Repeat 3 or 4 times.)

Now, be still and listen to God in your heart.

Feel the love and peace of the Holy Spirit.

Getting ready for Chapter 19

A choice of things to do at home

The Church Helps the World

The word *catholic* means "universal." By our very name we are called to reach out to others. This chapter examines how being Catholic changes the way we act in the world. The children will discover how the Holy Spirit works through the Church. They will learn how the Church community helps people in need, and how they can help others.

Make someone happy

Help your child make cheerful cards for children in a hospital or elderly people in a nursing home. Take the cards to the people, or give the cards to someone in your parish who will deliver them.

Help a helper

With your child, write a letter or e-mail a missionary order, such as Maryknoll, asking how you can help them in their work. Usually for a small donation, you will receive their magazine, which shows pictures of missioners helping people around the world.

Learn about others

Read a story with your child about someone from another culture. Talk about the similarities and differences. Explain how people who are different from ourselves enrich us.

A Prayer for the Week

We are your hands and feet
in the world today, Lord, and
we want to help others in your
name. Help us to be strong
and to follow the path
you made for us.
Amen.

FAMILY TIME

Something to Do . . .

On Sunday

Check your parish bulletin to find out what service projects are being done by your parish.

Through the Week

Each night, light a candle, and pray for those who work in church ministries around the world.

Visit Our Web Site

www.blestarewe.com

Something to Think About . . .

Recruiting Volunteers

As the number of disciples continued to grow, the Hellenists complained against the Hebrews because their widows were being neglected in the daily distribution.

Acts 6:1

The Apostles were wearing themselves out trying to preach, lead prayers, and celebrate the Eucharist, while making sure their followers had food, clothes, and places to live. They solved the problem by getting others to help. These helpers cared for the people's physical needs so that the Apostles could focus on their spiritual needs. Just as the disciples of Jesus had a mission to love and serve others, so do we. However, our works of charity should not keep us from spending time with our families. Take a cue from the Apostles and recruit more helpers.

Something to Know About . . . Our Heritage in Holy People

Dorothy Day was a convert to Catholicism who had a strong sense of the social call of the Gospel. She reached out to the poor and powerless and gave of herself with great dignity. She started Catholic Worker houses across the country, and encouraged people to follow Christ.

One group of people Dorothy ministered to was women prisoners. While she was visiting a West Virginia prison, an elderly inmate wanted to know why Dorothy was there. She replied that she had come to wash their feet. Dorothy Day died in 1980. She was a powerful witness to the Church's mission of serving the poor.

19 The Church Helps the World

Go into the whole world. Share the good news about Jesus with everyone.

Based on Mark 16:15

Share

Before we can help others, we must find out what they need. Look at these pictures. What do the people need?

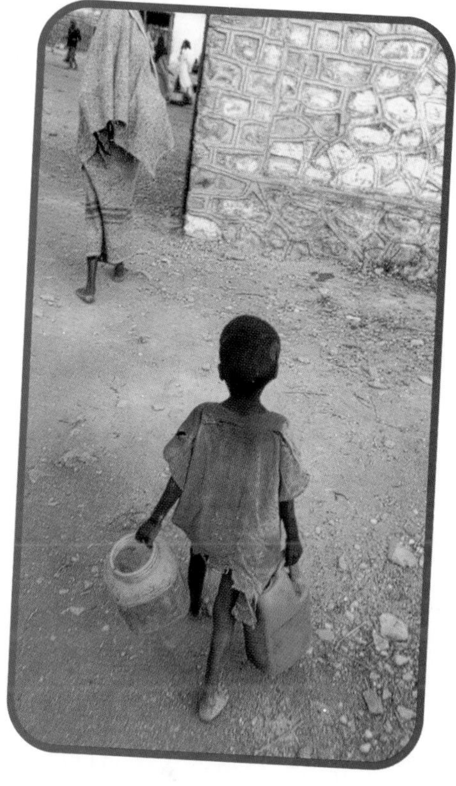

He needs

____

______________________________.

They need

____

______________________________.

She needs.

____

______________________________.

Why should Christians help people in need?

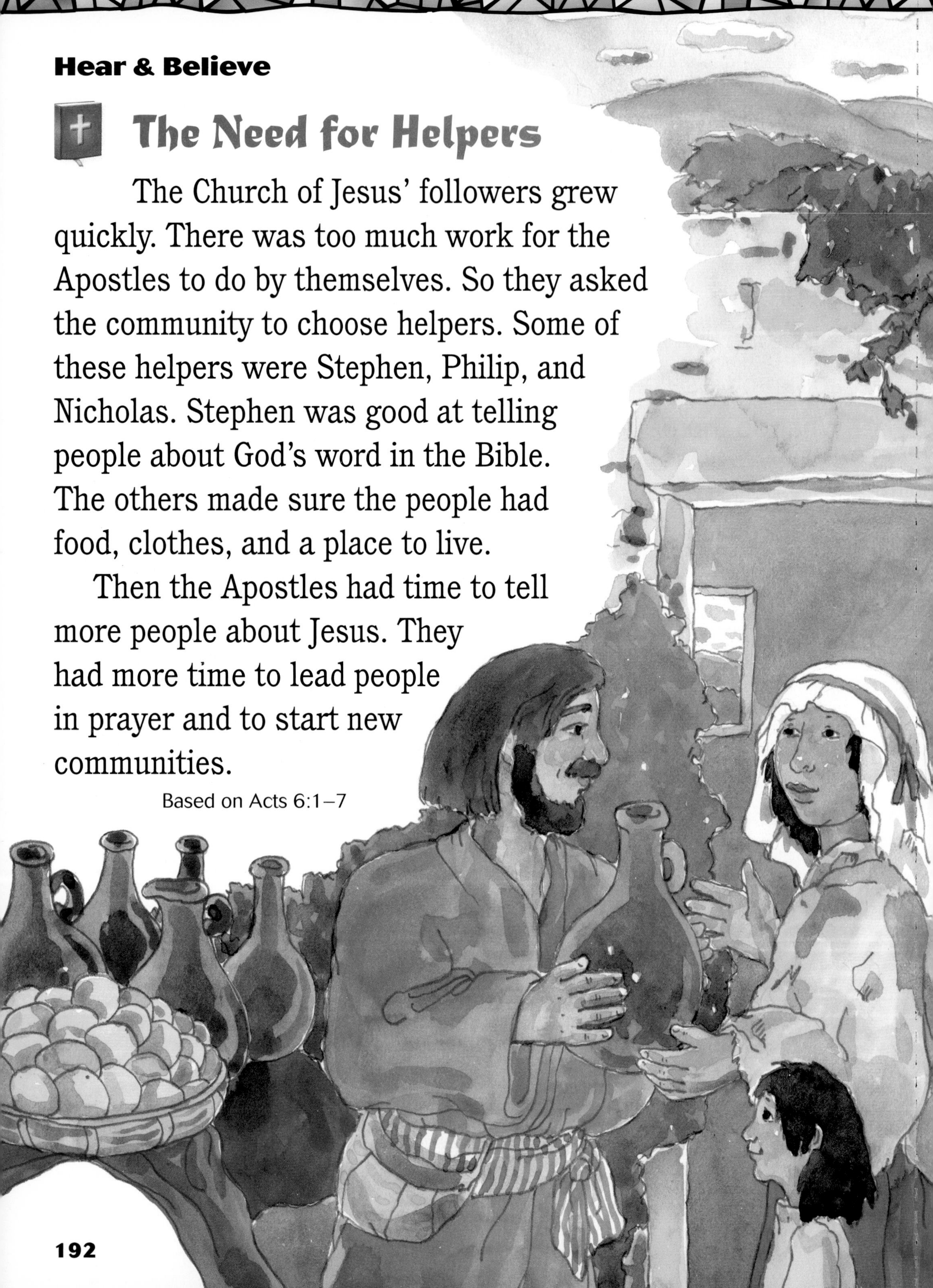

Hear & Believe

The Need for Helpers

The Church of Jesus' followers grew quickly. There was too much work for the Apostles to do by themselves. So they asked the community to choose helpers. Some of these helpers were Stephen, Philip, and Nicholas. Stephen was good at telling people about God's word in the Bible. The others made sure the people had food, clothes, and a place to live.

Then the Apostles had time to tell more people about Jesus. They had more time to lead people in prayer and to start new communities.

Based on Acts 6:1–7

Christian Service

The first Christians learned that God calls everyone to help and **serve** others. Helping others is our **mission**, or job, too. The Holy Spirit helps us serve others with love, peace, and joy. We try to take care of their needs. We try to follow Jesus.

We Believe

All people in the world are our brothers and sisters. That is why God asks us to help people in need.

Our Church Teaches

Each baptized person is called to choose a way to love and serve others. There are so many people around the world who need help. The Catholic Church has many ways for its members to become helpers.

Faith Words

serve
To serve means to help other people.

mission
A mission is a job that needs to be done. Our mission as Christians is to love and serve others.

How does the Church help people in need?

Respond

Christians Who Help

The Catholic Church helps people all over the world.

Some Catholics serve in countries far away. They help people by giving them food, clothes, and medicine. They teach people about Jesus.

Some Catholics teach children in Africa how to read and write. They also teach them about Jesus.

Some Catholics serve in our own country. They build houses for the poor. They teach people about Jesus.

? How can you help our Church's helpers?

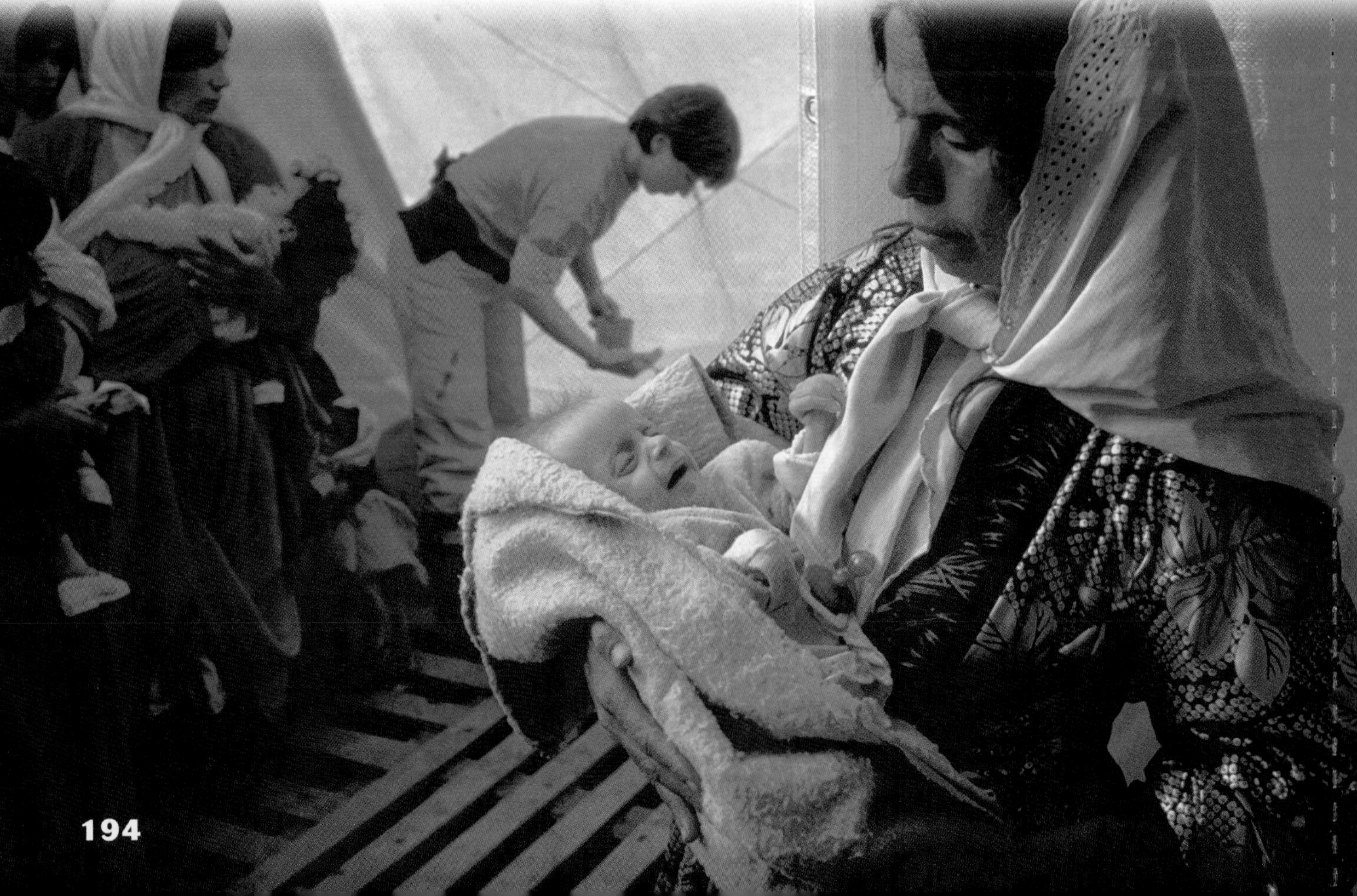

Activities

1. Draw how you will help someone in need this week.

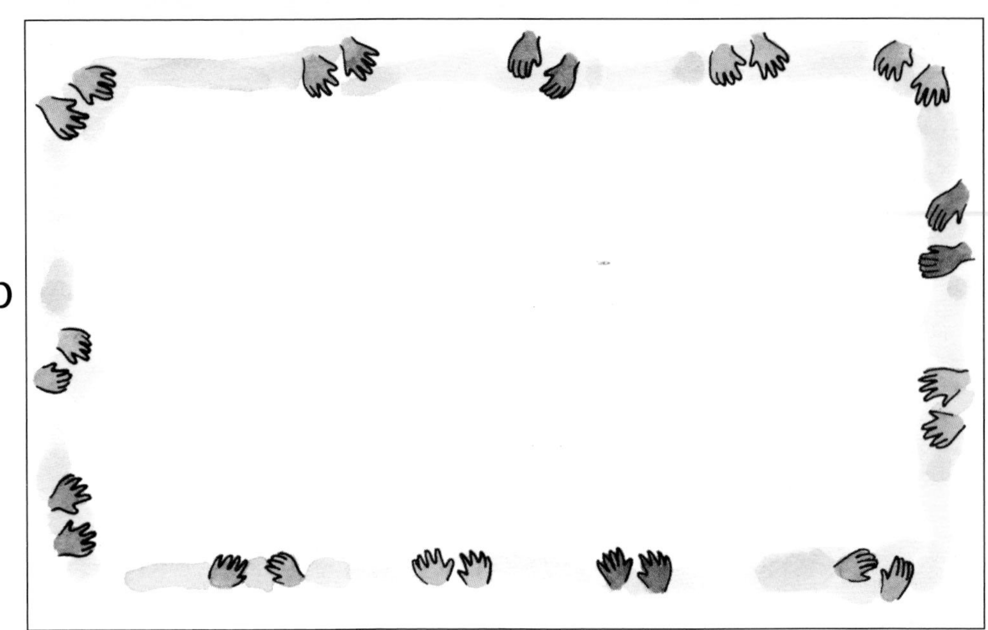

2. Write a prayer for church helpers who serve the needs of others.

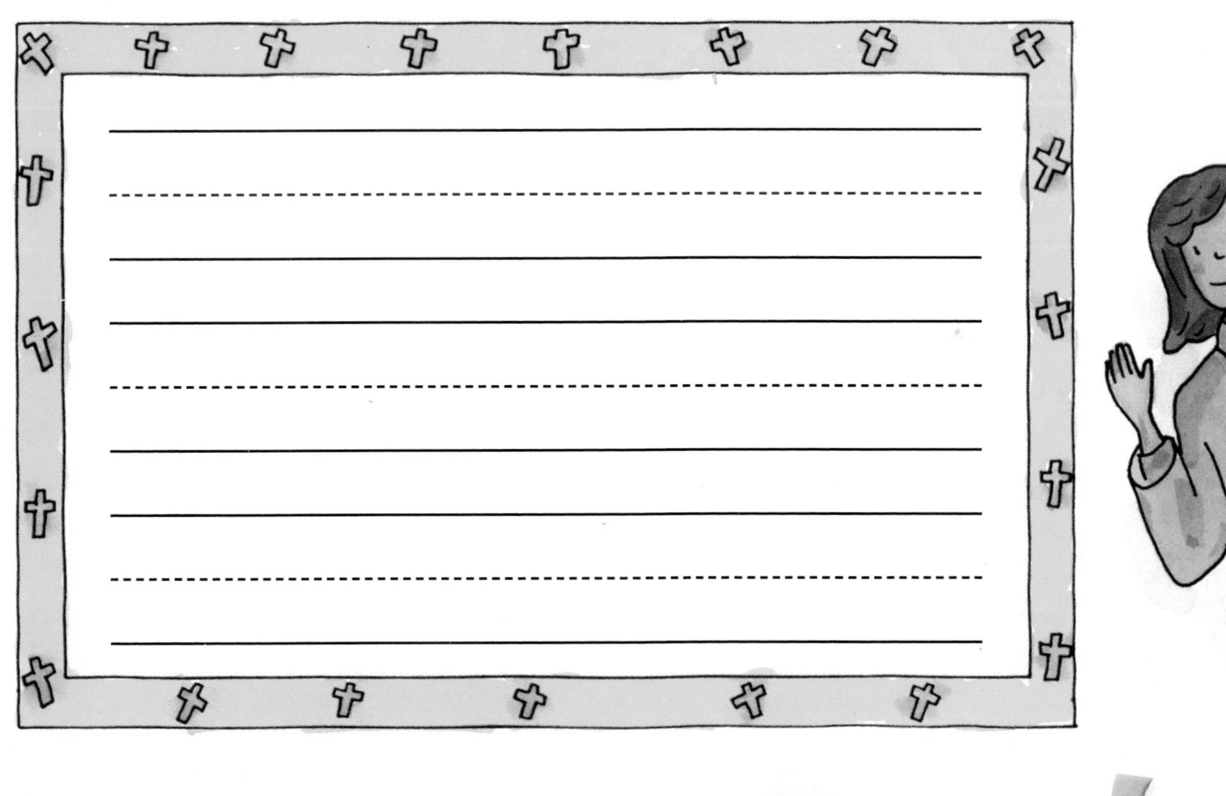

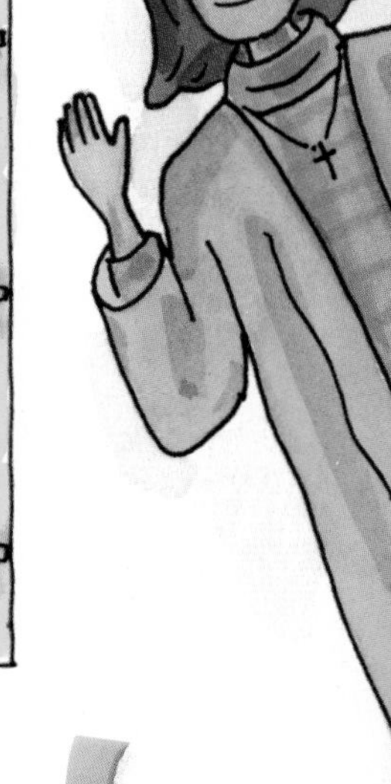

How can we get ready to be God's helpers?

Prayer Celebration

Listen for God's Call

As you grow up, God asks you to love and serve others. Are you listening? Are you ready to say "yes" to God?

Pray this prayer together about saying "yes" to God.

> God, our Creator,
> you called us by name
> to belong to your Church.
> When you call us as we grow up,
> help us, Lord, to hear your voice.
> Fill us with courage so that
> we may say "yes" to you.
> Amen.

Getting ready for Chapter 20

A choice of things to do at home

We Pray with Holy Songs

Music is an important part of our lives. Incorporating music into our prayer adds a new dimension to the way we pray, and the way we think about God. This chapter encourages the children to think of church music as an integral part of their worship experience. They will discover that holy songs are prayers, and that when we sing with our hearts, we pray twice. The children will also sing a song about peace, love, and service.

What's your favorite?

Have a discussion about your family's favorite songs. What do you like about each song? Is it the words? Is it the music? How do the songs make you feel? Compose a list of your family's top hits.

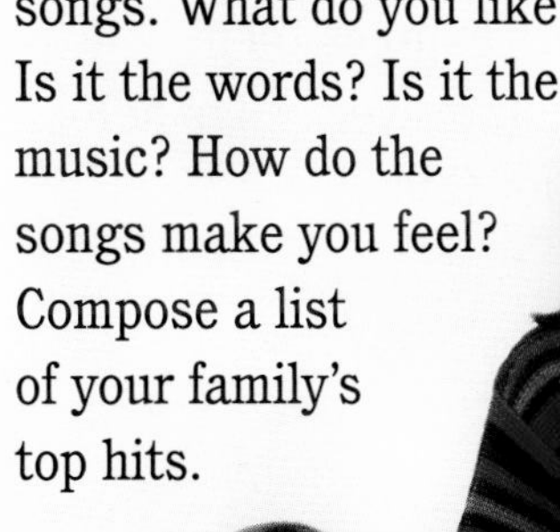

Sing grace

When your family prays grace before meals, try singing it. Use a familiar tune or have fun composing one of your own.

Feel the music

Play a song that your child likes. Have fun listening to the music and singing the words. Feel the music, and dance to it with your child, expressing how the song makes you feel.

A Prayer for the Week

Dear God, we thank you for the gift of music. It soothes us when we are sad and gives us a way to express our joy. We are grateful for the chance to pray to you in song. Amen.

FAMILY TIME

Something to Do . . .

On Sunday

Listen carefully to the hymns you sing at Mass. Discuss how they relate to the themes of the Scripture readings.

Through the Week

Choose one of your family's favorite hymns. Gather together and sing the hymn as a prayer.

Visit Our Web Site

www.blestarewe.com

Something to Think About . . .

Praying with Songs

Be filled with the Spirit, addressing one another [in] psalms and hymns and spiritual songs, singing and playing to the Lord in your hearts.

Ephesians 5:18-19

When the Holy Spirit filled the first Christians with joy, they sang. Religious songs provide us with another way to pray. Hymns drift through our minds and can be an occasion of grace. They console us when we are upset or frightened. For example, many people find the hymn "On Eagles' Wings," by Michael Joncas consoling when someone they love dies. Having music as part of our religious experience helps us deal with feelings that are difficult to express in words. Just as love songs help lovers express their feelings for each other; prayer songs help us express our love for God.

Something to Know About . . . Our Heritage in Music

Most of the African slaves in our country were not allowed to learn how to read or write. Many of these enslaved people were converted to Christianity. One way they kept their faith alive was by singing spirituals. These songs, based on Bible verses, helped to sustain the slaves in the same way that psalms sustained the Israelites during their captivity. The spirituals also gave the people a way to pass along their faith. They are now considered an art form and one of the original forms of music on this continent.

20 We Pray with Holy Songs

My heart is full of joy.
I sing praises to my God.

Based on Psalm 28:7

Share

People sing for many reasons.
Songs put babies to sleep.
Songs remind us of our country.

Songs take away our fears.
Songs celebrate happy times.

What is your favorite song?

____

____

Why do Christians sing?

Songs of the First Christians

When the first Christians celebrated the Eucharist, they did several things. They read the Bible. They prayed. They received the Body and Blood of Jesus. And they sang songs.

Why did they sing? Here is what Paul told the first Christians.

Be filled with God's Spirit. Sing psalms and **hymns** to God the Father. Sing your thanks and praise to God in the name of our Lord Jesus Christ.

Based on Ephesians 5:18–19

Praying with Holy Songs

The first Christians sang because the Holy Spirit filled them with joy. Singing is a good way to pray. We pray when we sing holy songs. Through song, we give God thanks and praise. We ask God for help. We tell God that we want to help others.

Our Church Teaches

Holy songs draw our hearts toward God. When we sing at Mass, we join in the Church's celebration. We sing about what we believe with our parish community.

We Believe

When we sing, we pray twice. We pray with our voices. We also pray with our hearts.

Faith Words

hymns
Hymns are holy songs about what we believe.

How can we sing our thanks and praise to God?

Respond

Amanda Loves to Sing

Amanda loves to sing at church. She sings as her parish community gathers to praise God. After the first Bible reading, she sings a psalm. She sings a hymn when people bring the bread and wine to the altar. She prays to God, our Father, when she sings the Lord's Prayer. Amanda sings at communion time. She also sings at the end of Mass.

Sometimes during the week, Amanda hums the songs from Mass. The music reminds her to give God thanks and praise. It reminds her to live in peace. It helps her love and serve others.

❓ What holy songs do you like to hum?

Activity

Use these words to complete the sentences.
Then write the words in the puzzle.

hymn **praise** **pray** **psalm** **thanks**

DOWN

1. We give God ______.
3. Singing is a ______ way to ______.

ACROSS

2. By singing, we ______ God.
3. A ______ is a song that is also a prayer.
4. A ______ is a holy song.

How can we celebrate our good year?

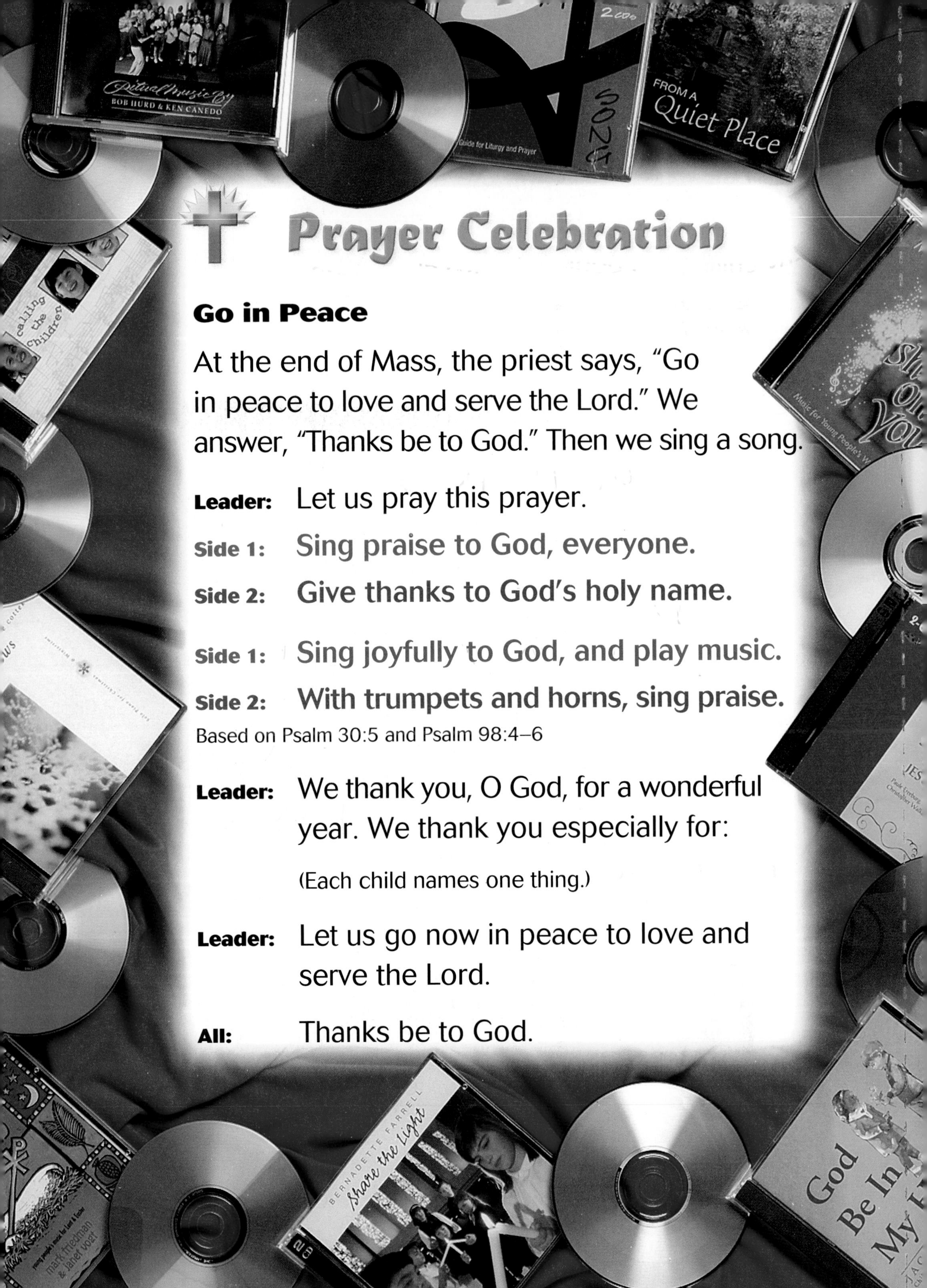

Prayer Celebration

Go in Peace

At the end of Mass, the priest says, "Go in peace to love and serve the Lord." We answer, "Thanks be to God." Then we sing a song.

Leader: Let us pray this prayer.

Side 1: **Sing praise to God, everyone.**

Side 2: **Give thanks to God's holy name.**

Side 1: **Sing joyfully to God, and play music.**

Side 2: **With trumpets and horns, sing praise.**

Based on Psalm 30:5 and Psalm 98:4–6

Leader: We thank you, O God, for a wonderful year. We thank you especially for:

(Each child names one thing.)

Leader: Let us go now in peace to love and serve the Lord.

All: Thanks be to God.

Collecting Pennies

Many children in poor countries are always hungry. Every day some children die of hunger. This is very sad. Just a few pennies can buy a meal of rice and beans. A few pennies a day can keep a child from starving.

The children in Louis's parish learned about the starving children in Ethiopia. Louis's class came up with an idea to help. First they got a large plastic jar. Then they made a sign about caring.

Each week the children put pennies into the jar. Many pennies came from their own piggy banks. Soon the jar was full. The class sent the money to a missioner to buy food for the hungry children.

How did the hungry children feel when they saw the food?

Think About It

What are your favorite snack foods? Do you buy some of your own snacks?

Circle your answer for each question.

About how many pennies do you spend on snacks each week?

0 10 25 50 more than 50

Would you give some of your pennies to feed a hungry child?

yes no

Learn About It

Our Earth can grow enough food for everyone. But we have to learn to share it. Jesus wants us to give food to people who are hungry. He wants us to help starving children in faraway lands. Jesus tells us that these children are our brothers and sisters.

Do Something About It

Ask your class to fill a jar with pennies. Choose a poor country. Send the money to a missioner to buy food for the hungry children.

Draw foods hungry children might like to eat.

UNIT 5 Organizer

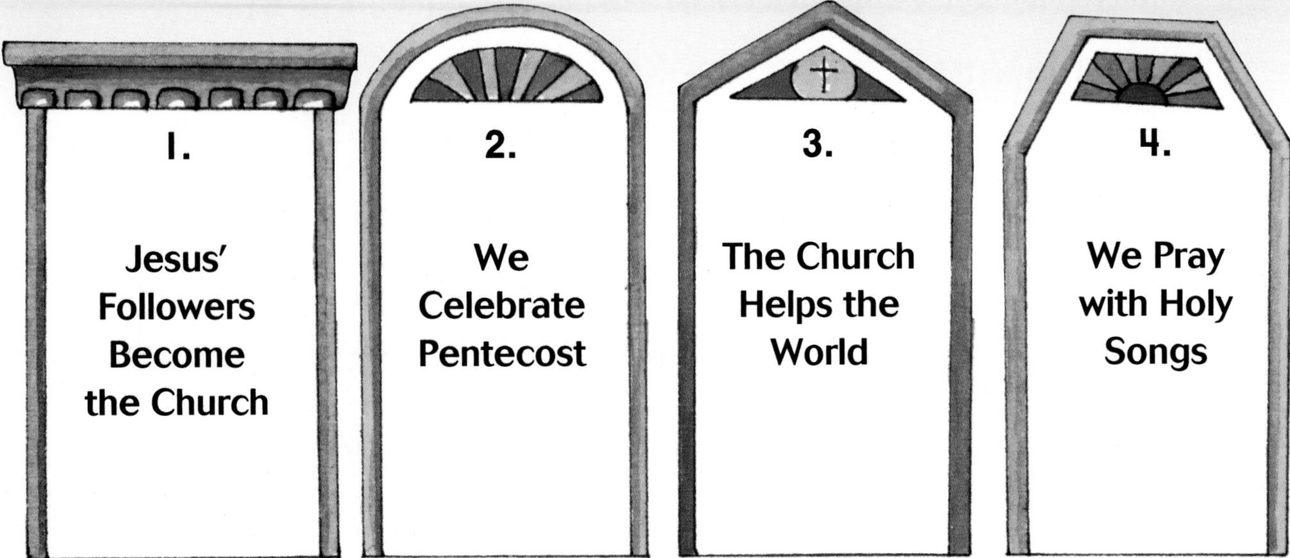

Read the titles on the doors.
The sentences below tell about things
you learned in one of the chapters.
Write the correct door number
on each knob.

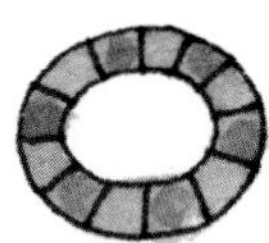

This day is the Church's birthday.
The Holy Spirit came on this day.

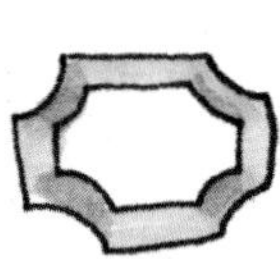

The first Christians grew in faith.
They prayed "Amen."

We pray with our voices and our hearts.
We sing praise and thanks to God.

The Church has many missions.
The Catholic Church needs helpers.

Review

A Find the letter hidden in each picture. Fill in the missing letter to make the word that means "Yes, I believe. It is true." Then color the letters and the pictures.

Find the letter hidden in each picture. Fill in the missing letters to make the word that means "belief and trust in God." Then color the letters and the pictures.

UNIT 5

Review

B Circle the correct word to complete each sentence.

1. We celebrate the birthday of the Church on ____.
   Pentecost **Christmas**
2. Pentecost celebrates the coming of the ____.
   Holy Bible **Holy Spirit**
3. When we get along with others we have ____.
   peace **fights**
4. The Holy Spirit helped the Apostles tell about ____.
   James **Jesus**

C Draw a line to the word that completes each sentence.

1. God calls each baptized person to help	•	• **Holy Spirit.**
2. "To help others" means to	•	• **mission.**
3. A job that needs to be done is called a	•	• **others.**
4. One who helps us bring joy to others is the	•	• **serve.**

UNIT 5

Review

D **Look at the words on the banner.**
Write the correct word to complete each sentence.

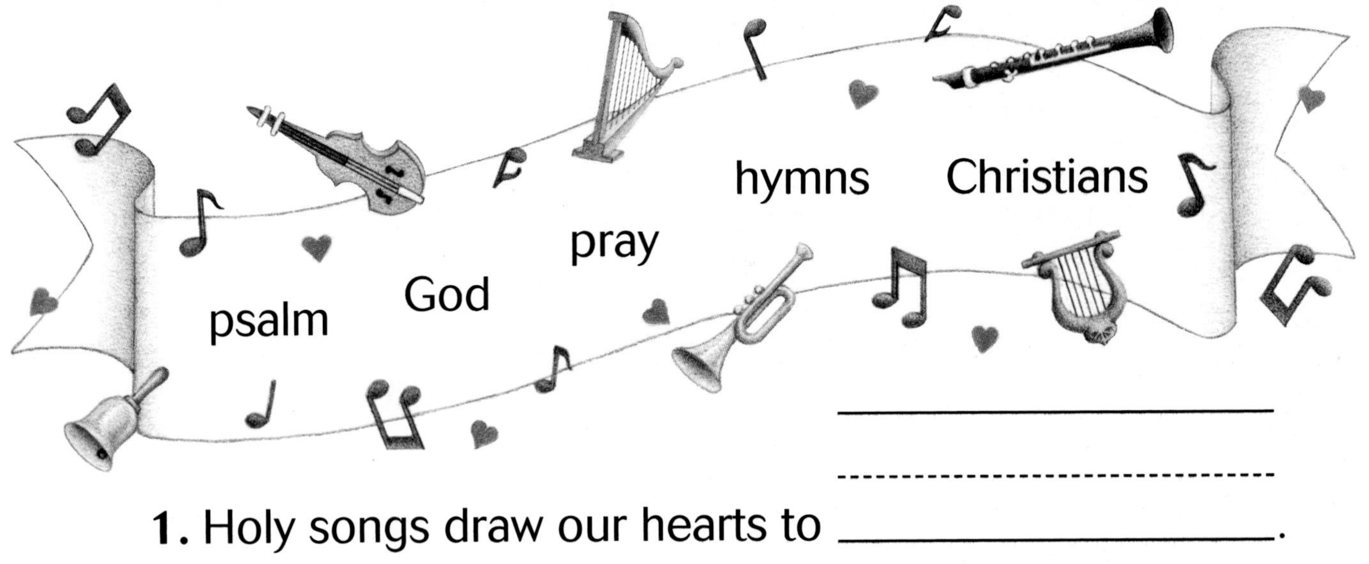

1. Holy songs draw our hearts to ____________________.

2. When we sing we ____________________ twice.

3. Holy songs about what we believe are called ____________________.

4. The first ____________________ sang because the Holy Spirit filled them with joy.

5. A ____________________ is a prayer that we can sing.

FEASTS AND SEASONS

The Liturgical Year

Holy Family
Epiphany
Baptism of the Lord
Christmas Time
Ordinary Time
Ash Wednesday
Christ the King
Advent
Lent
January
1 Mary, Mother of God
25 Conversion of St. Paul
February
2 The Presentation
22 Chair of St. Peter
December
25 Christmas Day
8 Immaculate Conception
November
1 All Saints' Day
October
4 St. Francis of Assisi
2 Guardian Angels
March
17 St. Patrick
19 St. Joseph
25 The Annunciation
Holy Week
Passion Sunday (Palm Sunday)
Holy Thursday
Good Friday
Holy Saturday
Easter Sunday
April
Easter Time
May
31 The Visitation
June
24 John the Baptizer
July
August
15 The Assumption
September
Ascension
Pentecost
Trinity Sunday
The Body and Blood of Christ
Ordinary Time

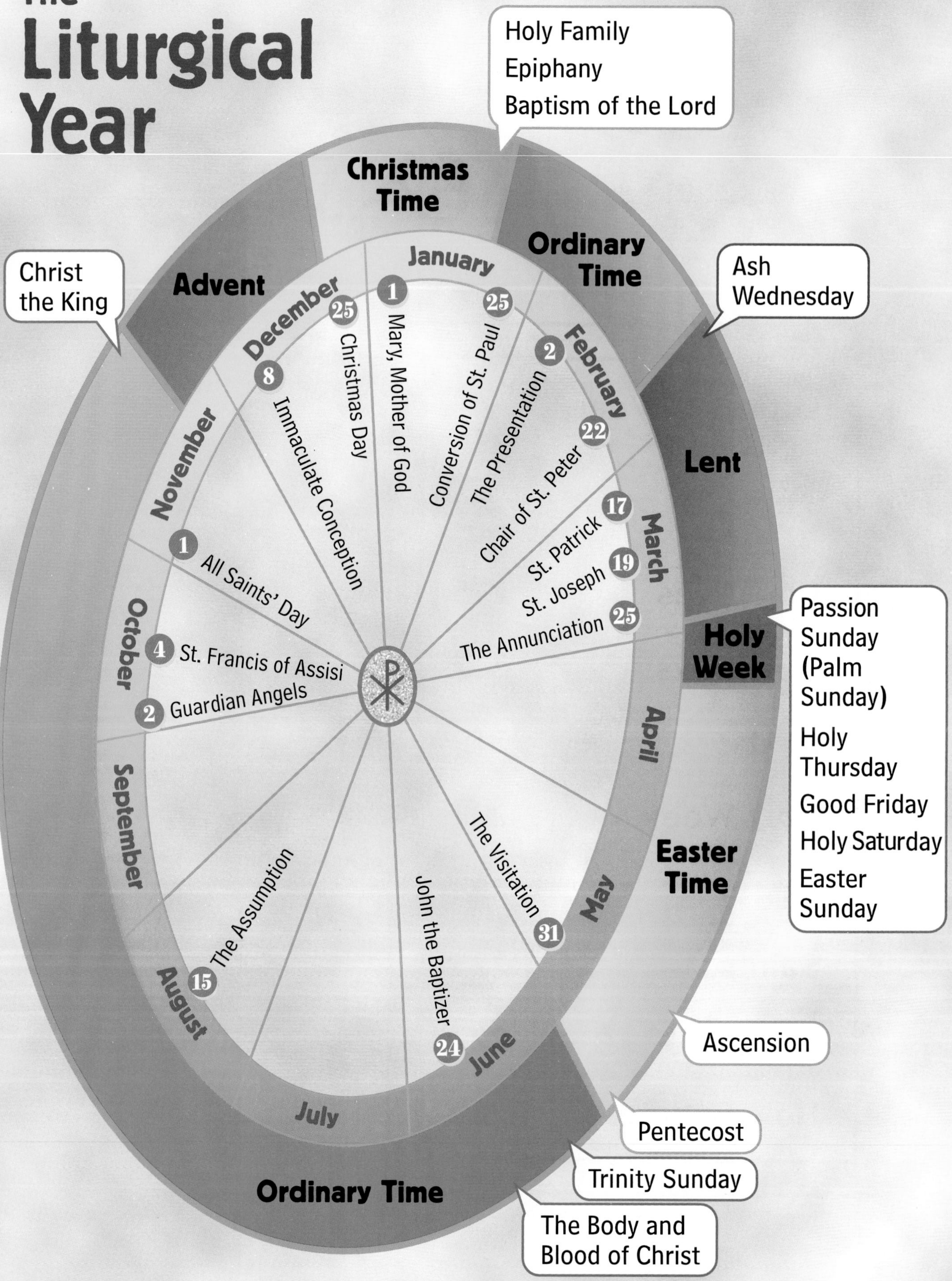

Advent

Make ready the way of the Lord.

Based on Isaiah 40:3

Welcome to Our Home!

Sometimes we welcome guests to our home. We want our guests to be happy. So we get ready to welcome them in special ways. A pleasant welcome makes our guests feel special.

Activity

Circle the pictures that show some of the ways your family welcomes guests.

A Time to Get Ready

During **Advent** we get ready to welcome Jesus. We prepare our hearts. We do things for each other to show we care.

These are some of the ways our Church prepares us to welcome Jesus.

Each Sunday we light another candle on the Advent wreath.

We read Bible stories about people who waited for Jesus.

We care for those in need.

Jesus,
help me get ready
to welcome you.
Amen.

Christmas

I have come from God to bring you good news.

Based on Luke 2:10

A Promise

"Guess what? My big brother promised to play soccer with all of us," said Sammy.

Sammy is very excited. He wants his brother to keep his promise.

Activity

Draw a picture about a promise that you made to someone.

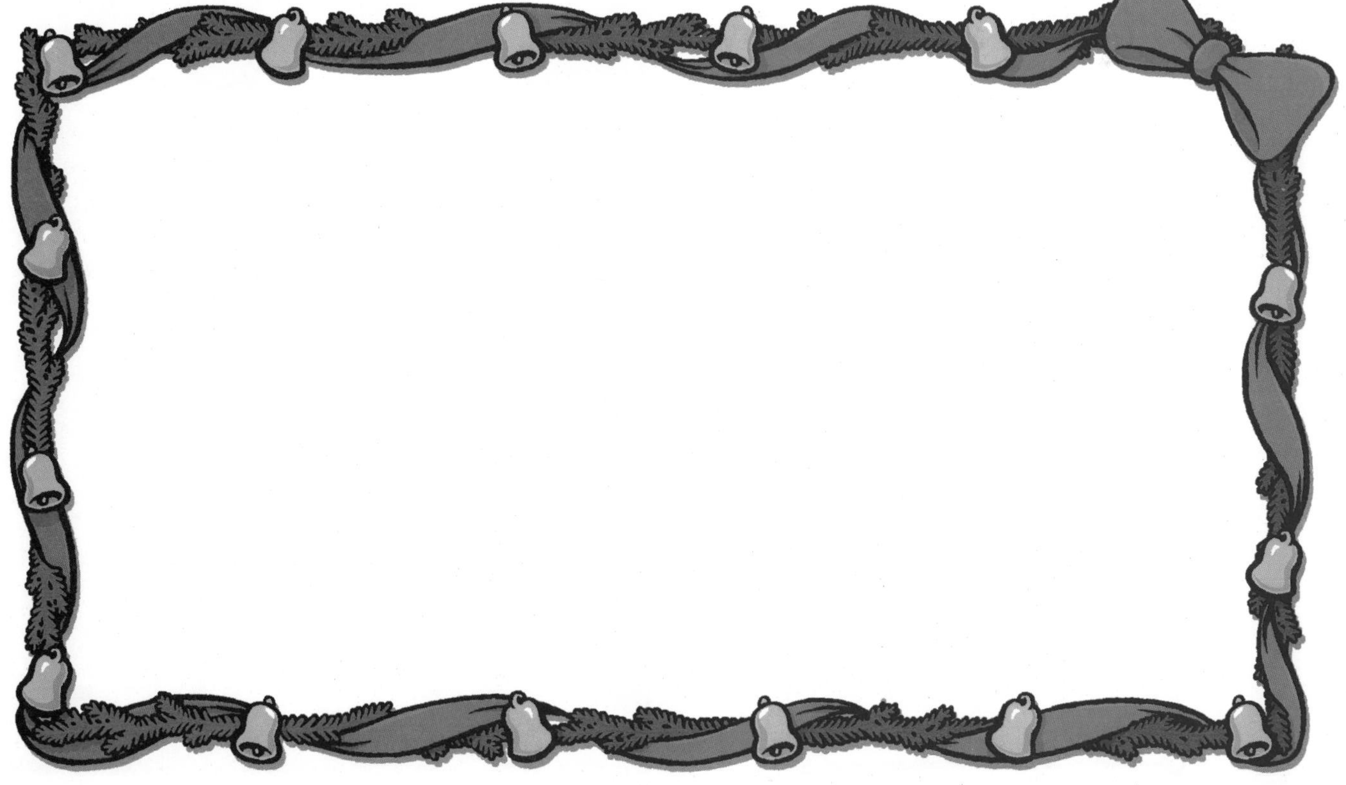

God Keeps a Promise

On **Christmas** we gather at Mass. We listen carefully to the Gospel story.

There were shepherds watching their sheep nearby. An angel sent by God appeared. The angel said, "Do not be afraid. I have come from God to bring you good news. God has kept his promise. Today Jesus has been born. You will find him lying in a manger." The shepherds ran and found Mary and Joseph, and the baby Jesus lying in the manger. They praised God for all they had seen.

Based on Luke 2:8–20

God our Father, thank you for keeping your promise and sending Jesus to be with us. Amen.

Holy Days

Happy are you who love God and walk in his ways.

Based on Psalm 128:1

What Does Holy Mean?

Do you know what it means to be holy? To be holy means to be like God.

What is God like?

God is full of love.
God brings peace.
God is kind and gentle.
God cares for us.
God forgives us.

Activity

God has made us to be holy.

Color the words that show what wonderful ways our families can act to be holy.

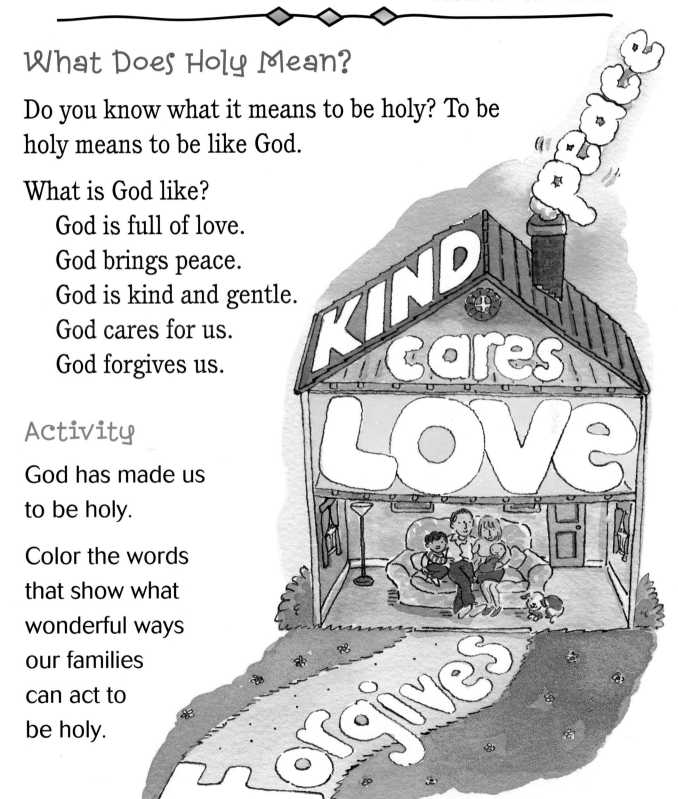

The Holy Family

The family of Jesus is called the Holy Family. Mary is Jesus' mother. **Joseph** is Mary's husband and Jesus' foster father. Jesus loved and obeyed Mary and Joseph. They were kind and caring to Jesus and each other.

Feast of the Holy Family

During Christmastime we celebrate the Feast of the Holy Family. We celebrate the love that the members of the Holy Family have for each other. We honor God's love for all families.

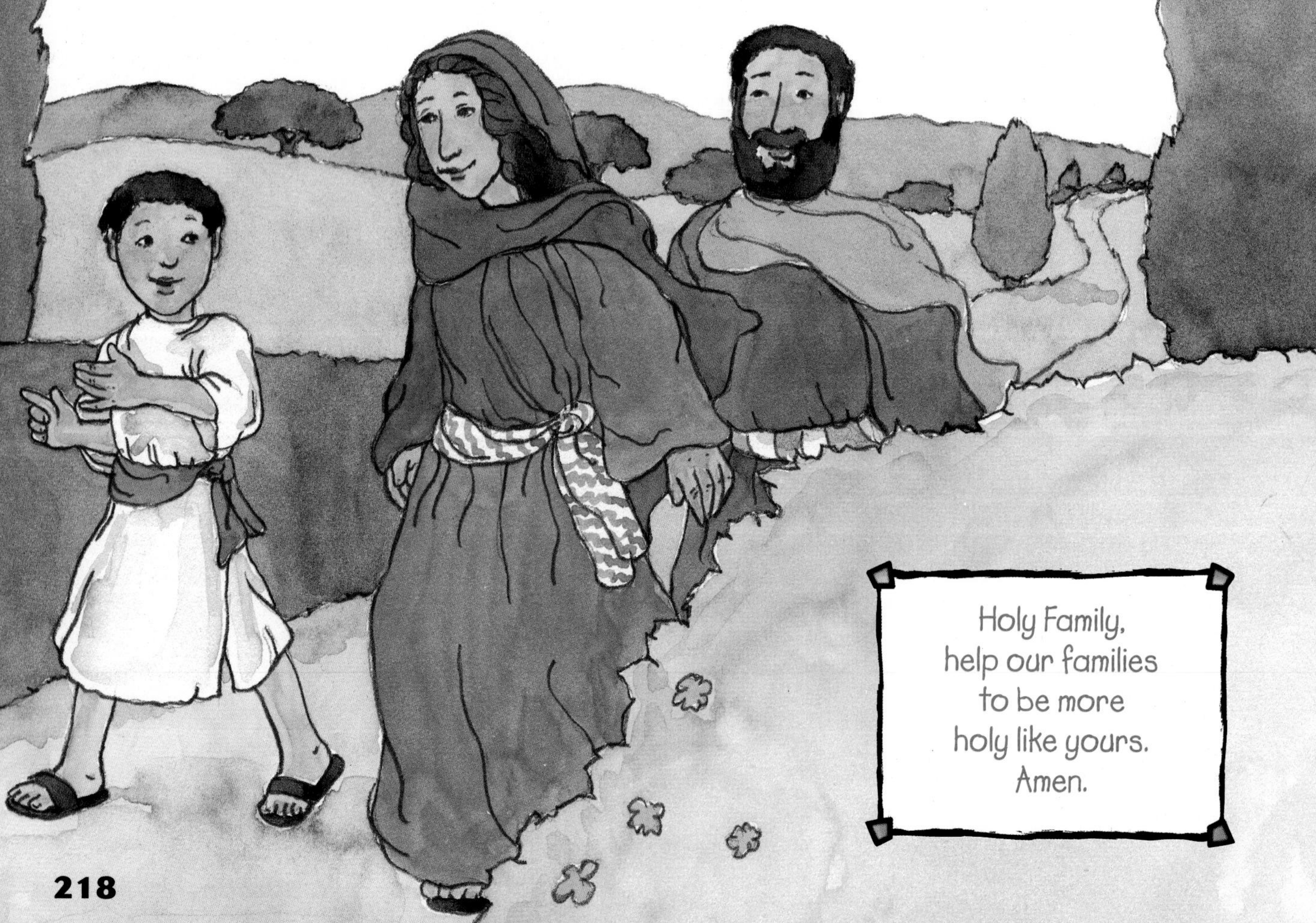

Holy Family,
help our families
to be more
holy like yours.
Amen.

Lent

Come! Follow me!

Based on John 1:43

More like Jesus

Every day we try to do what Jesus would do. To be followers of Jesus, we are called to live as Jesus showed us. We are called to love and care for each other.

Activity

You are a follower of Jesus. Draw yourself in the picture with the other followers of Jesus.

Lent

Lent lasts for forty days. During these forty days we get ready to celebrate Easter. We try to remember to become more like Jesus.

What Can We Do?

There are many things we can do during Lent to become more like Jesus. We can do some things with our parish community. We can do other things by ourselves.

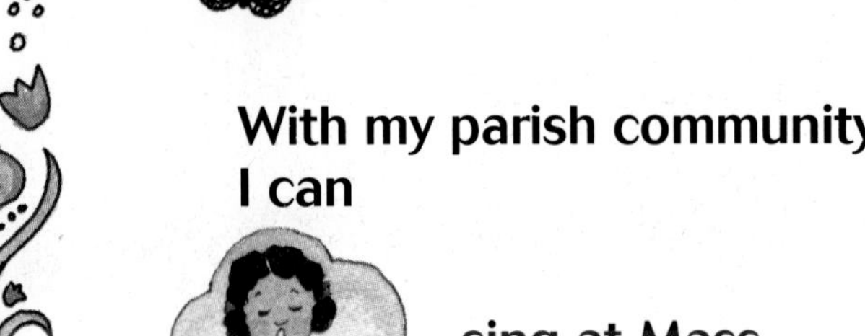

With my parish community I can

sing at Mass on Sunday.

care for the sick.

pray for others.

By myself I can

be helpful to my family.

obey my parents and teachers.

forgive others.

Jesus, I want to be more like you. Help me to be kind and forgiving. Amen.

Holy Week

Blessed is he who comes as our king!

Based on Luke 19:38

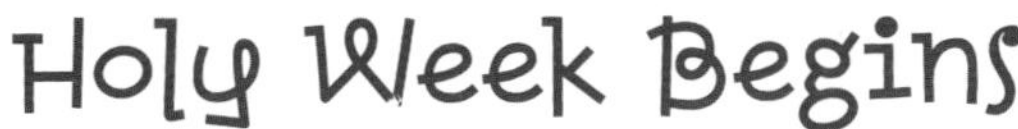

Holy Week Begins

Holy Week is the week before Easter. Jesus came to the city of Jerusalem during Holy Week.

Activity

Read the story below.
Use the pictures to help you.

Palms are branches of  .

Palm trees grow in hot,  places.

One day a crowd of people cheered and waved palms at  .

The people were  to see Jesus.

They had a great parade to honor Jesus.

Palm Sunday of the Lord's Passion

The Sunday before Easter is called Palm Sunday of the Lord's Passion. Palm Sunday is the first day of Holy Week. On Palm Sunday we remember the celebration that welcomed Jesus to Jerusalem. We carry palm branches. We walk into church with the priest and our church community. We say, "Blessed is he who comes in the name of the Lord" (Matthew 21:9).

We can take the blessed palm home. We remember that Jesus came in the name of the Lord. We say, "Hosanna!"

Jesus,
we welcome you
into our hearts
and homes.
Hosanna!

Easter

I have seen the Lord. He is alive!

Based on John 20:18

Signs of Spring

It is Sunday afternoon. The Sanchez family is going for a walk. The sun is shining. The breeze feels warm on their faces. The air smells clean and fresh. They see many signs of new life. It is spring!

Activity

Look at the picture.
Circle the signs of new life that you see.

Jesus Is Alive!

Jesus died on a cross. His followers were very sad. They felt scared and all alone. They missed Jesus very much. Three days later God raised Jesus from the dead. God gave Jesus the gift of new life. Jesus' friends were filled with joy. The Risen Jesus was with them again. They thanked God for raising Jesus to new life.

Easter

Easter is our greatest feast. We celebrate Jesus' new life. We believe that we will share new life with Jesus forever. On Easter Sunday we go to Mass. We sing joyful songs. We pray joyful prayers. We say, "Alleluia."

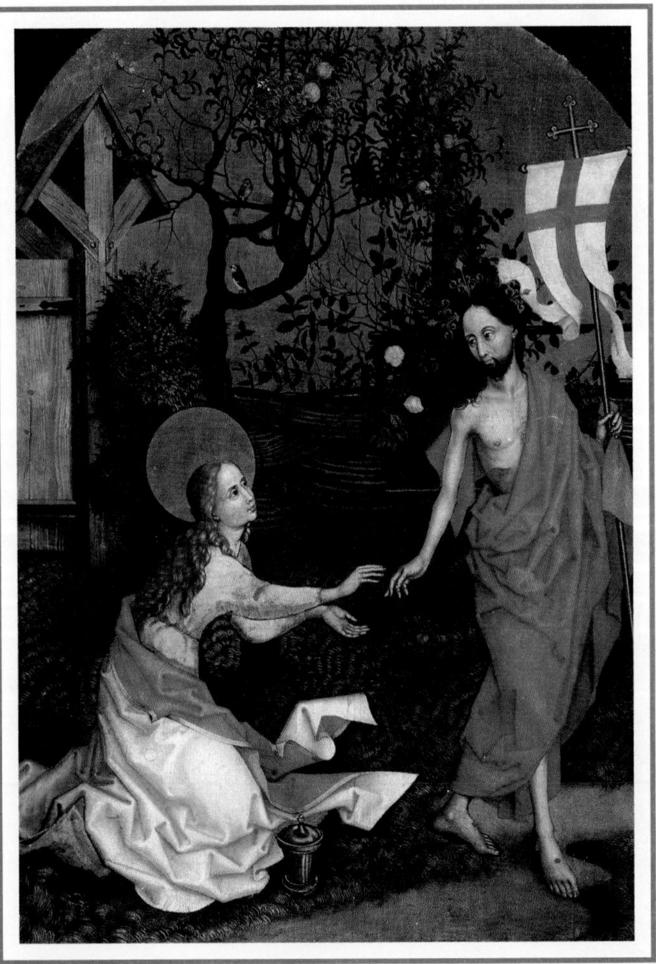

Risen Jesus,
help us share in your
new life. Alleluia!
Amen.

Saints

Be my follower by helping others.

Based on Matthew 19:21

Sharing

When you were a baby, you did not know how to share. Now you are older. You know it is important to share what you have with others.

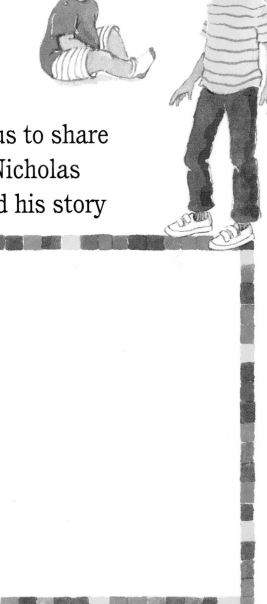

Jesus Asks Us to Share

Even when it is hard, Jesus asks us to share what we have with others. Saint Nicholas did what Jesus asks. You may read his story on the next page.

Activity

Draw your favorite toy.

Is it easy to share it with others?
Circle your answer.

Yes **No**

Saint Nicholas

When Nicholas grew up, he became a bishop. He saw many poor children and many children without families. He wanted to find ways to share his riches.

At night, when everyone was asleep, Bishop Nicholas went to the homes of poor children. There he left gifts of fruit, candy, and money on their doorsteps. Then he slipped quietly away. He did not want to be noticed!

Bishop Nicholas was a follower of Jesus. Nicholas shared what he had with those who had very little. We celebrate the life of Saint Nicholas on December 6.

Saint Nicholas,
help us share our
things with others.
Amen.

Mary

Hail Mary!
You are full of God's grace.

Based on Luke 1:28

Mary Cares for Jesus

Look carefully at the pictures on this page. Each picture shows how Mary cared for her son, Jesus.

Activity

Circle the picture of Mary caring for Jesus that you like best. Tell why you like the picture.

Mary, Mother of God

God chose Mary to be the mother of Jesus. We call Mary the Mother of God. Mary is very special.

Mary cared for Jesus. Jesus wants Mary to love and care for us, too. He gave her to us as our special mother. She loves us and cares for us. Mary prays for us. She prays to her son, Jesus.

Mary,
pray for us and
for all children.
Amen.

Holy People

Let the children come to me.

Based on Matthew 19:14

Gifts from God

God makes every child special. Every child is a gift from God.

Activity

You are a special gift from God.

Draw a badge that shows others what is special about you.

Mother Clara Hale

Mother Hale lived in New York City. She loved God very much. Mother Hale believed that every child is a special gift from God.

For many years, Mother Hale and her helpers cared for babies who were very sick. No one wanted these children, but Mother Hale did. She brought them into her home and cared for them. She fed them and gave them medicine. She rocked them to sleep when they cried.

Mother Hale loved these sick children as if they were her own. She knew that this was very special work. She knew that she was doing what God wants.

Jesus,
help me treat
everyone as a
child of God.
Amen.

OUR CATHOLIC HERITAGE

What Catholics Believe

How Catholics Worship

How Catholics Live

How Catholics Pray

WHAT CATHOLICS BELIEVE

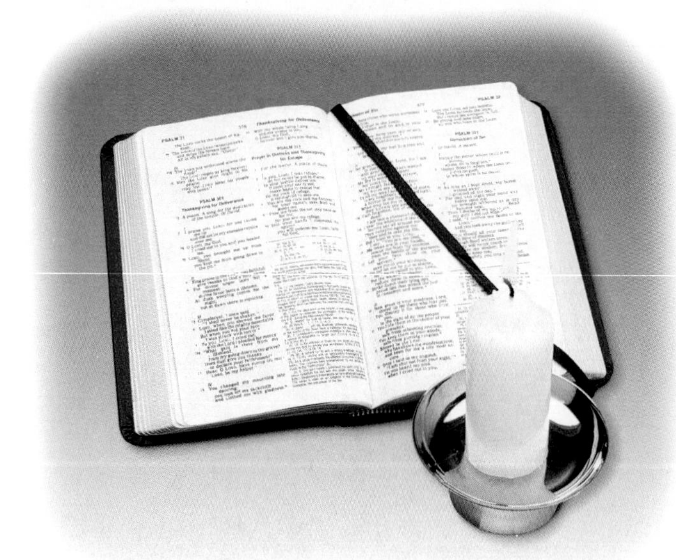

We can come to know and understand our faith in many ways.

ABOUT THE BIBLE

The Bible is a special book about God's love for us. It is one big book written by many people. God chose the people who wrote the Bible.

The Bible is God's word. In the Bible we can read many stories. We can read about God's Son, Jesus. We can learn about what Jesus said and did. Bible stories teach us how we can share our love of God.

Some Bible stories are from the Old Testament. That is the oldest part of the Bible. The stories in the New Testament tell us about Jesus' life.

ABOUT THE TRINITY

There is only one God.

There are three Persons in God—the Father, the Son, and the Holy Spirit.

We call the three Persons in God the **Holy Trinity**.

We Believe in God Our Father

God created all of us. God created us special. We are God's special children.

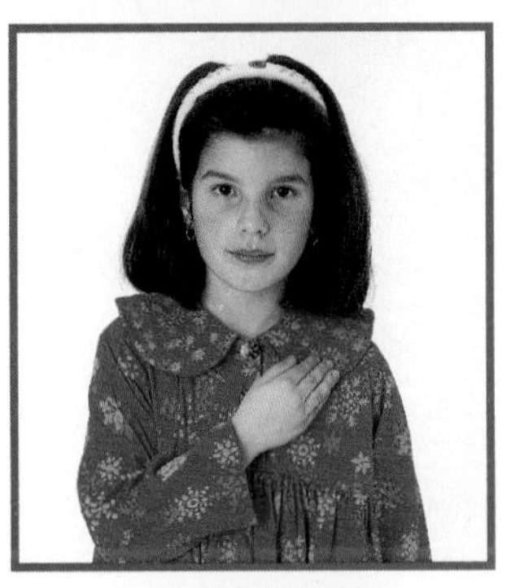

Jesus teaches us that God is our Father. Like a caring father, God watches over us with love. God wants us to watch over each other, too.

God created our world. Everything in our world is made with love. God wants us to take care of our world.

We Believe in Jesus Christ

Jesus Christ is God's own Son who became a man. God sent Jesus to teach us.

Jesus teaches us about God. Jesus teaches us how to show love. When we do what Jesus teaches us, we are followers of Jesus.

Jesus died on the cross and rose from the dead to save us from sin. Jesus Christ is our Savior.

Jesus is alive. He shares new life with us.

We Believe in the Holy Spirit

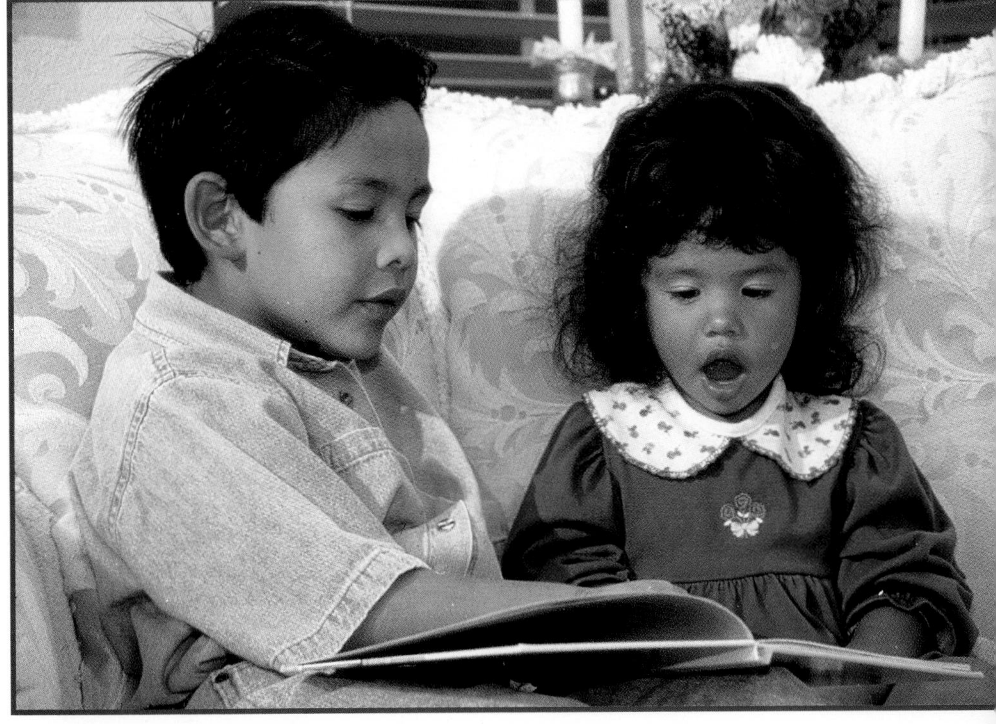

The Holy Spirit is God. The Holy Spirit is with us always.

The Holy Spirit gives us **grace** to help us live good lives. Grace is the gift of God's loving presence in our lives. Grace helps us live as Jesus teaches us. The Holy Spirit helps us be followers of Jesus.

ABOUT
THE CATHOLIC CHURCH

We are Catholics. We are followers of Jesus.

We celebrate the sacraments. We pray to God. We help others.

The pope is the leader of the Catholic Church. We call the pope our Holy Father.

The Church is the People of God. We pray with the other followers of Jesus.

The Church is our community. Our church community shares the good news about Jesus.

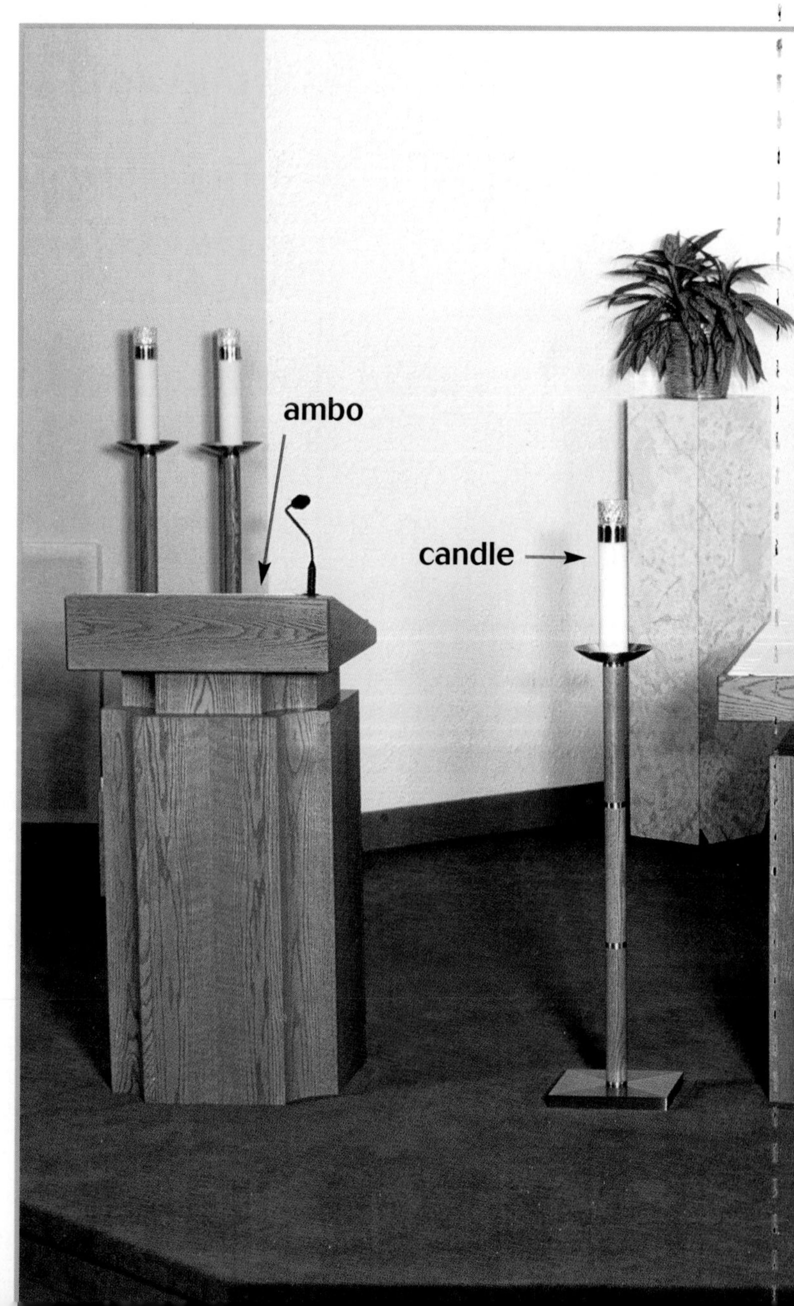

ABOUT
A VISIT TO CHURCH

A Catholic church is a very special place to visit.

We go to church to worship God. We go to church to pray. We go to church to be with our church community.

These are some things that we can see when we visit our parish church.

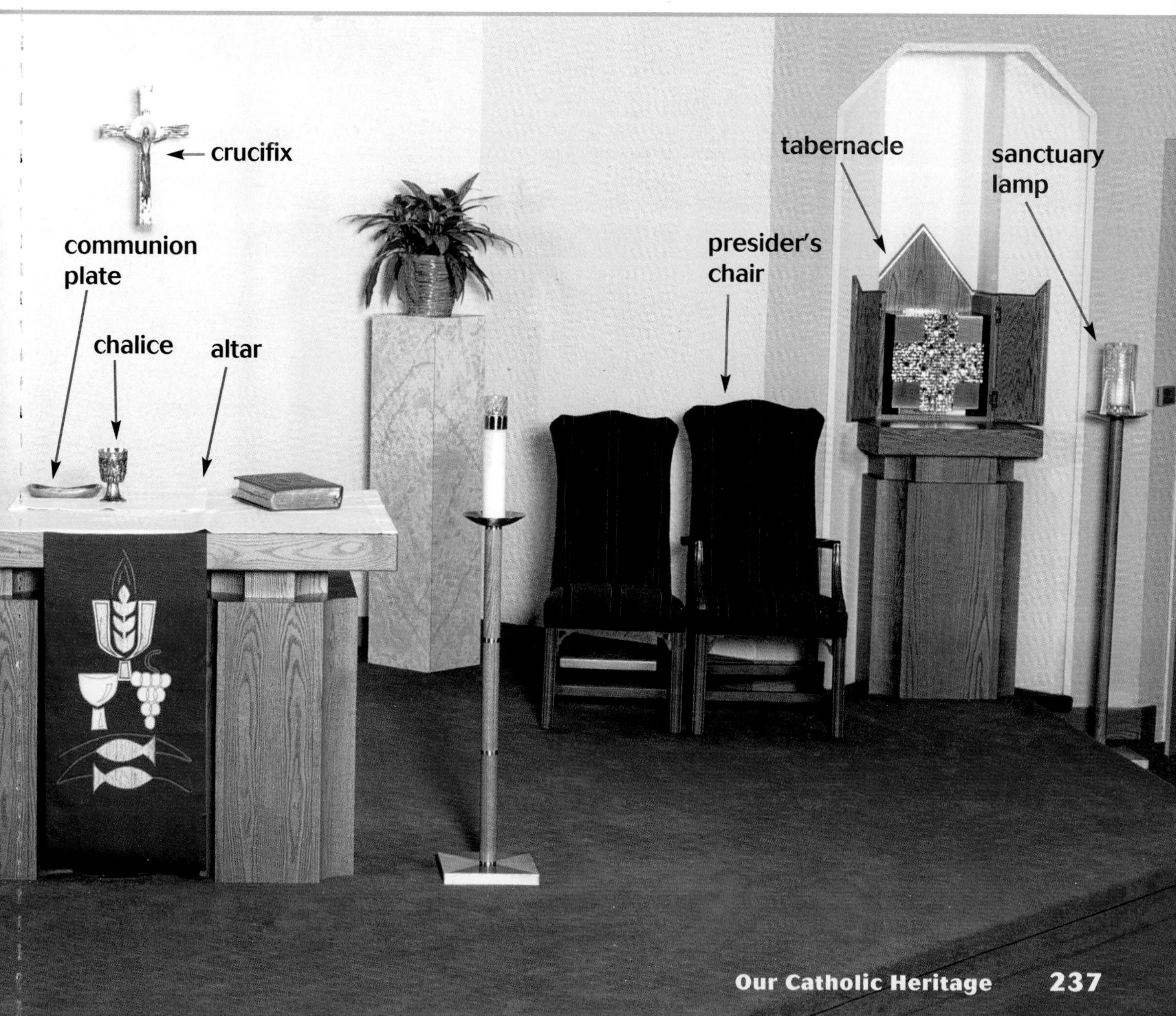

ABOUT MARY

Mary is the mother of Jesus. She was chosen by God.

Mary loved and trusted God. Mary loved and cared for God's Son, Jesus.

We call Mary our mother, too. Like a good mother, Mary loves and cares for us.

Mary is our greatest **saint**. The saints are special people. Saints show us how to follow Jesus. We honor Mary and the saints. We ask them to pray for us.

ABOUT NEW LIFE FOREVER

Jesus teaches us to act with love. When we act with love, we will be happy with God in heaven. Heaven is love that never ends. Heaven is happiness with God forever.

HOW CATHOLICS WORSHIP

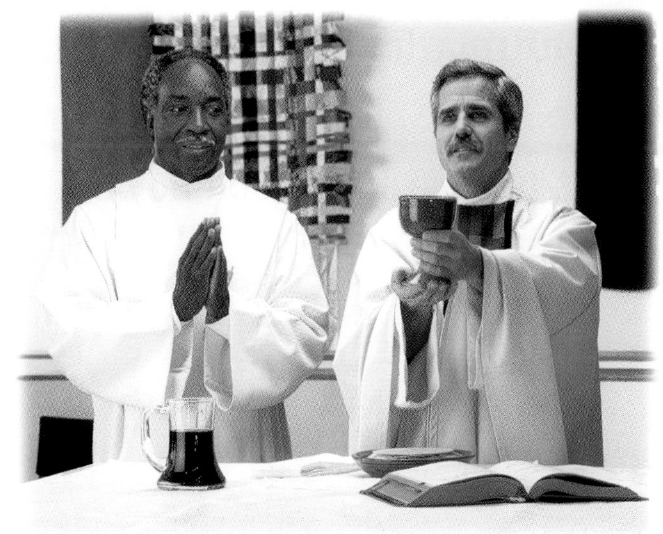

Worship is giving honor and praise to God. We worship when we pray and when we celebrate the Eucharist. We worship when we celebrate the sacraments.

ABOUT THE SACRAMENTS

The sacraments are celebrations of God's love for us.
We celebrate that we belong to Jesus Christ.
We celebrate that we share in his new life.

Baptism is the sacrament of welcome into the Church. At Baptism we receive the Holy Spirit. We are baptized with water. Baptism is a sign that we belong to Christ.

Confirmation is the sacrament of the Holy Spirit. The Holy Spirit helps us share the good news of Jesus.

In the **Eucharist**, Jesus gives himself to us as the Bread of Life. The Eucharist is a special meal we all share together with Jesus.

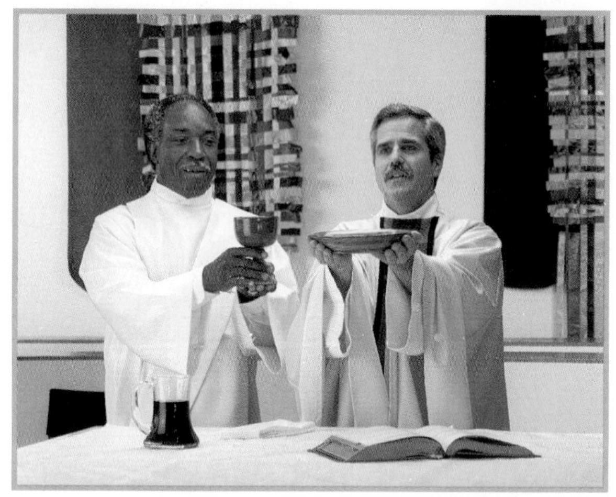

Reconciliation is the sacrament of forgiveness. We say we are sorry for our sins. We celebrate God's forgiveness.

The **Anointing of the Sick** brings the peace of Jesus to people who are sick.

The sacrament of **Holy Orders** celebrates priests, deacons, and bishops. These people are called by God to do Jesus' work in a special way.

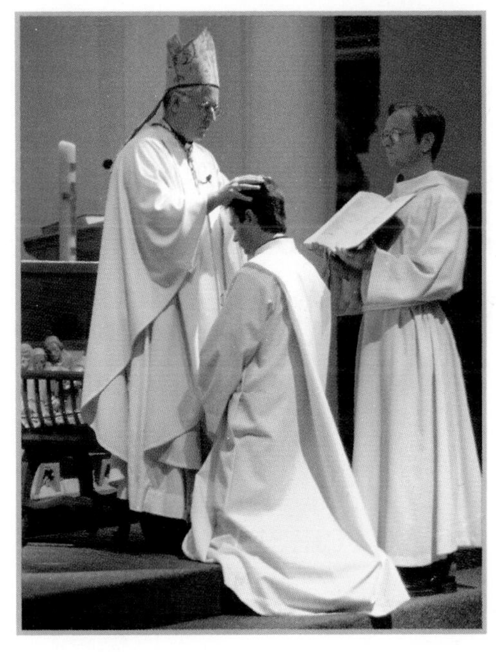

The sacrament of **Matrimony** celebrates the love that a man and a woman have for each other. They promise to be faithful. They are ready to begin their family life.

ABOUT
THE MASS

1. Our celebration begins. The priest and other ministers go to the altar. We stand and sing a welcome song.

2. We make the Sign of the Cross. The priest welcomes us with these words: "The Lord be with you."

3. We remember our sins. We ask God to forgive us.

4. We listen to God's word in readings from the Bible. After each reading we say, "Thanks be to God."

5. The priest or deacon reads the Gospel story. The word gospel means "good news." We stand and listen to the good news story of Jesus. We say "Praise to you, Lord Jesus Christ."

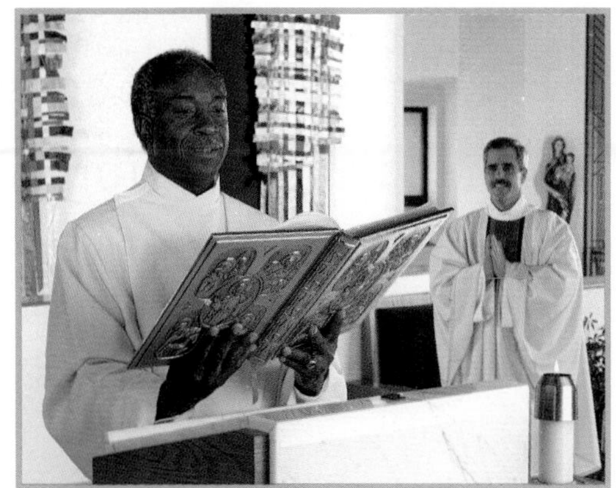

6. The priest or deacon helps us to understand Jesus' message in a special talk called the homily.

7. In the Prayer of the Faithful, we ask God to help the Church, our country, and all of God's people.

8. We bring the gifts of bread and wine to the altar for the special meal with Jesus. We remember that Jesus always loves us.

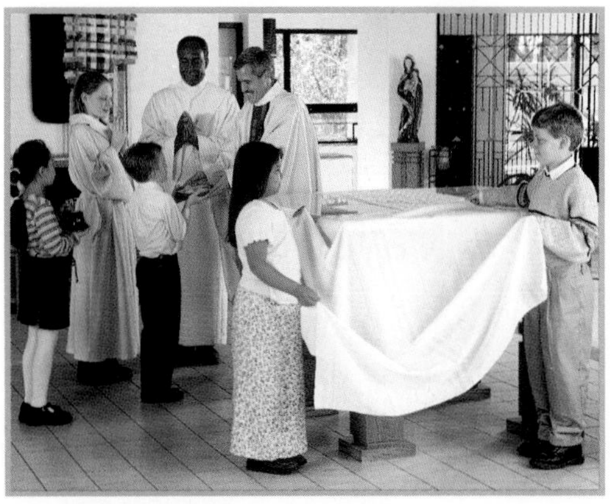

9. The priest offers our gifts of bread and wine to God.

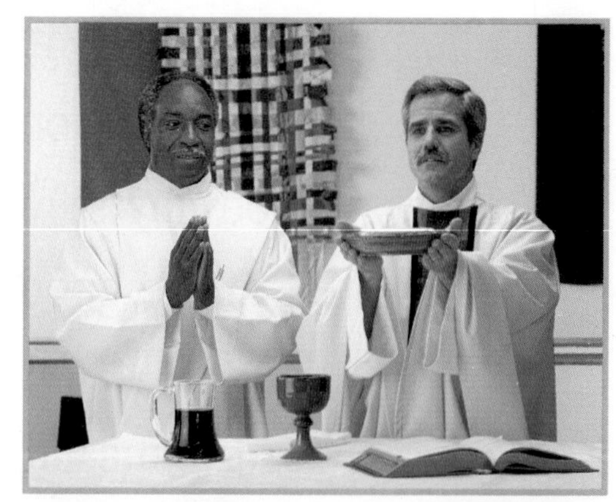

10. We thank and praise God for all of our blessings. We especially thank God for the gift of Jesus.

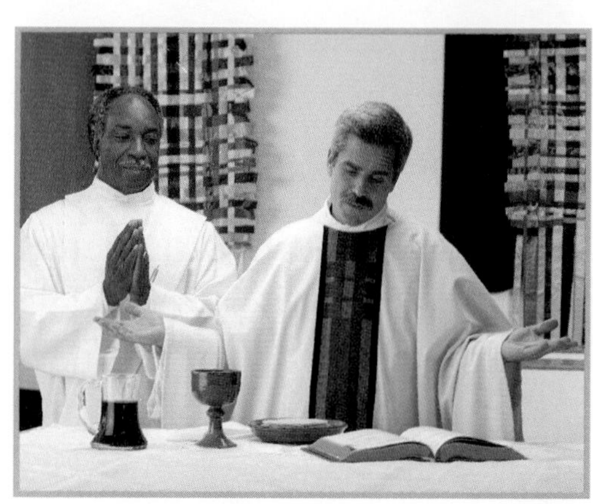

11. The priest prays as Jesus did at the Last Supper. Our gifts of bread and wine become the Body and Blood of Jesus Christ.

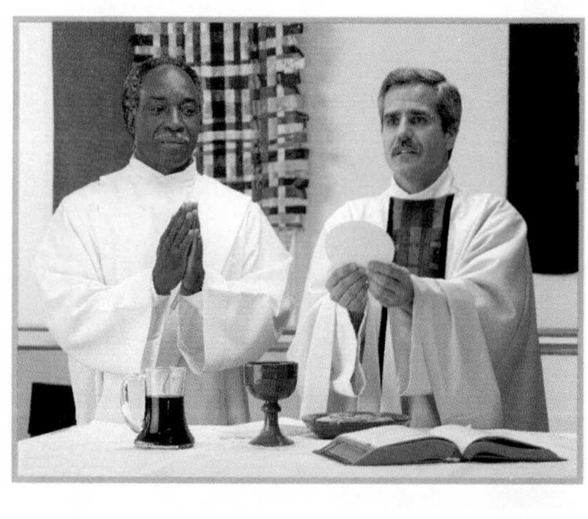

12. The priest holds up the Body and Blood of Jesus. He says a prayer to praise God. We answer, "Amen."

13. We say the "Lord's Prayer." This is the prayer that Jesus taught us to say.

14. We offer one another a Sign of Peace. This is a sign that reminds us to live as Jesus teaches us to live.

15. We receive Jesus in the Eucharist. Sharing Jesus' Body and Blood in a special way means that we are promising to act like Jesus.

16. We receive God's blessing. We answer, "Amen." We sing a song of praise. We go in peace to love and serve all people.

About Forgiveness

Jesus loves us. Jesus teaches us to love and care for others.

We can choose what is good and what is right. When we choose to do what is wrong, we sin. Sin is turning away from God. Sin hurts our friendship with other people.

We know that God will always forgive us. When others do wrong, we can forgive them, too. In the sacrament of Reconciliation, we think about our sins. We say that we are sorry. We promise to do better—and really mean it.

I can talk to Jesus. I can say "I am sorry" to Jesus. I can ask the Holy Spirit to help me do better.

"Dear Jesus,
I love you with my whole heart.
I have thought about the ways that I have sinned.
I am truly sorry. I do not want to sin again.
I am glad I have the Holy Spirit to help me.
I am glad you will forgive me.
I want to act like you showed us, Jesus.
I want to follow in your footsteps.
Amen."

HOW CATHOLICS LIVE

Jesus teaches us how to live. He gives us the Holy Spirit to help us. He gives us the Church so that we can pray with his followers.

ABOUT
THE GREAT COMMANDMENT

Jesus told us that God's laws are really one Great Commandment. Jesus said, "You must love God above all things and love your neighbor as yourself" (based on Mark 12:30–31).

The Great Commandment tells us how to love God and other people.

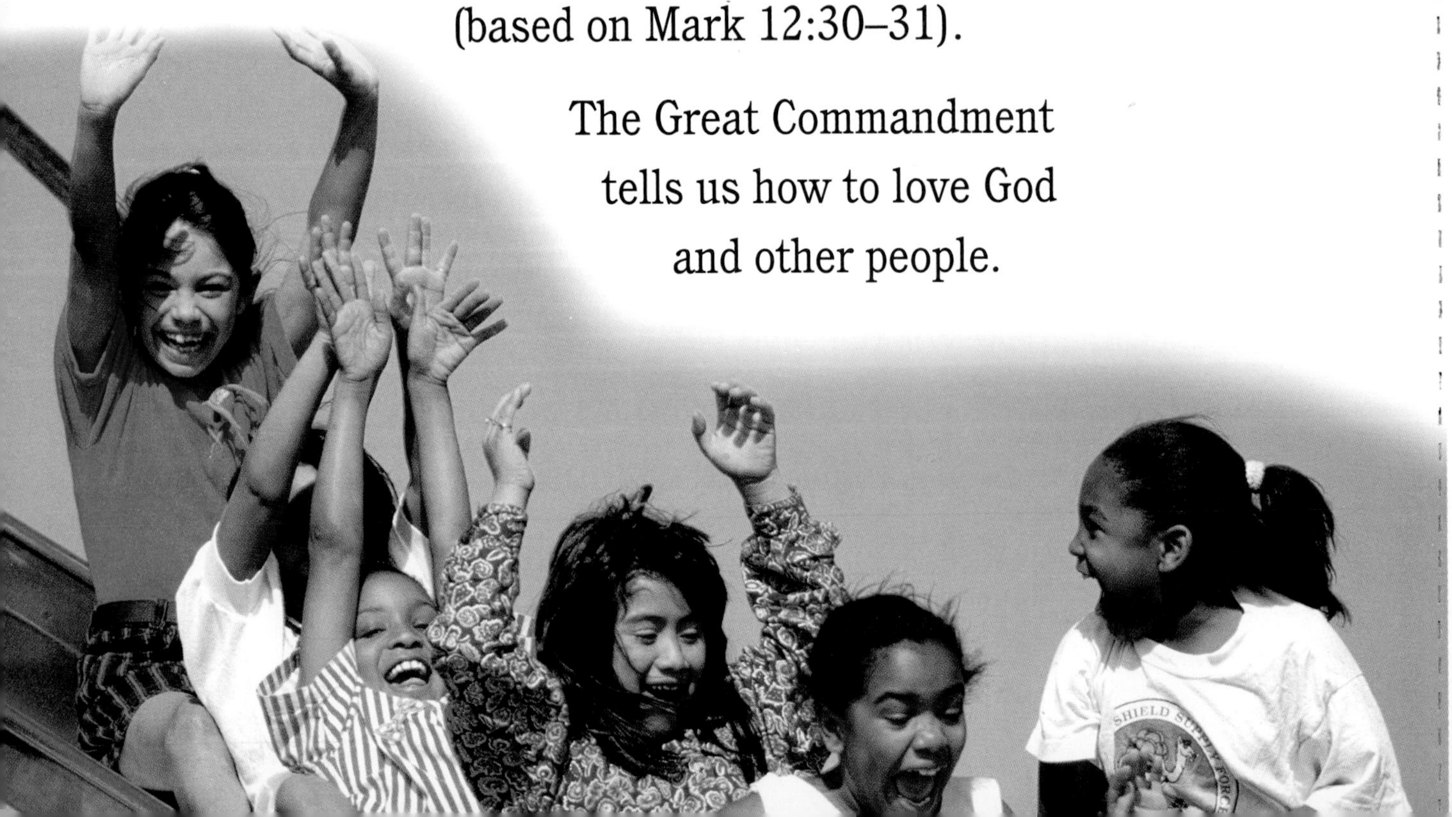

ABOUT

THE NEW COMMANDMENT

Jesus gave us a New Commandment. He said, "Love one another as I have loved you" (based on John 13:34).

We can show our love by caring for all living things. We can be fair and kind to all people. We can be helpful. We can be forgiving.

About
The Ten Commandments

We Live God's Law

We show our love for God.

1. We believe in God and love God.
2. We use God's name with love.
3. We pray with our Church community at Mass. We keep God's day holy.

We show our love for our neighbor.

4. We obey our parents and those who care for us.
5. We care for all living things.
6. We respect our bodies and the bodies of others.
7. We respect what is given to us and what belongs to others.
8. We always tell the truth.
9. We rejoice in the happiness of others.
10. We do not want more than we need.

ABOUT
SIN AND FORGIVENESS

Sin is doing something harmful on purpose.

The Holy Spirit helps us to say, "I am sorry. I was wrong."

> "God, I am sorry for what I have done wrong. I will try to do better. I will choose to love. I will ask the Holy Spirit to help me.
>
> God, you are so good. I am not afraid to come to you. I know you will always forgive me. I know you will always love me.
>
> Amen."

About Vocations

When we were baptized, we became members of the Catholic community. God calls each of us to live our lives in a special way. This is called our vocation.

God calls some people to a religious vocation. It is a call to a special way of life in the Church. Priests, deacons and religious sisters and brothers have a religious vocation.

Many Ways of Helping

God calls Catholics to help in the Church.

Catholics can help at Mass by reading the Bible, leading songs, or giving communion to people.

Catholics can teach others about God. They can teach Jesus' Gospel message.

Catholics can visit sick people who need help. Catholics can teach in schools.

Catholics who share the good news about Jesus' love are answering God's call.

God calls some people to help the Church in a special way. There are priests who do the work of Jesus by leading the parish community.

There are religious sisters and brothers who teach, help the poor, or help lead the parish.

There are deacons who work with the priest by leading the celebrations of marriage and of Baptism. Deacons can also take care of those who may need help.

As you get older, God will call you to a vocation. Then you will know how to serve God in your Catholic community.

About
Parish Ministers

We belong to our parish community. At church, we see many people who serve their Catholic community.

The priest is the leader of the parish. The priest does the work of Jesus by celebrating the Mass. The priest celebrates the sacraments with the people. The priest cares for God's people.

We may see religious sisters, brothers, and deacons. They help with the celebration of the Mass. They help with other needs of the parish community.

Religious sisters and brothers may be teachers in schools. They also might help by caring for the sick. They care for people who need help.

God calls all Catholics to share God's message. God calls all Catholics to share God's love.

HOW CATHOLICS PRAY

Prayer is talking and listening to God. We can pray anywhere and at any time. God is everywhere. God always hears our prayers.

ABOUT KINDS OF PRAYER

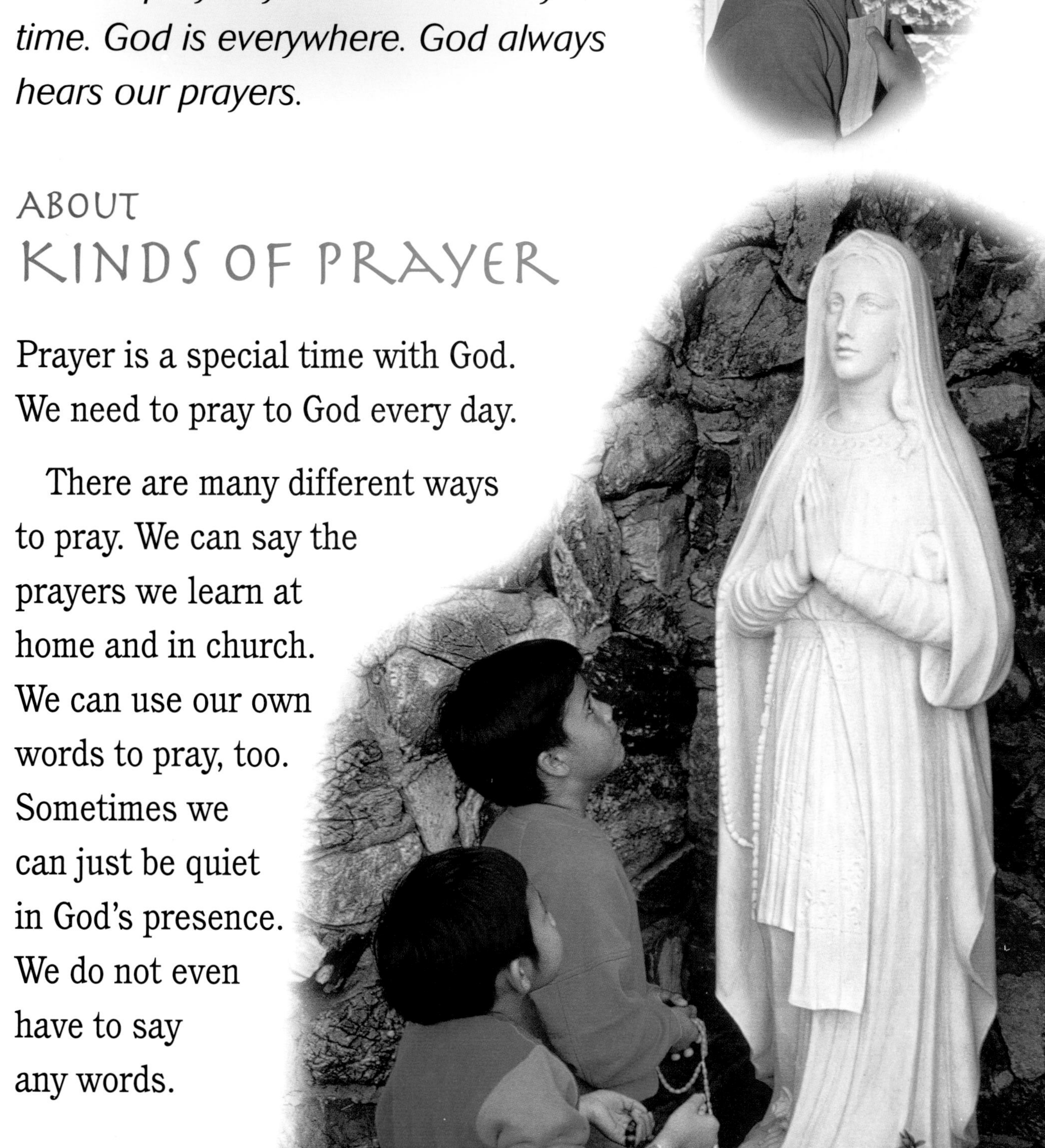

Prayer is a special time with God. We need to pray to God every day.

There are many different ways to pray. We can say the prayers we learn at home and in church. We can use our own words to pray, too. Sometimes we can just be quiet in God's presence. We do not even have to say any words.

Our thoughts can be a prayer. Our hopes can be a prayer. This kind of prayer is called meditation. In meditation we use our imagination to think about God. We think about what God wants us to do.

We can use our bodies when we pray. When we make the Sign of the Cross, we use our hands. Sometimes we kneel when we pray. We can even sing or dance as a prayer to God.

We are never alone when we pray. God hears our prayers.

ABOUT
THE LORD'S PRAYER

The Lord's Prayer is a very special prayer. Jesus taught us the words. In this prayer, Jesus teaches us to call God "our Father." We know that God watches over us.

Our Father, who art in heaven, hallowed be thy name;

God is our Father. We pray that everyone will say God's name with love.

thy kingdom come;

Jesus told us that God's kingdom is happiness with God forever. We pray that everyone in the world will know God's love.

thy will be done on earth as it is in heaven.

God wants us to live as Jesus taught us to live. We pray that everyone will live in peace.

Give us this day our daily bread;

God is good. God gives us everything we need. We remember to pray for our needs. We also remember to pray for the needs of others.

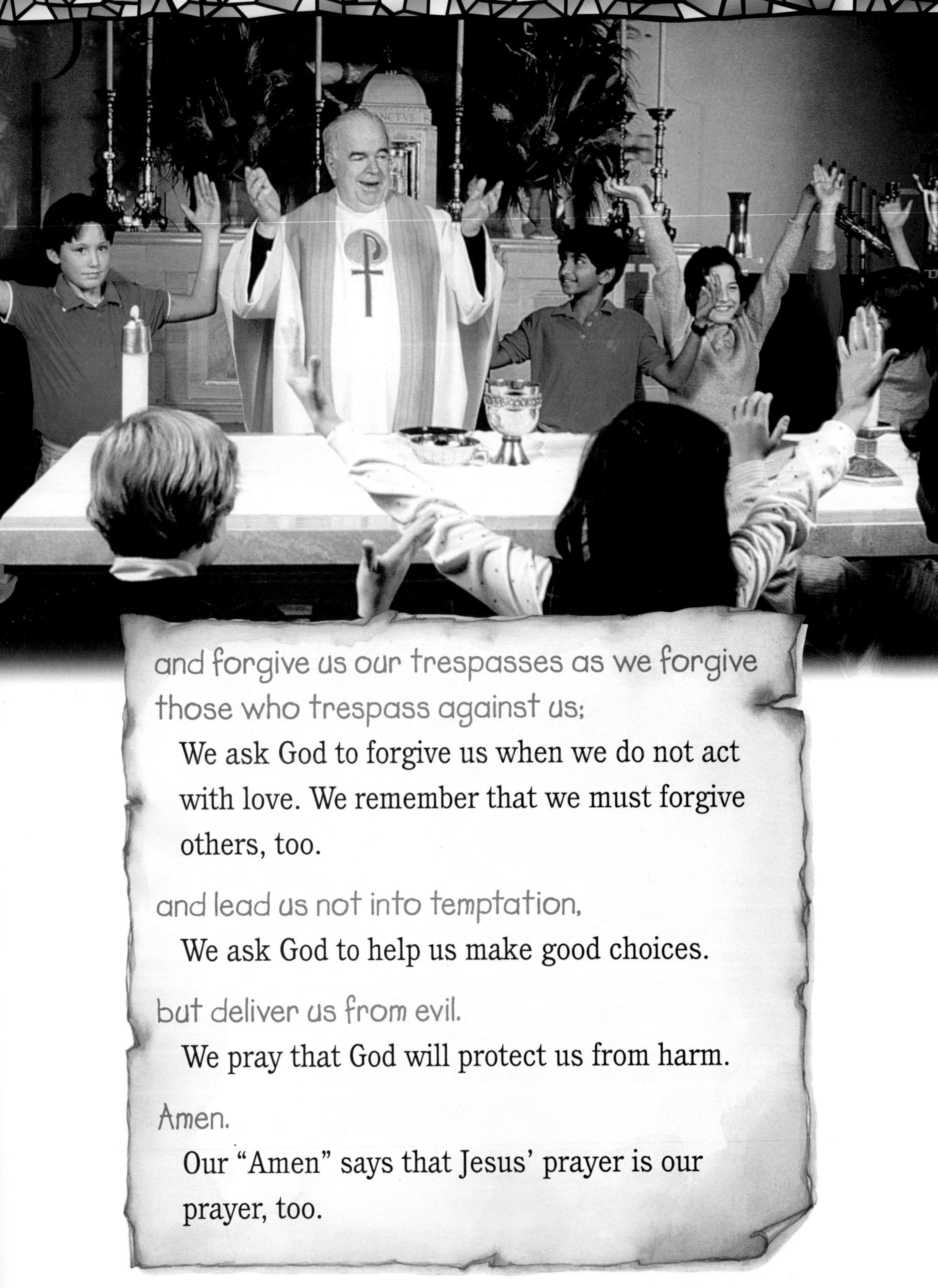

and forgive us our trespasses as we forgive those who trespass against us;

We ask God to forgive us when we do not act with love. We remember that we must forgive others, too.

and lead us not into temptation,

We ask God to help us make good choices.

but deliver us from evil.

We pray that God will protect us from harm.

Amen.

Our "Amen" says that Jesus' prayer is our prayer, too.

Write-In Glossary

Advent _______________ is the time before Christmas when we get ready to welcome Jesus into our lives.

Amen _______________ means "Yes, I believe. It is true." We often say "Amen" at the end of prayers.

angel An _______________ is a helper or a messenger from God. Guardian angels protect and guide us.

Anointing of the Sick _______________ **of the** _______________ is a sacrament that brings the peace of Christ to people who are sick.

Baptism _______________ is a celebration of welcome into the Catholic community.

Bible The _______________ is the written word of God. God chose special people to write the Bible.

blessing A _______________ is a gift of God's favor, or a prayer that asks for God's protection and care.

Catholic Church The ______________________ is the community of Jesus' followers to which we belong.

Christ ______________________ is another name for Jesus. It tells us that he was sent by God to save all people.

Christians ______________________ are people who love Jesus Christ and follow him.

Christmas ______________________ is the time when we celebrate the birth of Jesus.

church A ______________________ is a special place where Christians come together to pray.

community A ______________________ is a group of people who belong together.

Confirmation ______________________ is the sacrament in which the Holy Spirit makes our faith in Jesus Christ stronger.

Creator God made everything in the world. God is our ____________.

____

Eucharist The ____________ is a special meal that Jesus shares with us today. We receive the Body and Blood of Christ.

____

faith Our ____________ helps us believe and trust in God.

____

forgive To ____________ means to excuse or to pardon.

____________ ____________

fruits of the Holy Spirit The ____________ **of the** ____________

____

____________ are signs of the Holy Spirit's action in our lives. Some fruits are love, joy, peace, patience, gentleness, kindness, and self-control.

____

Gloria The ____________ is a prayer of praise to God said or sung at Mass.

good habit A ________________ is a way of acting for the good of others.

Gospel The ________________ is the Good News of Jesus. There are four Gospels in the Bible.

grace The gift of ________________ is God's loving presence in our lives.

hallowed To be ________________ means to be holy.

Heaven ________________ is happiness with God forever.

holy To be ________________ is to be like God.

Holy Orders The sacrament of ________________ celebrates God's call to become a deacon, priest, or bishop.

Holy Spirit The ______________________________ is the Spirit of God. This Spirit helps us follow Jesus.

Holy Trinity The ______________________________ is one God in three Persons—God the Father, God the Son, and God the Holy Spirit.

hymn A ______________ is a holy song about what we believe.

Jesus ______________________________ is the Son of God.

Joseph ______________________________ is Mary's husband and the foster father of Jesus.

Last Supper The ______________________________ is the special meal that Jesus shared with his friends. Jesus changed bread and wine into his Body and Blood.

Lord's Prayer The ______________________________ is the prayer that Jesus gave us. One time we pray the Lord's Prayer is during Mass.

Matrimony The sacrament of ______________________ celebrates the love that a man and woman have for each other.

Mary ______________ is the mother of Jesus.

Mass The ______________ is a special meal that Jesus shares with us.

mercy God's ______________________ is his loving forgiveness. We are called to show mercy to others.

mission A ______________________ is a job that needs to be done. Our mission as Christians is to love and serve others.

parish A ______________________ is a community of Jesus' followers who belong to the same local Catholic church.

peace To be at ____________ means to get along with others.

Pentecost On ____________ we celebrate the coming of the Holy Spirit and the birthday of the Church.

petition Prayers of ____________ are asking prayers. We ask God to give us the things we need.

praise A prayer of ____________ celebrates God's goodness.

Prayer ____________ is listening to and talking to God.

Psalms ____________ are prayers from the Bible that people often sing.

Reconciliation ____________ is the sacrament that celebrates God's forgiveness.

sacraments The ______ are special signs of Christ's love and presence.

saint A ______ is a special person who lived a holy life. The life of a saint shows us how to follow Jesus.

Savior The ______ is Jesus, the Son of God. He helps us and saves us.

serve To ______ means to help other people.

sin A ______ is a choice to do something we know is wrong.

tabernacle A ______ is a container in church where the bread of the Eucharist is kept.

Temple The ______ was a special building in Jerusalem. Jesus prayed in the Temple and learned about God.

Index

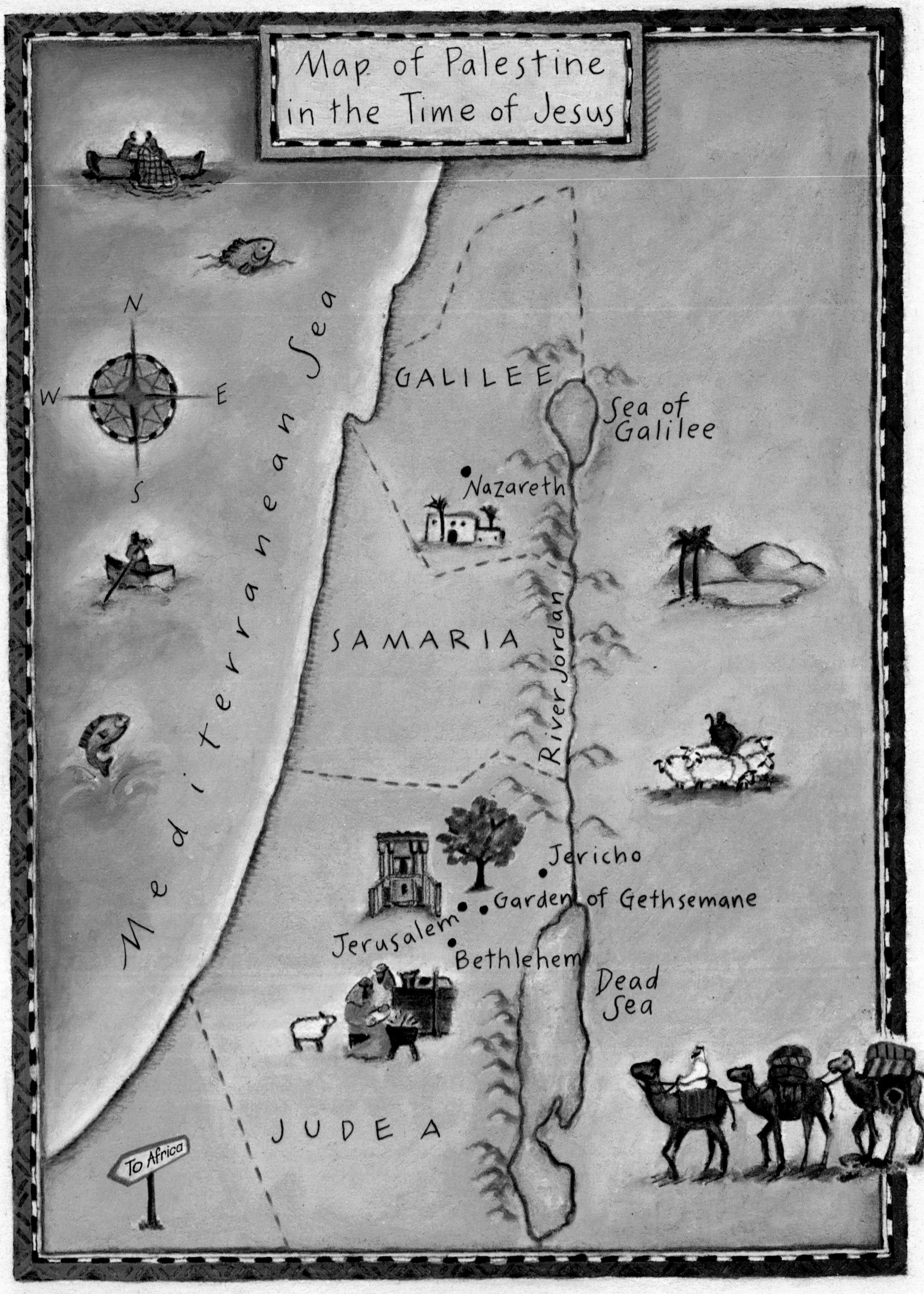

Map of Palestine in the Time of Jesus

N
W
E
S

Mediterranean Sea

GALILEE

Sea of Galilee

Nazareth

SAMARIA

River Jordan

Jericho

Garden of Gethsemane

Jerusalem

Bethlehem

Dead Sea

JUDEA

To Africa